— THE LAST TO DIE —

THE LAST TO DIE

RONALD TURPIN, ARTHUR LUCAS, AND THE END OF CAPITAL PUNISHMENT IN CANADA

ROBERT J. HOSHOWSKY
FOREWORD BY PETER C. NEWMAN

DUNDURN PRESS
TORONTO

Editor: Tony Hawke
Copy-editor: Andrea Waters
Designer: Jennifer Scott
Printer: Tri-Graphic Printing Ltd.

Library and Archives Canada Cataloguing in Publication

Hoshowsky, Robert J
    The last to die : Ronald Turpin, Arthur Lucas, and the end of capital
punishment in Canada / Robert J. Hoshowsky.

Includes bibliographical references.
ISBN 978-1-55002-672-6

    1. Turpin, Ronald, 1933-1962. 2. Lucas, Arthur, d. 1962. 3. Hanging--Ontario--History--20th century.
4. Capital punishment--Canada--History--20th century. 5. Murderers--Ontario--Biography. I. Title.

HV8700.H68 2007   364.66092'271   C2007-900084-3

1   2   3   4   5   11   10   09   08   07

We acknowledge the support of the **Canada Council for the Arts** and the **Ontario Arts Council** for our publishing program. We also acknowledge the financial support of the **Government of Canada** through the **Book Publishing Industry Development Program** and **The Association for the Export of Canadian Books**, and the **Government of Ontario** through the **Ontario Book Publishers Tax Credit** program and the **Ontario Media Development Corporation**.

Care has been taken to trace the ownership of copyright material used in this book. The author and the publisher welcome any information enabling them to rectify any references or credits in subsequent editions.

J. Kirk Howard, President

Printed and bound in Canada

www.dundurn.com

Dundurn Press	Gazelle Book Services Limited	Dundurn Press
3 Church Street, Suite 500	White Cross Mills	2250 Military Road
Toronto, Ontario, Canada	High Town, Lancaster, England	Tonawanda, NY
M5E 1M2	LA1 4XS	U.S.A. 14150

Table of Contents

FOREWORD
by Peter C. Newman

There's really only one good reason to read this book: it's a fascinating story told by a great storyteller. Robert Hoshowsky has masterfully reconstructed the lurid tale of the two low-lifes who became the last two criminals hanged in Canada. The devil is in the details, and he digs them out fearlessly, including much new information that reveals new and unexpected nuances about the crimes.

Ronald Turpin's murder of Toronto police officer Fred Nash is minutely reconstructed, as is the double slaying by Arthur Lucas of a key witness due to testify against American drug runners and his prostitute common-law wife. The author has not only interviewed all of the survivors but dug deep into hitherto unseen archives on the case, which brought to an end nearly one hundred years of capital punishment in this country. Their double hanging on December 11, 1962, at the Don Jail was an epochal event that deserves book-length recognition — and this is it. My hesitation in investing valuable reading time in such a gruesome subject soon dissipated. Not only is this a dramatic retelling of the actual events, but Hoshowsky has demonstrated the rare ability of writing a book that is more than the sum of its parts. I wish I could forget his hard-ass description of the details of the hangman's art, but it will never leave me …

Acknowledgements

The last hangings in Canada remains a sensitive subject for many, especially those connected to Ronald Turpin and Arthur Lucas, and to their victims, Toronto police officer Frederick John Nash, Therland Crater, and Carolyn Newman.

I would like to express my deepest gratitude to those who granted me interviews, sometimes resurrecting painful memories in the process. I remain especially grateful to members of the Nash/Kryskow family for sharing their stories about Frederick Nash, their late father, husband, and brother. Individuals I interviewed for this for this book include: Donald Bitter, Jackie Clausen, Ron Clifford, John Costello, Jim Crawford, Karen E. Davis, Bram Everitt, Dorothy Kryskow, Alison MacKay, Jim Majury, Nancy Morrison, Harold Nash, Julian Porter, Stephen Posen, Judy Ring, and Gwyn "Jocko" Thomas.

In preparing *The Last to Die: Ronald Turpin, Arthur Lucas, and The End of Capital Punishment in Canada*, I consulted primary source material whenever possible, beginning with the trial transcripts of *Regina vs. Arthur Lucas* and *Regina vs. Ronald Turpin*. While they remain an invaluable source of information, they remain factual and colourless by their very nature. Newspaper accounts from the *Toronto Star*, the *Globe and Mail*, and the *Telegram* helped add necessary emotions and detail.

No work of non-fiction is possible without extensive research, and I wish to thank the following for their assistance and encouragement: Peter C. Newman, staff at the Toronto Public Library, the City of Toronto

Archives, the Archives of Ontario, Library and Archives Canada, the Ontario Realty Corporation, Major David Pitcher (retired) and Karl Larson at the Salvation Army Archives, Canada and Bermuda Territory, Sharyn Devine from Don Heights Unitarian Congregation, Jenny Seeman at the Anglican Church of Canada, Susan Lewthwaite from the Law Society of Upper Canada, the Tennessee Department of Correction, the Mount Pleasant Group of Cemeteries, Jack Batten, Edward McGill, Gary and Lisa Cripps, the Metro Toronto Police Pensioners' Association, and Norina D'Agostini at the Toronto Police Museum.

Special thanks to my friend of twenty-five years, George Serhijczuk, for his invaluable research and suggestions on this and other projects.

A work like this is not possible without access to protected files. A number of documents from the Federal Bureau of Investigation on Arthur Lucas were made available through the U.S. Freedom of Information/Privacy Acts, while other materials on Lucas and Turpin — such as psychiatric reports, Don Jail log books, and appeal notes — were obtained through Canada's Freedom of Information and Protection of Privacy Act. Other materials consulted in preparation for this book include archival television footage, documentaries, radio transcripts, and photos and documents from privately held collections.

I wish to thank my wife, Elizabeth, for her love and patience, and my parents, Ann and Morris Hoshowsky, for teaching me never to be afraid to ask a question, no matter how strange it might be. I dedicate this book to them.

One final note: a number of people I contacted asked that their names not be used in the book, and I have abided by their requests. I thank them for their time nonetheless, and respect their wishes to remain private, and for their past actions to remain in the past.

List of Major Characters

In many cases, individuals referred to in *The Last to Die* used different spellings of their given names, or assumed an alias. Often, court records and newspaper accounts provide variations on spelling of names as well. To maintain consistency, birth names are used and maintained throughout the book.

Alexander, Irvine: *Toronto Detective Sergeant of Homicide*
Bassett, John Henry: *Toronto Detective Sergeant of Homicide*
Bitter, Donald: *Early lawyer to Ronald Turpin*
Boykin, Lillian (alias Laura Jean Wilson): *Girlfriend to Arthur Lucas*
Bull, Henry: *Crown prosecutor in the Lucas case*
Burns, Della (alias Della Naomi Stonehouse, alias Doreen Clarke): *Friend of Ronald Turpin*
Chipps, Delores Jean (alias Mrs. Roy Martin, alias Delores Eddington, alias Jean Lewis, alias Joan Martin): *Wife to Arthur Lucas*
Clifford, Ron: *Toronto police officer*
Cotnam, Harold Beatty: *Chief coroner*
Crater, Therland (alias "Checkerboard"): *Murder victim*
Crawford, Jim: *Toronto Detective Sergeant of Homicide*
Diefenbaker, John George: *Prime Minister of Canada 1957–1963*
Everitt, Cyril: *Salvation Army chaplain*
Fisher, Lizzie: *Sister of Arthur Lucas*
Fleming, Donald: *Minister of Justice 1962–1963*

Fry, Lois: *Friend of Ronald Turpin*

Gale, George Alexander: *Judge presiding over Turpin trial*

Hartt, Patrick: *Turpin appeal lawyer*

Hills, W.H.: *Don Jail physician*

King, Harold: *Basement tenant at 116 Kendal Avenue*

Klein, Arthur Otto: *Crown prosecutor in Turpin case*

Knox, Wesley Glascoe (alias "Kid" Knox): *Friend of Arthur Lucas*

Ladd, Margaret (wife of Harold King): *Basement tenant at 116 Kendal Avenue*

Lucas, Arthur (alias Jesse Miller, alias Jessie Miller, alias Luke): *Convicted killer*

MacKay, Ross: *Lawyer representing Ronald Turpin and Arthur Lucas*

Mackey, James P:. *Metropolitan Toronto Chief of Police 1958–1970*

Majury, James Frederick: *Toronto detective and sketch artist*

McCorkell, Gary Alexander: *Convicted child-killer and death row inmate*

McGuire, Frank Paul: *Post office employee and tenant at 116 Kendal Avenue*

McRuer, James Chalmers ("Hanging Jim"): *Judge presiding over Lucas trial*

Morrison, Nancy: *Law student*

Nash, Dorothy: *Wife of Frederick John Nash*

Nash, Frederick John: *Toronto police officer killed by Ronald Turpin*

Nash, Harold: *Toronto police officer, brother of Frederick John Nash*

Newman, Carolyn Ann (alias Carol Crater, alias Debra Randall, alias Jean Rochelle): *Murder victim*

Pearson, Lester Bowles: *Prime Minister of Canada 1963–1968*

Penrose, Orval William (also alias used by Ronald Turpin): *Friend of Ronald Turpin*

Porter, Dana Harris (father of Julian Porter): *Chief Justice of Ontario*

Porter, Julian: *Lawyer, assisted Walter Williston with Lucas appeal*

Posen, Stephen: *Lawyer, assisted Ross MacKay during Turpin trial*

Saunders, Gus: *Detroit narcotics trafficker*

Steiner, Marion: *Friend of Ronald Turpin*

Thomas, Gwyn "Jocko": *Toronto Star crime reporter*

Thomas, Morris Edward (alias "Red", alias "Polkadot"): *Friend of Therland Crater*

Thurston, Herbert Stanley: *Inspector in charge of Morality Squad*

Turpin, Ronald (Born Donald Arthur Neumann. Alias Orval Penrose,

alias Ronnie Pemrose, alias John Blanche, alias Mr. A.
   Bromley): *Convicted killer*

Turlinski, Zygmunt B.: *Owner of 116 Kendal Avenue*

Webster, John Davidson ("Jack"): *Detective Sergeant of Homicide*

White, Lillian (born Lillian Wysinski, spellings include Lilyann
   Wysynski. Alias: Mrs. A. Bromley): *Girlfriend to Ronald Turpin*

White, Willie: *Mysterious acquaintance of Arthur Lucas*

Williston, Walter: *Lucas appeal lawyer*

A Brief Overview of
Capital Punishment in Canada

When Ronald Turpin and Arthur Lucas plummeted to their deaths on the gallows at Toronto's Don Jail on December 11, 1962, no one could say for certain they would be the last to die by judicial hanging in Canada. Just one year earlier, in 1961, amendments had been made to the Criminal Code, and murder had been divided into capital and non-capital murder. Capital murders were planned or deliberate, used violence, or resulted in the death of a police officer or prison guard. While capital punishment would not be abolished for another fourteen years following the deaths of Turpin and Lucas, the notion of putting a man or woman to death had been losing favour with politicians for decades. This was not the case early in the country's history.

Prior to Canada's Confederation in 1867, public executions were not uncommon. In 1797, American spy David McLane was killed in one of the most gruesome ways imaginable in Quebec. After McLane was publicly hanged, he was beheaded, *then* disemboweled. In 1869, Patrick James Whelan was hanged during a blinding snowstorm before a cheering crowd of five thousand in Ottawa for the murder of politician and Father of Confederation Thomas D'Arcy McGee.

From 1867 until the hangings of Turpin and Lucas in 1962, a total of 710 people met their ends on the gallows, 697 of them men and 13 of them women. Following the British system, which employed the noose, all were hanged. No other method of execution was used in Canada from the time of Confederation, unlike the United States, which continues to use hanging, the firing squad, the electric chair, the gas chamber, and lethal injection.

The laws regarding capital punishment in Canada changed over the years, and the variety of offences that resulted in the ultimate punishment grew smaller. Previous to 1867, it was possible to be hanged in Canada for murder, rape, treason, robbery with wounding, buggery, arson, administering poison, and displaying false signals that could endanger a ship. Just two years after Confederation, hanging offences were reduced to three: murder, rape, and treason. Early in Canada's history, many found the idea of putting a man or woman to death repugnant, and efforts were made over the years to rid the country of capital punishment.

In 1914, 1915, and 1917, Member of Parliament Robert Bickerdike introduced private members' bills for the abolition of capital punishment. Despite his best efforts, all bills were soundly defeated. In the 1920s, Canadian politician, clergyman, and journalist William Irvine also introduced a bill favouring abolition, which was similarly defeated.

In the years that followed, hangings in Canada became less and less of a public spectacle. Newspaper reporters, once called upon to not only cover the story but also act as witnesses, were no longer welcome at hangings. Increasingly, executions, which were once held outdoors in a carnival-like atmosphere, were moved inside thick-walled stone jails and conducted at midnight in near-secrecy. One botched hanging was largely responsible for ending the era of public hanging in Canada.

Along with several others, Mrs. Thomasina Sarao was found guilty for the murder of her husband, Nicholas Sarao, in 1935 and sentenced to die. Hangman Arthur Ellis[1] arrived early at the women's jail in Montreal to calculate her measurements, especially her height and weight, crucial when conducting a hanging. The precise weight was needed to calculate the length of rope required. Too short a rope usually resulted in strangulation, instead of a clean break. Rather than being allowed to meet Mrs. Sarao, the executioner was given a slip of paper with her weight written on it. At seventy-one years old, the hangman had performed or assisted at hundreds of hangings in Canada, the Middle East, and England. Upset at not being permitted to weigh the woman, the hangman was forced to rely on the numbers provided.

Unknown to the hangman, Sarao had gained about forty pounds while in jail. As Frank W. Anderson wrote in *Hanging in Canada*: "Two seconds after the bolt was drawn, hangman Arthur Ellis and the tense spectators knew something disastrous had taken place. The noose flew up through the trap, slapped against the overhead beam and fell back through the hole. Then it swung back and forth in hypnotic fashion. Sarao had been decapitated."[2]

For the hangman, the bungled hanging was a disaster, and it would be his last. No one would hire him for the rest of his life, and Ellis, old, feeble, and suffering from malnutrition, died in poverty in 1938.

Although decapitations were relatively rare, careless mistakes on the gallows were not. It was not uncommon for condemned men to die a slow and agonizing death at the end of the rope, sometimes kicking and flailing in mid-air for minutes.

In 1950 and 1953, Saskatchewan Member of Parliament Ross Thatcher, like Bickerdike and Irvine before him, introduced private members' bills against capital punishment, with additional bills following in the ensuing years to limit capital punishment to treason.

By 1956, recommendations were made in Parliament to exclude juveniles from the death penalty and to provide mandatory appeals. That same year, the federal government recommended retention of capital punishment, but recommendations were made to distinguish between a condemned man or woman facing death or life imprisonment. This came into effect in 1961, when amendments were made to Canada's Criminal Code and murder was divided into capital and non-capital murder.

Capital murders, such as Ronald Turpin's murder of police officer Frederick John Nash, carried with them the sentence of death. In other cases, even if an individual was sentenced to die — as was the case with child-killer Gary Alexander McCorkell — the judge presiding over the case asked the jury if they wanted to make a recommendation for mercy. In McCorkell's case, the jury recommended mercy for the nineteen-year-old killer in the strongest possible terms. No such recommendation was made for Ronald Turpin or Arthur Lucas.

By 1967, a moratorium was placed on the use of the death penalty, effectively limiting its use to the murder of policemen and corrections officers.

In June 1976, Prime Minister Pierre Trudeau delivered an impassioned speech in the House of Commons rallying against capital punishment. He reminded members that "eleven men are being held in Canadian prisons under sentence of death for the murder of policemen or prison officials," and that if the bill to rid Canada of the death penalty were defeated, it would again place the hangman's noose around some person's neck:

> To make that quite clear: if this bill is defeated, some people will certainly hang. While members are free to vote as they wish, those who vote against the bill for whatever reason, cannot escape their personal share of responsibility for the hangings which will take place if the bill is defeated.
>
> It is in that context, Mr. Speaker, that I wish to place my remarks on the issue before us. Any discussion of capital punishment must begin with the identifications of its intended purpose, which is clearly the security of society, the protection of innocent people against the ultimate criminal violence. It is not that goal which divides us. It is a goal we all share. What divides us is the question of the appropriateness of state execution of murderers as a means of achieving that goal.[3]

Trudeau's speech would prove to be a turning point in the fight against capital punishment just one month later, when a free vote — with members free to vote as they wished, not according to their party's official position — was held in the House of Commons on July 14, 1976. By a razor-thin margin of just seven votes, Bill C-84 was passed 131 to 124, and capital punishment was removed entirely from Canada's Criminal Code. It was replaced by a mandatory life sentence without the possibility of parole for twenty-five years for all first degree murders. Capital punishment did remain in the Canadian National Defence Act for serious military offences, such as treason and mutiny.

The abolition of capital punishment was not without controversy. Some members of the House alleged the vote was not entirely free, while others, like Progressive Conservative Member of Parliament John Reynolds, said the debate should have been a national referendum, since the majority of the Canadian public at the time was still in favour of capital punishment.

In a strange twist of fate, the United States Supreme Court *reinstated* the death penalty within days of its being abolished in Canada.

While many hoped the issue of capital punishment in Canada was a closed one, the debates were far from over. Many were angered over the slim margin favouring abolition, and just a few months later, another bill was introduced for the reinstatement of capital punishment. Soon, other private members' bills followed, and by the 1980s, a push was on to have capital punishment reinstated in Canada.

Under the Conservative government of Prime Minister Brian Mulroney, members of Parliament again voted on the reinstatement of the death penalty in 1987. This time, the vote against reinstatement was 148 to 127. Public support for the noose remained strong, at 73 percent.

Even though capital punishment no longer exists in Canada, the subject of resurrecting hanging still comes up, as it did in 1991 at a Conservative national conference. Public polls are still conducted on the subject. A 1995 national poll revealed 69 percent of Canadians "moderately or strongly favoured the return of the death penalty." However, an Ipsos-Reid poll conducted six years later found support for the death penalty had gone down to 52 percent. The findings revealed numerous reasons for the decline, such as guilty parties being cleared by DNA evidence, increased publicity of the wrongly convicted, and "controversy with respect to the death penalty in the United States."[4]

On December 10, 1998, the last traces of capital punishment disappeared from Canada when it was removed from the National Defence Act, thirty-six years to the day after Ronald Turpin and Arthur Lucas were preparing themselves to die on the gallows.

Introduction

"After almost half a century, why would you want to write about the last hangings in Canada?" is a question I heard over and over again during the five years it took to research and write this book. It was, and remains, a valid question. After all, the judicial executions of Ronald Turpin and Arthur Lucas took place a long time ago, back in 1962. It was the same year Hollywood sex symbol Marilyn Monroe was found naked and dead in her bed, the victim of a depression-driven suicide (or a massive cover-up involving everyone from the Kennedy clan to organized crime, depending whose story you choose to believe). It was also the year astronaut John Glenn made history when he orbited the earth, and the year legendary rock band the Rolling Stones formed in England. In that year, two men died in Toronto's Don Jail, bringing an end to almost one hundred years of the death penalty in Canada.

My reasons for writing this book are many, ranging from an almost obsessive need to learn more about who these two men were to finding out what became of those connected to them, from the lawyer who represented them to the Salvation Army chaplain who comforted them in their final days and stood alongside them when they were hanged on December 11, 1962.

The main inspiration for this book comes from my mother, but not in the sentimental way one might expect. When I told her I wanted to write a story for *Maclean's* magazine on the fortieth anniversary of the last hangings back in 2002, I was surprised to hear her say, with unwavering certainty, "The last ones to die were Steve Suchan and Lennie Jackson, members of the Boyd Gang."

While this would not elicit much of a reaction in most families, I was stunned — crime, criminals, murder, and mayhem were standard subjects of conversation at our dinner table. To appreciate my reaction, one has to understand my mother, a woman possessing a carved-in-stone knowledge and immediate recollection of facts, trivia, dates, and events from not only her own life growing up as a child of Ukrainian immigrants in Rosa, Manitoba, but also from the sometimes sanitized panorama we call Canadian history. An obsessive reader, my mother's regular fare included the *Toronto Star*, the *Telegram* (later the *Toronto Sun*), and magazines ranging from *Life* to *National Geographic*. She never much cared for the *Globe and Mail*, and still doesn't. "Too many business stories, and not enough about people," she'd complain of Canada's national newspaper.

If my mother was wrong, surely the editor I initially approached at *Maclean's* would know precisely who the last two people executed in Canada were, along with details about the crimes they'd committed and why they were found guilty. As it turned out, the editor *also* thought members of Boyd's colourful bunch of 1950s-era bank robbers were the last to meet their deaths at the end of the rope. I soon realized that most people I spoke to — with the exception of retired police officers and true crime zealots — either thought Suchan and Jackson were the last to drop from the gallows or had no idea whatsoever.

Perhaps the greatest question remains: why should it matter? After all, capital punishment in Canada was abolished in 1976, and dead was dead, no matter which way you looked at it. As I began researching my piece for *Maclean's*, my interest in the lives of Arthur Lucas — a pimp from Detroit — and Ronald Turpin — a small-time Canadian career criminal — *did* become an obsession. Borrowed moments between working on story ideas and fact-checking other people's articles while working in the Research Department at *Maclean's* were consumed with Internet searches, reviewing hundreds of pages from various archives and old microfilmed newspapers, and, most important of all, tracking down and interviewing anyone connected in some significant way to Turpin and Lucas.

Immediately after my article came out in the December 2002 issue of the magazine, I began receiving very strange calls at work. Some were hang-ups — the really irritating kind, where people seem to listen on the other end for an eternity before hanging up — but others were messages from older-sounding gentlemen. I remember one in particular, which was along the lines of, "If only people *really* knew what happened the night of the hangings. You should find out, and tell them," followed by a *click* and the electronic drone of a disconnected telephone line. The fact that people would react thus to a history piece about two men put to death forty years earlier made me want to investigate the lives of these men further, and to sort out fact from fiction, perhaps the biggest challenge of all.

Many of the men and women I interviewed while researching this book were forthcoming about their involvement with the last hangings in Canada. Others I spoke to preferred to remain anonymous, but directed me to sources who would talk on the record. All expressed tremendous interest in seeing a book on Turpin and Lucas written before everyone connected to the trials passed away, their stories dying with them. Even the sharpest memories fade over time, and details that seemed insignificant at the time can expand to enormous proportions. It's like the archetypal "big fish" story, where the fish keeps getting bigger and bigger with every retelling of the tale. This book incorporates those stories against the backdrop of factual material from trial transcripts, notices of appeal, psychiatric evaluations, newspaper archives, crime scene photos, and original police reports. I like the "big fish" story as much as the next person, but in writing this book, I was always mindful of making sure the minnow didn't turn into a whale.

Admittedly, part of the reason for writing this book is to reintroduce to readers the fact that Canada *had* the death penalty. While this might seem a bit of an exaggeration — how can people simply "forget" that our country put more than seven hundred men and women to death between the time of Confederation in 1867 and 1962? — we remain unlike other countries that abolished the ultimate punishment, and we do very little to bring the subject back into public consciousness. In Australia, for example, Ronald Ryan remains a household name to this day. The last man executed in that country in 1967, he continues to be the subject of books, articles, documentaries, plays, university classes, and more.

Our nearest neighbour, the United States, rages on about the legality and morality of putting people to death who are mentally unstable, too young, too old, too infirm, too hampered by lack of money for adequate legal representation, or simply of the wrong race. In America, the death penalty remains a popular subject in university classrooms, books, and films like *Capote*, *The Green Mile*, *Dead Man Walking*, and *The Executioner's Song*, to name a few. Women even have their own class of Hollywood death row films, like *Monster*, *Last Dance*, and the Susan Hayward classic *I Want to Live!*

In England, the names Peter Anthony Allen and Gwynne Owen Evans, the last men to be executed in 1964, remain very well known, as do the names of Britain's executioners. In a country where capital punishment is something of a national obsession, new books and feature films appear every year about England's long-dead hangmen, like members of the Pierrepoint family, James Berry, and William Calcraft.

Some British authors, like former yeoman Geoffrey Abbott, have made solid writing careers penning books about executioners and the grisly mistakes they sometimes committed. Abbott's books feature colourful and gruesomely descriptive titles like *The Executioner Always Chops Twice: Ghastly Blunders on the Scaffold*; *Lipstick on the Noose: Martyrs, Murderesses and Madwomen*; *William Calcraft: Executioner Extra-ordinaire!*; and what is quite possibly the longest title ever for a book on the ultimate punishment, *What a Way to Go: The Guillotine, the Pendulum, the Thousand Cuts, the Spanish Donkey, and 66 Other Ways of Putting Someone to Death*. No one can ever accuse Abbott of not giving the British book-buying public what they want and telling them exactly what they're going to get.

The same acknowledgement of hangmen and capital punishment does not exist in Canada. Britain has its infamous Tyburn Tree — the site of countless public hangings — and the nine-hundred-year-old Tower of London, but many Canadians remain unaware that their local jail was where men and women were "hanged by the neck until dead." There remains remarkably few books on the subject of capital punishment in Canada. Most of the books that have appeared are either long out of print, and therefore unavailable, or based on statistics, with few details of the crimes and fewer still about the perpetrators and their victims.[5]

Arthur Lucas and Ronald Turpin continue to remain virtual unknowns, with respected sources of information — ranging from encyclopedias to official government documents — getting vital facts wrong, even details of the crimes: who they killed, why they killed them, even their names; one source states that the last to die were "Turgsin and Lumas." Even Canada's Department of Justice calls Ronald Turpin "Robert," and states the two were hanged on December 10, 1962, instead of the correct date, December 11.[6] While these errors may seem trivial to some, they made me wonder: if the Department of Justice can get details wrong about the last hangings in Canada, what else out there is incorrect? As I found out, a great deal.

Unlike other nations, which pride themselves on the fact they no longer have the death penalty, the end of judicial hangings in Canada remains widely unacknowledged and uncelebrated by both the anti- and pro–death penalty movements, often appearing only as a footnote in the literature for either cause.

As respected criminologist and historian Dr. Carolyn Strange writes:

> In sharp contrast, the last people executed in Canada are essentially forgotten men, whose cases have proved barren ground for the cultivation of public memory and political agitation. Unlike Ryan, Arthur Lucas and Ronald Turpin found no powerful or popular champions, neither at the time of their trials nor in subsequent decades. Interest in what turned out to be the last executions in Canada was nothing out of the ordinary in 1962; no politicians were out to get them, and no sympathetic observers lobbied for mercy.[7]

At the time they committed their crimes, little if any sympathy was felt for either Turpin or Lucas. A small-time hood with convictions for non-violent crimes like escaping lawful custody, auto theft, mail theft, cheque forgery, and shopbreaking, Turpin shot and killed veteran Toronto police officer Frederick John Nash during a traffic stop following a break-in he'd just committed. Lucas, a black pimp from Detroit, was sentenced to death after coming to Toronto and killing Therland Crater, another American, who was scheduled to be a key witness in an upcoming American drug trial. Crater's common-law wife, prostitute Carolyn Newman, witnessed the murder, and was brutally killed along with Crater. Both had their throats slashed from ear to ear, and Crater had four bullets pumped into his body.

As far as the Canadian public was concerned at the time, the lives of a cop killer and a black pimp who killed another black pimp and his hooker girlfriend were of little consequence. The crimes both men were convicted of were considered hideous, and rightfully so. The degree of violence used on both victims in the Lucas case was extreme, and Newman, just twenty years old at the time of her murder, was nearly decapitated.

The brutal killings of Crater and Newman were the first double homicide in the city of Toronto in at least eight years, and they took place at a time when the Canadian government's Royal Commission on Crime was investigating the criminal activities of U.S.-based gangs moving into Canada, bringing theft, drugs, prostitution, and gambling along with them. With his lengthy criminal record for armed robbery, forgery, gambling, and living off the avails of prostitution, Arthur Lucas was the right man to prosecute at the right time.

Like Lucas, Ronald Turpin was far from a sympathetic character in the eyes of the public, and of the police. Just twenty-eight years old at the time he shot and killed officer Nash on Danforth Avenue that frigid February night in 1962, Turpin had spend most of his life in and out of foster homes, the Children's Aid Society, reformatories, and jails. The product of a broken home, Turpin's early childhood saw him living with a violent, abusive, sexually promiscuous mother whose primary concern was not her child, but getting drunk as often as possible. Unwanted by his own parents, Turpin soon found the same demons that fed his mother, drinking bottle after bottle of whisky a day. A classic juvenile delinquent, Turpin turned to crime to get by, racking up several convictions by the time he killed Nash. The killing of a police officer — someone who represents the thin blue line between the average citizen and the criminal element — is repugnant, and superseded only by those who abuse and kill children.

Even today, there is little about Turpin or Lucas that tugs at the public's heartstrings or imagination when compared to other Canadian criminals, like members of the bank-robbing Boyd Gang. With his dark hair, neat moustache, and ready smile, gang leader Edwin Alonzo Boyd bore a striking resemblance to swashbuckling Hollywood screen actor Errol Flynn. The subject of countless articles, books, movies, and documentaries, the Boyd Gang continues to captivate the public, who regard Boyd himself as more of a folk hero than a criminal.

In sharp contrast, Turpin was viewed as a troublesome and scrawny little ferret of a man, a cop-killing career criminal who spent his miserable life in and out of jail and deserved what was coming to him. The public's opinion of Lucas was certainly no better. A hulking black man from Georgia's Bible Belt, Lucas went back to Detroit after killing his quarry and was quickly extradited to Canada, a move that would be unheard of today. Juries did not find the lives of either Lucas or Turpin worth saving and did not recommend mercy in either case, which could have resulted in life imprisonment instead of death.

The events leading up to the crimes committed by the two men are as important as what happened the night of the hangings. It is vital to view Turpin and Lucas as more than just a footnote in Canada's history. They were real-life flesh and blood, and through interviews and psychiatric reports, I have attempted to let the reader know where they came from and how they justified their crimes — as Turpin did with claims of self-defence — or denied committing them entirely — as was the case with Lucas.

Most of the people who witnessed the double execution, including hangman Arthur Ellis, the Don Jail physician who listened to their dying heartbeats, the coroner who pronounced them dead, and the chaplain who saw them through to the end, are long gone. The original section of the Don Jail, where Turpin and Lucas spent the last ten months of their lives, closed on December 31, 1977. An active jail for 113 years, the Don was used as a location for movies and television shows, and was threatened with demolition countless times.

The gallows where Turpin and Lucas died was long ago dismantled, following a controversial order by a correctional services minister who wanted them destroyed. Fearing that pieces of the structure would end up in the possession of souvenir hunters with a taste for the macabre, he believed he was fulfilling a promise that the gallows would never become part of a historic restoration project. Tragically, he kept his word, and it is unlikely any bits and pieces of the gallows still exist. All that remains of the place where seventy people died at the end of a rope is a grey silhouette painted on the brick wall of the execution chamber. Thankfully, the Don Jail has been designated a historic site under the Ontario Heritage Act by the City of Toronto. Its life spared once again, the jail will soon assume a new identity as office space for a hospital. I am grateful to all at Dundurn Press, especially Tony Hawke, Editorial Director (Non-Fiction), and President and Publisher Kirk Howard, for allowing me to publish my work before all traces of Turpin and Lucas are covered with drywall and a new coat of paint.

CHAPTER 1
Salvation

They had a signal with the hangman, at a certain word.
— Bram Everitt

Snow crunched beneath the wheels of the mud-splattered Ford van as it slowly crept along the road towards the bolted gates of Prospect Cemetery, rolling to a gentle stop just inches from the entrance. From inside the vehicle, the stark beam of a flashlight flicked on and off, signalling the gatekeeper of their arrival. A bundled figure appeared out of the darkness, and the massive metal doors — nearly frozen shut from the December cold — slowly creaked open. As the van passed through the gates, other cars followed, their occupants wearing thick overcoats buttoned to the top. Although no one spoke, the same thought was on everyone's mind: three o'clock in the morning was not the normal time to conduct a funeral.

The procession soon came to a halt in Section 13, a flat, nondescript area of the cemetery bordered by an old stone fence on one side and a huge storage shed on the other. The area was common ground, used mainly for burying the poor and those anonymous souls lost to their families and friends over time. The city of Toronto paid for these burials, and the cemetery assigned each plot a numbered block made of grey concrete to take into the afterlife, instead of a name. Other areas of Prospect were far more scenic, landscaped with rolling hills and vistas lined with magnificent old oak and maple trees. Since opening in Toronto's west end in 1890, the cemetery has become the final resting place to legions of First World War soldiers and respected figures like hockey goalie Vernon "Jumpin' Jackie" Forbes and Group of Seven artist J.E.H. MacDonald. In the next few minutes, the cemetery would become home to the last men executed in Canada.

Opening the van's rear doors, attendants began unloading two plain pine coffins. Although both were the same dimensions, one was noticeably heavier, which made the task of carrying it more difficult, especially over the slippery, snow-covered ground. Above them, a full moon illuminated the bluish black sky, as shadows danced and swayed from bare tree limbs and tombstones. Flashlights slashed away at the darkness to light a path over the remains of loved ones buried in the frozen earth. Winding past headstones and over flat markers, they made their way to two fresh, open graves that lay side by side like the empty eye sockets of a skull, waiting for these newest arrivals.

The two boxes were set down, and the men waited for the funeral to begin. Some turned their collars up to keep the cold wind off their necks, while others rubbed their gloved hands together to stay warm. Of all the religious ceremonies Salvation Army Chaplain Cyril Everitt had presided over, this was the most unusual. A gentle, soft-spoken man who provided words of encouragement and spiritual guidance to inmates at the Don Jail, Everitt was at home accompanying Sunday hymn groups on the organ, not conducting funerals in the middle of the night two weeks before Christmas.

Before he began the service, the chaplain surveyed the faces of the police officers, witnesses, and funeral home director Jack Jerrett. It had been a very long night for everyone, especially Everitt, who hadn't slept well for weeks leading up to the executions. In the shadows, a few cigarettes glowed on and off like crimson fireflies. A servant of God and a man of extreme patience, Everitt nevertheless sounded slightly irritated as he asked the men to put out their cigarettes, which they did, one by one. It is likely no one present at the funeral, save Everitt, was sad to see Arthur Lucas or Ronald Turpin meet their maker, especially the police officers, who'd had one of their own killed by Turpin in a gunfight ten months previously. No matter what anyone thought of the men in the simple wooden coffins, they had a great respect for Chaplain Everitt, who believed it was far more effective to help others through his actions than by being a talky Bible-thumper. Through the chaplain's daily visits to death row, Lucas and Turpin not only found God but made a friend in Everitt, perhaps the only real friend either man had ever known. Months earlier, he promised the two that if it came to this — if all the appeals to save them from the gallows failed and they were going to die — he would be with them at the end. Everitt kept his promise.

"All of you know how these men came to their deaths a few hours ago," said the chaplain, his breath condensing in the cold. "Their bodies have been separated from their souls, and we therefore commit their bodies to the grave." Flashlights illuminated the coffins as they were lowered into the black earth, and Everitt began reading from the Book of Common Prayer, the ritual for the dead. Upon reaching the line, "as it has pleased Almighty God," Everitt suddenly paused, substituted another phrase lost in time, and continued praying. He knew in the depths of his heart he couldn't bring himself to say those words, since he didn't believe the hangings of Turpin and Lucas pleased God, or himself.

As the coffins touched the bottom of their graves, Everitt couldn't get the image out of his mind how the remains of his friends were treated more like trash taken to the curb than human beings who had been alive just a few hours before. Once they had been pronounced dead, the ropes around their necks were cut, and the bodies of Turpin and Lucas were covered with white sheets and placed on metal gurneys. They were wheeled into a clammy room on the ground floor of the Don Jail, where a jury of strangers looked at the bodies and signed a sheet attesting to the fact that they were dead, as was customary following a hanging. No friends or family were there to say their final farewells, and Everitt was especially upset that neither man was embalmed before being placed into his simple casket, still wearing the jail-issued grey shirt and blue trousers in which they died. It was a picture that would trouble him for the rest of his life.

The burials were finished in five minutes. Afterwards, some of the policemen went to a fellow officer's house for drinks, while Everitt just wanted to go home to his wife and son. As the spiritual advisor and confidant to Lucas and Turpin for almost a year, he was physically and emotionally drained, unable to stop his mind from retracing the last twenty-four hours. On their final day, he sat with them talking about sports, shared their last steak dinner, sang hymns, prayed, and even had a laugh or two. Then, at one minute to midnight, the footsteps of the hanging party were heard outside their cells, and soon their lives were over.

By the time Everitt arrived at his Randolph Road home, it was almost five in the morning, and the snow-covered streets were silent, except for the steady *crunch-crunch-crunch* as he ascended the front steps. In their bedroom, his wife, Olive, was sound asleep, but their only child, nineteen-year-old Bram, was still awake. He had been answering phone calls all night from reporters desperate to talk to his father, eager to get a juicy quote or two about what really happened in those final moments at the Don Jail. Did Turpin and Lucas beg for mercy at the end? Did they spit in the hangman's eye in a last fit of defiance, or faint like the cowards they were and have to be carried to the gallows? These and other questions would have to wait, and some — like what really happened to Lucas as he plunged through the scaffold — would remain a secret Everitt would reveal only before his own death in 1986.

When the door opened, Bram knew his father would be exhausted, but he was shocked at how much he seemed to have aged, his eyes sunken, his skin a pale, lifeless grey. The chaplain's son knew his father had spent the entire day and night with the two men, praying with them in their cells in the hours leading up to their executions and standing right by their sides as the black hoods, then the nooses, were slipped over their heads and around their necks. Bram asked his father how he was, and the chaplain responded in a barely audible voice, "It was awful." Bram knew his father had become friends with the two condemned men, and assumed that it was awful because they were both dead. Everitt didn't tell his son anything else about that night at the Don Jail, except for one thing as he headed upstairs: "There was blood everywhere." Something happened, thought Bram, something went terribly wrong, but what? This was a hanging, after all — why would it be bloody? It was a secret the father would share with his son only when the time came, many years later.

The next morning, Bram awoke to find his father still asleep in bed. It would be the first, and only, time he remembered his father staying in bed all day.

CHAPTER 2

Ronald Turpin and Arthur Lucas:
Two of a Kind

His early formative years were chaotic with lack of guidance, lack of love and affection, and rife with unstable, argumentative and physically-violent parents. He was exposed to all sorts of sexual activities at a very early age and seemingly skipped the early teenage development entirely.
— Dr. W. Arthur Blair on Ronald Turpin

We are dealing with a pathological personality, a man with lowered intellect and an I.Q. of 63. He has little moral or civic concept and probably never will.
— Psychiatrist David P. Phillips on Arthur Lucas

Although they committed separate crimes, and met for the first time in the Don Jail less than a year before dying on the same scaffold, Ronald Turpin and Arthur Lucas shared much more than the dubious distinction of being the last two men hanged in Canada. Different in almost every way — from race to physical appearance, from age to country of birth — Turpin and Lucas had one thing in common: each carried into adulthood the deep scars of a childhood rampant with tales of abandonment, physical and emotional abuse, a severe lack of education, and an unhealthy exposure to sex.

In 1933, the world was in the midst of the Great Depression. In Germany, Adolf Hitler was appointed chancellor, a fateful move that led to the carnage of the Second World War. In the midst of this turbulent decade, a baby boy was born in Ottawa, Canada's capital city, on April 29. Instead of being a joyous occasion, the birth of Donald Arthur Neumann had a black mark against it from day one.

The infant's parents, who had married just two years earlier, fought bitterly and were separated at the time of Donald's birth. In an effort to further distance himself from his estranged wife, Alvin Harold Neumann stated categorically that this newest addition to the world was not his son. This did nothing to help the troubled marriage of Alvin and Edith, which continued to disintegrate until the young couple could take no more, finally divorcing in 1935. In no time at all, young Donald's mother, Edith, was back on the market. She found a man and married him less than a year after her separation. Far from wedded bliss, her marriage to Emil Turpin, like the one to Alvin just four years earlier, quickly escalated to physical and mental cruelty set against the stinging backdrop of poverty. It was not uncommon for little Donald to become trapped in an argument between Edith and Emil, and later to be disciplined by his mother with a wooden coat hanger.

In numerous psychiatric evaluations, Turpin revealed his earliest memories of childhood, almost all of them bad. With few exceptions, domestic abuse, screaming matches, and even fistfights were daily occurrences. When backed into a corner in a filthy, cramped apartment, almost any object can become a lethal weapon. One day during dinner, Edith was upset with her husband for one reason or another, so she reached over the table, grabbed a fork, and rammed it with all her strength into his arm. Another time, Emil Turpin armed himself with a knife and hacked his wife's face so severely that she was almost permanently blinded. It was a lose-lose situation from the beginning, and the young Turpin grew more and more violent, fighting with other boys in the schoolyard, or on the way home after class. "If he ended up the loser he was beaten by his mother and if he ended up the winner, he was once again beaten by his mother."[8]

Tiring of the constant bickering and looking for a way to escape, Emil left home, often for days at a time. Edith Turpin, a self-confessed party girl, went on wild alcoholic binges, pawning whatever she could to buy alcohol, even her husband's cherished hockey equipment. Strange sexual innuendos were common in the household, and one of

Edith's favourite tricks to play on her son — especially when he was being bathed — was to tease him about his penis, playfully suggesting that she should cut it off.

As her dependency on booze increased, Edith would cruise the bars and take any willing partner back to her bed. While he was still a child, Turpin remembered a man — not his father — staying over. One evening, he walked into his parents' bedroom and saw his mother and the stranger in the middle of having sex. Instead of covering herself in embarrassment or ordering him out of the room, she tossed her curly-haired little boy a dollar "and told him to go on to a show." This type of behaviour didn't come as much of a surprise to Turpin, who remembered sleeping in his parents' bed one night, sandwiched between his mother and a female friend of hers. At one point during the night, the woman grabbed the young boy by his hair, "pushing his head towards her own genitals," trying to force him to perform cunnilingus on her.

One of the most crushing incidents of his early childhood was yet to come, involving not his mother, but his stepfather. Arriving home early from school one day, Turpin was shocked to discover his stepfather in bed with someone other than his mother, "a rather large, sloppy woman." He knew his mother behaved badly, but he couldn't comprehend how Emil could act the same way. He knew his mother's moods were often stormy and unpredictable, especially during her bouts of binge drinking, which saw her temperament change in mere moments from that of a warm and caring woman to an alcohol-fueled monster who beat her son without hesitation.

In an uncharacteristic act of kindness one day, she offered her young son his choice of a kitten. Pick one, she said. Go ahead. The boy hesitated, and couldn't decide which one he wanted to keep as a pet. As if a switch flipped in her brain, his mother gathered all the mewling little cats, stuffed them into a bag, and threw them in a river in front of her son, the cries fading as the bag sank to the bottom. Years later, Turpin told a psychiatrist that seeing his mother drown a sack full of helpless animals wasn't especially cruel of her, but it certainly was "unusual."

Up to this time, the youngster's short life had been full of rage, torment, and emotional neglect, but even worse was yet to come. Unable or unwilling to take care of Donald and his half-brother, their parents placed them with relatives who looked after the boys for a time — until they got fed up and pawned them off on another one of their uncles or aunts. It was around this time that two of Turpin's aunts, aged sixteen and eighteen, "played with him, and tried to have sex with him." Turpin readily admitted he wasn't always a passive victim in these strange situations, and later told psychiatrists he felt his entire childhood was coloured by sexual incidents, although he vehemently denied ever having any homosexual experiences.

Soon, Turpin's life changed yet again. At age eleven, he was transferred from the care of family, becoming a ward of the Children's Aid Society. For the young boy, it was the ultimate betrayal by his parents, especially his mother. Although she was neglectful and often cruel to him, he still loved her and was able to forgive her for her emotional instability and physical cruelty. Any remaining attachment he had to her evaporated when she abandoned him at Children's Aid, and their relationship was permanently shattered.

Turpin spent the next few years in and out of an endless string of foster homes, each one worse than the last. In his early teens, Turpin took to calling himself Ronald instead of Donald, for reasons unknown. An early placement was on a farm about twenty miles outside Ottawa, Ontario, which was soon followed by another farm, and another after that — after a while, Turpin lost count. Sometimes he disliked the family he was staying with, sometimes they complained to the foster supervisor about his behaviour; either way, the young Turpin was often moved from one place to another, or ran away before he could be transferred, only to be caught and placed with another group of strangers. Turpin told psychiatrists that, although they could be trouble, farmers preferred youngsters from Children's Aid since they could be used as cheap labour.

As a child at one foster farmhouse, Turpin remembered walking into a barn one morning and being taken aback when he saw a boy about his age having "intercourse with a cow." Turpin kept running away whenever possible, and he stole, cheated, and did whatever was necessary to try to make it on his own, far away from the foster homes that treated cattle better than they did children. Soon, the troubled Turpin was caught and sent to the Bowmanville boys' reformatory for petty theft and playing hooky. The word used by authorities at the time to describe him was "uncultured," and although he escaped from the reformatory three times, Turpin somehow managed to learn how to be a bakery chef, and attended, but not completed, Grade 10.

Over the next few years, Turpin was in and out of reformatories and jails in Canada and the United States for a number of offences. By 1952, Turpin's string of crimes landed him in the infamous Guelph reformatory.

A place for juvenile delinquents, the reformatory was full of tales of abuse, beatings, rape, and even medical experimentation. The year Turpin arrived was the same year the facility faced a full-scale riot, one of the worst in the history of Ontario's penal system. An institution designed for rehabilitation and discipline as opposed to a full-scale prison, the reformatory was seriously damaged when at least six hundred inmates — who outnumbered guards thirty to one — set fires and threw jagged chunks of concrete, iron pipes, cans of food, and anything else they could find at guards. The most violent rioters were younger than nineteen-year-old Turpin, boys barely into their teens who had been placed in the reformatory because of their constant attempts to run away and total lack of discipline. To control the violence, guards were joined by police, who sprayed rioters with water from high-pressure fire hoses and threw tear-gas canisters into the mob. Miraculously, no one was killed, but the reformatory was left burned and broken, with walls and windows shattered from sledgehammers and crowbars nabbed by the rioters from the store room.

Armed with rifles, police and guards rounded up rioters and ordered them to walk to the centre of the compound, hands clasped behind their heads. Some were told to start cleaning the mess they'd just made, while others were ordered back inside the wrecked building. A decade later, while testifying at his own trial for the murder of Constable Frederick J. Nash, Turpin recalled the incident for the jury. Soon after the doors of the reformatory closed behind him, Turpin and others in his group were stripped naked.

"Guards were standing there with picks handles, bats and clubs," Turpin told the jury. "The place was a shambles. The windows and everything were all broke, the toilets were all smashed — there was glass all over the place — and we were told to run down a corridor, and when we got to the end of the corridor we were told to turn and continue down to what they called the 'reception' and I was the first in line."

The passageway was lined on both sides with provincial police and guards wielding billets and bats. While running down the hall, which Turpin called the "Indian gauntlet," he was struck by a superintendent armed with a pick handle. "We had to run down the centre of it, through the glass and so forth, and when we got to the end — if you did get to the end — you were thrown in a cell and left there. I was left in that cell for two days." Some never made it to the end of the corridor and were left unconscious on the cold floor beaten and bleeding.

It was while Turpin was in solitary confinement at the Guelph reformatory that he learned of his mother's death. When told by staff that she was gone forever, Turpin was "detached" about her sudden passing. As a child, he had remained close to his mother, despite her abusive behaviour. But when she allowed him to be abandoned to Children's Aid, he lost all feeling for her. In a pathetic end to her short life, his mother, Edith, died on her thirty-ninth birthday. She was celebrating when a car rammed into her as she walked across the road, a case of beer in her hands. She was drunk at the time of her death.

Over the next few years, Turpin was in and out of the Guelph reformatory and Kingston Penitentiary, a massive fortress-like structure that has been in operation since 1935 and was home to one of Canada's worst prison riots. His lengthy criminal record reveals a variety of offences, ranging from auto theft (eighteen months in jail) to mail theft in Danbury, Connecticut (two years; part served in Danbury, part at the Federal Penitentiary at Lewisburg, Pennsylvania). Back in Canada in 1959, he was convicted of three counts of escaping lawful custody and was sentenced to six months. Still, for all his convictions, none involved violence or guns. Turpin often said the reason he never carried one was because "if you live by the gun, you'll die by the gun."

When he wasn't behind bars, Turpin was living on his own, sleeping on friends' sofas, at the local YMCA, in cars and garages, or moving from one dirty motel room to another, leaving just before the bill came due. His financial situation was always dire, as he chose to steal instead of work for a living. On those rare occasions when he secured legitimate employment, he never lasted very long, choosing instead to adopt a "live for the moment" attitude. His job at a jewellery store was cut short when the owner discovered a shortage of petty cash one day, and Turpin was accused of the theft. He lasted about six months as a pressman at Runge Press Printing before the job came to an abrupt end. While working as a $23-a-week usher at the Centre Theatre, he simply got fed up one day and left, never to return. When he moved to Toronto in the early 1960s, Turpin worked as a rental agent who placed people in furnished apartments, with furniture supplied by Union Furniture and Showroom Company, and he made $250 to $400 a week on commission as a salesman for Union Furniture on Spadina Avenue.

Unfortunately for Turpin, he couldn't escape the shadow of his mother's alcoholism. Like Edith, he drank heavily and he drank often. On an especially tough day, Turpin could swig two, sometimes even three, twenty-six-ounce bottles of cheap whisky. He used to tell friends his nerves were "unsteady," and he couldn't drive a car unless he had at least three or four shots in his system before getting behind the wheel. And like his mother, Ronald Turpin avoided lasting, meaningful relationships. He could be charming, even charismatic, but he preferred to keep things with women light and superficial. Sex was okay, commitment was not. One article described him as "quiet, polite, dapper, a non-bully, a big spender and generous tipper, a little guy with big ideas." Others, however, considered him shifty and always on edge, his mind racing to get to the next big score. Maybe it was the years he spent behind bars that made Ronald Turpin more than a little paranoid, especially when it came to the subject of cops: he always felt they were hounding him, beating him down, and just waiting for him to slip up.

Like Ronald Turpin, Arthur Lucas got off to a bad start in life. He was born on December 18, 1907, in Cordele, Georgia,[9] a muggy little place that briefly served as the capital of Georgia during the final days of the American Civil War. Located about one hundred miles from the Florida state line, Cordele is the self-proclaimed watermelon capital of the world, a predominantly black city where Lucas spent his childhood suffocated by poverty. Both his parents were African-Americans from the deep South, hard-working individuals who held strong religious beliefs. The boy's mother, Sue, belonged to the Baptist church and was an attendant, while his father, Ed, was a section hand for the railroad. Both parents struggled to give Arthur and his younger brother, Henry, food and shelter, and to provide a strict but loving home guided by God and morality.

Tragically for the two boys, their poor but relatively stable home life was shattered when both parents died within a few years of one another, their father from pneumonia and their mother from typhoid fever. By the time he was eight, Arthur and his brother were living with different aunts and uncles, sometimes on large farms, other times in strange cities, hundreds of miles apart from one another. Arthur stayed with an aunt named Sue in Detroit until she, too, died when he was just twelve years old. It was around this time that he was baptized in a Georgia mill pond by a relative during a week-long revival meeting.

From there, the young boy lived with a cousin in the city. At the tender age of fourteen, he was entirely on his own, in squalid boarding houses. Years later Lucas, who had a fondness for sports, especially baseball, would tell psychiatrists one of his only good childhood memories was seeing fellow Georgia native Ty Cobb, "The Georgia Peach," at bat.

With no stability in his life, the young Lucas was only able to achieve a Grade 8 education before dropping out of school. It was at this time that he started associating with criminals, and learned how to survive in the company of con men, pimps, and whores.

"Lucas is the product of a marginal income working-class home," stated one memorandum. "At fourteen years of age he left home and since that time, for the most part, has lived off the proceeds of criminal activities. He has a long criminal record in the United States, including convictions for forgery, theft, armed robbery, vagrancy, pandering (living off the avails of prostitution), and lesser offences."[10]

Still in his teens, Lucas was in and out of prison for a multitude of crimes, and soon acquired an alias, Jesse Miller, sometimes spelling it Jessie. In May 1927, he was charged with vagrancy; by July and August of that year, he had also racked up convictions for unarmed robbery and grand larceny. The God-fearing boy who started life in Georgia as the son of loving, hard-working parents was fast becoming a career criminal with the massive build of a heavyweight boxer, but retaining the limited mental capacity of a child.

A report prepared by a psychologist for the classification board at the State Prison of Southern Michigan on Lucas was brief and cutting, even cruel. It pegged his IQ at 63, labelling him, "Intellect of moron. Deficient personality. Anti-social. Suggestible." Other prison doctors considered the young black man "feeble-minded" and "psychoneurotic." One evaluation prepared by a psychiatrist from the infamous penitentiary at Leavenworth, Kansas, was slightly more charitable, describing Lucas as being of "dull normal intelligence. Good personality. No evidence of nervous or mental disease." The Bureau of Prisons summed him up in one word: "unsalvageable."

Throughout his early life Lucas, like Ronald Turpin, held few legitimate jobs; any real skills he had were acquired in prison while doing time for one crime or another. Incarcerated in Jackson Prison, Lucas worked as a millwright for a brief time, until he was transferred to another facility for an unexplained behaviour problem. When he got out of jail, his employment at a Detroit meat market ended after just two months, when he abruptly quit. He enjoyed working as a coremaker for auto manufacturer Ford, until he was arrested on a conspiracy charge. Over time he tried many odd jobs, from working in a shoe factory to helping out in a bakery. He didn't stick to any of them.

Under leisure time activities, one prison report said Lucas "spent much time in idle loafing." He was considered sexually promiscuous, and cited for associating "with persons of sporting and questionable reputation." Since no legitimate job outside of jail held any appeal for Lucas, he soon turned his attention to the world's oldest profession: prostitution.

In the United States, Arthur Lucas's criminal activities were serious enough to garner the attention of the Federal Bureau of Investigation. In previously suppressed documents, it was revealed that the FBI maintained a lengthy file on him in the mid-1950s, when it was headed by controversial director J. Edgar Hoover. Lucas was investigated under the White Slave Traffic Act, better known as the Mann Act, named after American legislator and Illinois congressman James Robert Mann. Created in 1910, the Mann Act prohibited the interstate transportation of women and girls for "immoral purposes,"

THE LAST TO DIE

namely prostitution. Few persons were more deserving of investigation than Arthur Lucas, who was responsible — in the words of the FBI — for "transporting girls from Detroit, Michigan, to Chicago, Illinois, to prostitute."[11]

The FBI's files contain Lucas's criminal record back to 1927, when — using the alias Jesse Miller — he was first arrested in Detroit. This was soon followed by numerous other arrests for armed robbery in 1928, 1935, and 1938, forgery in 1940, and numerous other convictions for mail theft, pandering, and other offences. The file contains several pages that end with the sentence — ominously capitalized and underlined in the original — "In view of previous arrest for armed robbery, subject is considered armed and dangerous."[12]

The FBI kept Lucas under surveillance for keeping prostitutes in rented hotel rooms, a charge he was not unfamiliar with, since he had been arrested in February 1946 for pandering, with his wife held as a police witness against him. Ten years later, in March 1956, Lucas was again arrested for armed robbery. In January 1957, Assistant United States Attorney Robert E. DeMascio, Eastern District of Michigan, Detroit, declined to prosecute Lucas "due to the unavailability of competent witnesses and the reluctance of the Victims to testify."[13] Lucas was a big man with a violent temper, and he wasn't afraid to let it show when necessary, even when it came to intimidating a witness.

In the words of Detroit police, Arthur Lucas was a man "addicted to violence," and an active player in drug trafficking, numbers, and prostitution rackets. These were ruled by the American underworld, who got their way no matter what. If threats didn't work, then a beating or a broken leg or two might persuade someone to come around.

Although he denied it, documents reveal Arthur Lucas was notoriously hard on girls working for him as prostitutes and kept a hawk-like watch on them at all times. He lived common-law with some of his girls, and got at least one of them pregnant. In 1953, Lucas married Delores Jean Chipps, a woman who had a staggering eleven abortions before she bore Lucas's child. Soon after the boy's birth, Lucas packed his bags and left her for his girlfriend, Lillian Boykin, who claimed Lucas often beat her with baseball bats, chains, or his massive fists, fingers clad in heavy rings made from silver or gold.

By 1961, Lucas was fifty-four years old, overweight, with knees that were starting to give out on him. It was at this time that a friend in Detroit asked him to take a drive to Toronto to take care of some business for him. It would be the last time his taste for fine jewellery got him into trouble.

CHAPTER 3

The Cop Meets His Killer

Well, that's the way it goes. You've got to go sometime.
— Ronald Turpin to patrol sergeant Albert Williams,
after being told Constable Nash was dead

The evening of February 11, 1962, started out no different from most other nights for Toronto police officer Frederick John Nash. This particular Sunday was spent like most other Sundays at the Nash household: dinner with the family, kids doing the dishes before heading off to bed, and Fred's wife, Dorothy, silently walking upstairs to check on their latest addition, two-month-old baby Karen.

Once the house was quiet, Nash cracked open the books and got in a couple of hours of study time for two correspondence courses he was taking. Although he had been a police officer for almost eleven years, radio and television interested Nash, who wanted to keep his mind open to new things. Some men stayed on the force until the day they retired, while others switched careers after putting in a number of years with the police department. Who knew what could happen in the future?

With his thirty-second birthday just one week away, Fred Nash — better known as Jack to his family and friends — had a lot to be proud of. He was married to the same woman, the former Dorothy Allen, for twelve years, and they had four great kids together: Jackie, Patricia,

Judy, and newborn Karen. Friends, especially fellow cops, joked with him about his wife having yet another girl, but he loved them all the same and provided for his growing family.

Just two years earlier, the Nash family had purchased their home on Lakeland Drive in Thistletown, a Toronto suburb. A semi-detached house with seven rooms, it had to be large enough to accommodate the needs of the growing family now and as the children grew up into teenagers. Like most other couples, Dorothy and Fred needed to buy all the necessities that came with home ownership, like a washing machine and dryer. None of these things came cheap on a police officer's salary, and the couple still had a long way to go paying off their mortgage, about $12,000 of the $14,700 they'd paid for their home.

The upcoming weeks were going to be busy ones. Valentine's Day, a favourite of the girls, was just around the corner. The next day was Patricia's eighth birthday, and daughter Judy was turning six soon after that, on February 22. Invitations had been handed out weeks earlier for Patricia's birthday party, which would see the house filled with her friends and school chums, providing a nice diversion for the kids from the blistering cold outside. As a police officer for over a decade, lousy weather was something Nash knew all too well, and he made a point of donning a thick grey woollen sweater and long underwear before setting out on the night shift. Even driving the city streets in a patrol car, it was bloody cold on a February night in Toronto.

Dorothy was still upstairs with baby Karen when Fred called up to her at 10:30 that evening. It was getting late, and he wanted to leave a little earlier than usual. Snow was coming down, so he wanted to give himself extra time to report to the station for his shift, which started at quarter to midnight. The temperature outside was far below average for that time of year, well into the minuses, and the roads were icy. As he was closing the door, Dorothy called back to him, and he left to report for his late shift. It was one of the few times he left the house without kissing his wife goodbye.

Reporting on time for duty at No. 25 Division, Constable Nash left the police station in scout car 610, a grey 1961 Ford. Like many other nights, he was alone in the car as he patrolled Toronto's east end. Driving through the deserted streets, his headlights caught wisps of snow snaking across the black asphalt roads. It was another quiet night in the city as Nash drove, eyes scanning the road in front of him.

At 12:20 a.m., the same time Nash was patrolling the city, Ronald Turpin was using his well-worn crowbar to crack open the back door of the Red Rooster Restaurant. For Turpin, breaking in wasn't a big deal — all that was required were steady nerves as he forced the flat edge of the metal bar between the doorknob and the wooden frame, rocked it back and forth a few times, and listened to the wood as it splintered with a sharp crack into toothpick-sized pieces. Busting into a deserted restaurant in the middle of the night in the dead of February was no big deal for someone like Turpin, who had been doing it for years.

There was nothing special about breaking in to the Red Rooster. In fact, getting in the back door late at night, with no one around and darkness concealing his every move, made the job a lot easier than some of the places he'd broken into over the years in Ottawa and Toronto. For a twenty-seven-year-old, his criminal record was a long one. Turpin knew what he was doing, making mental notes about the restaurant ahead of time and checking out the easiest and fastest way to get in without getting caught. Besides, he'd eaten there before, and the food wasn't half bad.

Turpin knew the owners of the Red Rooster would still have the weekend's earnings on the premises, probably in the basement office, since it was Sunday and they couldn't deposit the money until the next business day. That's what Turpin counted on, and he was right. The haul was a good one, $632.84 in cash and coins. By his own estimate, the break-in took about an hour. Not the fastest burglary he'd committed, and not the slowest.

Smiling at his good fortune, Turpin stuffed the stolen money into a brown paper bag before he strolled out of the restaurant's basement office. On the way out, it is likely he took the time to enjoy a quick beer, as police crime scene photos later revealed an empty bottle of O'Keefe Extra Old Stock Ale sitting on a ledge near the basement office, a place an empty beer bottle wouldn't normally be found. Grabbing a free drink or two whenever possible was certainly within Turpin's nature — as it was, he went through bottles of cut-rate booze every day of his adult life. His credo was the opposite of "Don't drink and drive." Unless Turpin had a few to steel his nerves, he couldn't drive a straight line. First drink, then drive. That was the way to do it.

Once outside the scene of his latest break and enter, Turpin walked over to his rusty white truck, which was parked close to the deserted restaurant. On a cold night like this, why would you leave your vehicle far away? At that late hour, with a light snow coming down, who would notice, or care, about some truck parked near an empty restaurant?

He got inside the vehicle, turned the ignition, and started driving. Fortunately for Turpin, the Red Rooster was just a few doors down from the Andrews Motel on Kingston Road in Scarborough. The Andrews was one of the low-cost places he stayed at when he was in the city, along with the Seahorse on Lakeshore, the Selby, the Isabella, and the Metropole Hotel. Most of them were nondescript dumps where the service was lousy and the beds were lumpy, but they respected your anonymity. "Don't ask, don't tell" was the unofficial motto at the front desk, when you'd see middle-aged men check in for a couple of hours with some woman or another, the wedding ring noticeably absent from his left hand. They were also perfect hideouts for small-time hoods like Turpin, who made a point of keeping a low profile.

Still, these places weren't running a charity, and they let Turpin know it. He owed the Andrews Motel $166 in unpaid bills, and kept dodging the owners, hiding behind corners or running up the fire escape to another floor whenever he saw them. Although he was a lifelong criminal, Turpin was also a scrawny little guy and didn't like getting into confrontations with anyone, especially someone a lot bigger than himself. When he did leave his room, it was only to duck out for a few hours to meet friends for drinks downtown, or to take his dog Shep for a late-night pee in the motel parking lot. Turpin had had the German shepherd since it was a puppy, and he loved his dog, feeling more attached to the canine than he did to most people.

There was another reason Turpin didn't like to venture outside much those days, and that was the cops. In the past few months, his anxieties about being caught and beaten by the police had bordered on paranoia. Only Turpin knew if his fears were genuine. He was wanted for questioning in the murder of small-time hood Lorne Gibson the year before. It was a known fact in Toronto's underworld that Gibson got out of hand one day with one of Turpin's closest female friends, a woman named Della Burns, and left her beaten and bloodied. Soon after bashing Burns to a pulp, Gibson was found shot to death in a local laneway, brains leaking out of the three bullet holes neatly placed in the back of his head, his murder unsolved.[14] It was believed at the time that Gibson was killed not because somebody wanted to keep him quiet but because someone wanted to even the score. Toronto police also wanted to talk to Turpin about a shooting that took place during a party at Della's downtown apartment the previous October. According to guests, someone burst in and a gun went off. Fortunately, the only victim struck by a bullet that night was Della's lampshade.

Once his friends told him the police were coming by their apartments asking questions and looking for him, Turpin left Toronto, sneaking back to the city occasionally. He'd spend one night, maybe two, on a buddy's couch before hightailing it back out of the city. The police had been contacting his associates over the past few months, either by phone or just dropping in unannounced, to ask if they had seen or heard from Turpin. The frequent surprise visits from police didn't make him any less fearful, and if he knew his mug shots and his alias, John Blanche, had been posted on half a dozen Metropolitan Toronto Police "Today's Most Wanted Persons" bulletins in the past few months, he'd have been downright terrified.

The mug shots of Ronald Turpin — one revealing his right profile, the other full-face — are not terribly flattering. In the side view, his receding chin is evident, while the portrait shows him wide-eyed, head slightly cocked to one side, collar turned up on his tweed overcoat in a tough-guy persona that comes across more as a John Dillinger wannabe than anything else. His hair is also a dead giveaway: dark brown curly locks falling over his forehead, making him look more like a tough teenager than a hardened, streetwise criminal. Still, appearances are deceiving, and Turpin was wanted for Shoot with Intent. The other three men on the sheet, which was plastered all over bulletin boards in police stations across Toronto, were wanted for armed robbery, theft and possession, and escaping from a penitentiary. A lightweight, Turpin was under six feet tall. He may have been the second smallest and least sinister-looking of the wanted men, but he would soon prove he was no less dangerous than the rest of them.

When it came to Turpin's looks and the ladies, it was an entirely different story. Although he was often described as "ferret-like" by men, women found Turpin friendly and outgoing, even charismatic as he looked at them with his big blue eyes. Girlfriends were never in short supply, and he liked to keep things light and easy when it came to relationships, instead of long, complicated, and committed. Sex was rarely a problem. He fathered at least three children that he knew of, including a boy when he was about nineteen, a girl when he was twenty-four, and another child not long before that had died at just two months of age while in probationary adoption. Even though he wasn't active in the lives of any of his children, he bragged incessantly to whoever would listen about how proud he was to be a father.

Turpin's steady supply of female friends included Lois Fry (a tall, sassy redhead who liked wearing cropped faux fur jackets, black pumps, and short skirts that showed off her long, shapely legs) and Della Burns — women with lengthy criminal records that included convictions for forgery, narcotics, vagrancy, theft, and prostitution — but the one he was closest to was Lillian White; in fact, the truck he drove the night of the break-in was a gift of sorts from White. A tiny, pretty, wide-eyed brunette, White — whose real last name was Wysynski — was Turpin's on-again off-again girlfriend.

It was at White's apartment that Turpin often stayed, and the two travelled together out of town across the border to Buffalo. Just over a week before Turpin broke into the Red Rooster, White spent $50 on a deposit for a gift for Turpin, a 1954 Pontiac model sedan delivery truck she purchased from a place called Car-Ville Motors on St. Clair Avenue West. Her heart was in the right place, but even $50 was too much money for the vehicle.

The rusting truck was in appalling shape, and it was amazing it even worked at all. It looked like it had been whitewashed by a gang of imbeciles, and both the passenger and the driver's side doors had lettering scrawled on them — the names of former owners — which was smeared over with black paint, as if someone had crossed items off a grocery list. The name and address of one man, Ivan Smith, could still be seen through the lousy paint job. Below the rapidly disintegrating body of the vehicle, three out of four hubcaps were missing, and the whitewall tires were nearly bald.

The worst thing about the truck was the right front headlight. Barely clinging to the rest of the vehicle by thin strips of black electrical tape, it resembled an eyeball that had been knocked out of its socket and hurriedly set back in almost the right place. Astonishingly, both of the vehicle's headlights actually worked. It was a truck that would nab the attention of anyone seeing it as Turpin drove along Danforth Avenue that night, the grayish purple sky dusting the city with a fine white layer of snow. Although it was a major thoroughfare for the city of Toronto, Danforth Avenue was almost deserted that time of night — it was far too late and much too cold for most decent folk to be outside. Ronald Turpin wasn't like most people.

As the truck chugged along, stolen cash and coins from the restaurant break-in rattled and chattered in the brown paper bag underneath his seat. Turpin must have been happy. Over $600 was a great haul — more than enough cash to get the hell out of Toronto for a good long time, and still have some left over.

However, the bag of stolen money wasn't the only thing tucked under the driver's seat. Next to the paper sack was a gun, a 7.65-mm Beretta semi-automatic pistol loaded with .32-calibre ammo. For a couple of months, Turpin's girlfriend Lillian White had kept the thing hidden in the laundry room of her downtown apartment on Isabella Street. It had been under one of the washing machines since the previous October, and she wasn't thrilled about having a handgun around; in fact, it made her nervous as hell, and she wanted it gone. Since she was moving out of the apartment, White told Turpin to get rid of it, once and for all. She didn't tell him when she slipped the gun into the truck, only mentioning it to him later. Turpin said he was leaving town, no place in particular, just heading "up north" somewhere. The deep, dark forests of Northern Ontario would be the perfect place to dump a weapon for good or bury it in a box someplace he could remember, just in case he felt the need to get it back. Since none of his earlier crimes involved weapons, it is likely Turpin would have gotten rid of the Beretta permanently.

It was just after 2:00 a.m. when Turpin's dilapidated truck rumbled west along Danforth Avenue, passing Constable Nash in his scout car. For many years, it was not known if the police officer first noticed the unsafe condition of the vehicle and its wobbly headlight, or if he recognized Turpin's face. The officer began driving behind Turpin's Pontiac, flashing his headlights on and off, signalling him to pull over. As Turpin slowed to a stop near the intersection of Danforth and Dawes Road, Nash pulled his police car along the left side of the truck, stopped, and walked over to the beaten-up vehicle, leaving his scout car parked on the streetcar tracks.

With his Radar-Lite in hand — a powerful six-volt flashlight — Nash shone the beam inside the front of the truck, and saw Turpin was alone. A gentle snow swept through the bitterly cold night as Turpin rolled down the window. The light hit Turpin in the face, nearly blinding him. "Let's see some identification," said the officer. "Of course," replied Turpin, who handed over an operator's licence. The only problem was, the licence wasn't in Turpin's name but was stolen from Orval Penrose, an old friend of his. To Turpin's surprise, the police officer didn't say a thing about the robbery he'd just committed at the Red Rooster. Turpin's momentary relief turned to apprehension when Nash asked him to get out of the vehicle, and as he complied, the burly constable reached over and pulled the keys out of the ignition.

Turpin remembered some details of what was to follow, while other parts were a blur. According to his later testimony in court, Nash asked him for another piece of identification, then began looking under the driver's side seat of the truck, where he found not the brown paper bag of money but the loaded Beretta semi-automatic pistol.

"Your name isn't Penrose," said Nash, looking up at Turpin.

Carrying Turpin's pistol and the flashlight in his left hand, and his own black Webley .38-calibre revolver in his right, Nash ordered Turpin to walk to the back of the truck. The size difference between the two men was enormous. At 6' 1" and 230 pounds, Nash had the build of a former athlete: fit, but starting to pack on the pounds around the belly, like many men with a job, a house, and a family to support. Although he wasn't active in sports, Nash prided himself on keeping in shape by "pounding the beat." Turpin was another matter, at just 5' 9" and 160 pounds. Nash had a solid seventy pounds over the slight, younger man.

What happened next between the two would become a key part of Ronald Turpin's defence strategy during his fifteen-day trial some three and a half months later. According to Turpin, Nash shoved him onto the back fender of the police car face first. Startled, Turpin turned around to face Nash.

"What the fuck are you doing?" demanded Turpin, and he raised his arms as Nash brought the butt of his police revolver down to strike him.[15]

In a blinding white flash, a gun went off, and a bullet tore through Turpin's left arm. Stunned, he grabbed his injured arm. Staggering back from the car, Turpin claimed the gun then went off right in his face. "There was a flash of flame come out of the gun," he later testified in court. "It was that long [indicating]. It got me right dead in the face. I didn't know if I was dead; I didn't know where I was."[16] Turpin knew he had been shot, but the blast of light from the gun stunned him. In court, he would later testify he couldn't remember what happened next, if he'd grabbed the gun or tried to run.

In a matter of seconds, both Turpin's semi-automatic Beretta and Nash's police revolver went off. Nash fired six shots in total, three of them hitting Turpin, one in each forearm and one slicing open his left cheek. Nash's wounds were much more serious, with bullets striking him in the left thigh and in the chest.

Before the shooting started, Leonard Boreham, a seasoned driver for the Oakridge Taxi Company, was parked in his cab next to the south curb of Danforth Avenue. Sitting behind the wheel, Boreham was taking a break that night, sipping coffee and reading the *Globe and Mail* when he looked up and saw Nash and Turpin on the road about fifty feet away. The two men were struggling, and the cabbie saw Nash let go and drop to the pavement. He said this was quickly followed by gun blasts and flashes as three or four shots were fired.

Without looking back, Boreham hit the gas and made a quick U-turn. He called the dispatcher on the two-way radio, gave his dispatcher number, and bellowed, "This is an emergency. An officer has been shot to death at the corner of Danforth and Dawes. Call No. 10

station right away."[17] He then raced to the station, about half a mile from the scene of the shooting.

Even though it was after two o'clock in the morning, the taxi driver wasn't the only one around to hear the gunfight. Others living above stores and businesses in the area, like John Ough, looked out their windows after hearing the shots. A partner in the Hallowell Funeral Home, Ough lived in an apartment above the home and was getting ready for bed when he heard about three loud bangs, followed by two more. To his ears, it sounded like a car backfiring. A few seconds later, a streetcar from the Toronto Transit Commission rolled onto the scene. Driver John Wrycraft had no passengers at that late hour, and he was approaching Dawes Road when he saw the police car blocking the tracks. When he stopped, he saw the wounded police officer struggling to get to his feet, and he got out to help him. The next thing he knew, Turpin was standing in front of him, his gun pointed at him. In a quiet voice, he said, "Get into the car our I'll shoot you." Sensibly, Wrycraft stepped back inside his streetcar.

Leaving the TTC driver behind, Turpin raced back to his truck and got in. It is not known if he recovered his ignition key, but he was unable to get the truck going. In a panic, he got behind the wheel of Nash's cruiser. For several desperate moments, Turpin tried to get the vehicle to work, and the sound of gears grinding and mashing carried through the night. The car didn't move an inch, and Turpin was still frantically trying to get the police car going when officer John McDonnell arrived at the scene. He saw Nash face down on the ground, and could tell from his uniform that he was a police officer. When he looked over at Nash's car, he saw Turpin trying to get it going, and knew from his appearance that he wasn't an officer. Revolver in hand, McDonnell immediately ran over to the police car and placed Turpin under arrest.

When McDonnell ordered Turpin out of the police car and told him to put his hands up in the air, his reply was, "I can't, I've been shot in both arms." He then told Turpin to lean against the scout car on his elbows. "I give up," said Turpin. "I haven't got the gun. The gun is in the car. Look after the officer."

As McDonnell asked the streetcar driver to call an ambulance on the car radio, funeral home owner John Ough came by with his ambulance. Both Nash and Turpin were driven to East General Hospital, Nash by ambulance, Turpin by police car. On the way to the hospital, several officers heard Nash say, "He shot me first." Nash was in agony, and was losing massive amounts of blood from his wounds.

By the time the ambulance reached the hospital's emergency room, Nash was going into shock. His face was cold and white, and his pulse was so faint it could no longer be felt at his wrists or ankles, only at his neck. Struggling to breathe, his lips turning blue, he tried to get off the stretcher and had to be held down by two other police officers while doctors and nurses fought to save his life. Knowing he wasn't going to make it, he grabbed the arm of one young officer and pleaded, "My girls, take care of my girls." Doctors quickly put the officer on oxygen and administered blood transfusions as he moaned, "Put me under, put me under." Although the doctors and nurses did everything they could, Nash died at 3:05 a.m.

Back at the Nash household Dorothy and the girls were awakened by someone knocking at the door. The couple had rarely talked about the dangers of Fred's job, but Dorothy instinctively knew it was the worst possible situation when she heard the word *shot*. Friends and relatives came over to look after the four girls while Dorothy raced to East General Hospital. By the time she arrived, her husband was gone. Somebody had to tell Fred's parents their son was dead and identify his body, a responsibility that fell to Dorothy and her brother-in-law, Harold Nash, Fred's younger brother, also a Toronto police officer.

While a team of doctors in one room of East General Hospital were struggling to save Nash's life, doctors in another emergency room were attending to Turpin's bullet wounds. "They hurt like hell," complained the gunman. Once Nash was dead, the same doctor who tried to save the police officer then went to work on the man who took his life. Although Turpin moaned and groaned to anyone who would listen, his injuries were superficial and were treated with anaesthetic before being sutured. Soon, Turpin would learn that being shot that night was the least of his problems.

It was Turpin's odd attitude more than the bullet holes and cuts in his arms and cheek that surprised hospital staff and police officers guarding him in the emergency room. When nurse Jenny Zolopa saw him the night of the shooting, Turpin was sitting in a chair near the window, his wounded arms hanging by his sides. To Zolopa he appeared pale but still coherent. When she asked him his name, a routine question, one of the officers on guard turned to her and stated, "Turpin." The gunman then turned to look at Zolopa, laughing, "Lots of luck, lady." Confused by Turpin's comment, Zolopa shook her head slightly, declining to say anything about it.

Moments later, as she was preparing a syringe for Turpin, it made a slight popping sound when she separated the parts. "I'll have some of that champagne!" said Turpin, chuckling at his own joke. The nurse found nothing funny about Turpin, or his bizarre remarks. Considering he had just been in a gunfight, and the police officer he shot was lying dead in the next emergency room, Turpin struck Zolopa as being nonchalant about everything.

"He had the air of a braggart, and was quite unconcerned," she later testified. "He didn't appear to be at all worried about what he had done. I do not think that he knew that the officer was dead. Turpin appeared to be sober. I have seen a lot of people under the influence of alcohol and he certainly didn't appear to have been drinking."[18] He later seemed genuinely surprised when told Nash was dead, callously remarking, "We've all got to go sometime."

As the Nash family dealt with the shock of Frederick Nash's murder, Toronto newspapers were scrambling to get as many details as possible about the early morning shooting. Nash became the first member of the Metro Police Department to be slain in the line of duty since the department was established in January 1957 with the city's amalgamation, and the media was all over the story, trying to get hard facts whenever possible and reporting what they heard other times, even if it wasn't confirmed by the police. Murder was big news, but the murder of a police officer and father of four was even bigger news.

The front cover of the February 12, 1962, issue of the *Telegram* blazed the headline: "Dying, He Fires 3 Bullets Into Gunman, Officer Shot Dead on Street." It was a headline that would come back to haunt Turpin at his trial. Newspaper photos included one of a police officer wheeling the wounded Turpin down a hospital hallway on a gurney, opposite an older family photo of Nash with his wife and three of his four daughters (two-month-old Karen wasn't born when the photo was taken). Inside, the *Telegram* and the *Toronto Star* published large black and white images of Mrs. Nash holding her girls, taken just a few hours after the shooting, the children smiling slightly for the camera, not quite comprehending the reason why their picture was being taken.

In a rush to print, newspapers were not hesitant about stating the "facts" of the case as it suited them, sometimes drawing a conclusion about what happened that night on the Danforth before the police fully investigated the crime scene, gathered evidence, and interviewed witnesses. The *Telegram* described the shooting for their readers:

> One bullet knocked Const. Frederick John Nash, 32, to the pavement. Then his attacker stood over him and pumped three more shots at him. One missed. Mortally wounded, Nash pulled his service revolver and fired until it was empty. Three bullets hit his assailant in both arms and the neck. Moments later as Nash lay on the road he gasped four words to Const. Robert Butler — He shot me first. Ronald Turpin, 27, a man of many addresses, is in fair condition in East General Hospital. He is charged with capital murder.[19]

To the outraged citizens of Toronto, it really didn't matter how many bullets were fired, who stood where during the gunfight, or if Turpin was shot in the face instead of the neck. These were all slight, inconsequential details compared to the fact that a Toronto police officer — a man who represented the thin blue line between hard-working citizens and the criminal element — was shot and killed on duty, leaving his wife a widow and his four little girls without a father. And it was all because of Ronald Turpin.

"There is no doubt that Nash died a hero's death," Toronto Chief of Police James Mackey told the press. "He was dying himself as he shot this man. We always preach to our men in training that you shoot only in self-defence. That's why the other man got the shots in first."[20]

At the scene of the shooting on Danforth Avenue, police were busy sealing off the area, taking flash photos, and collecting evidence, the sky above them dark and frozen. The snow had slowed down to a few flakes here and there, coating the roads with a thin layer of treacherous black ice. Uniformed policemen were already there when seasoned homicide detectives and partners Jim Crawford and Irvine Alexander arrived at the scene. For both detectives, that long, sleepless night would be just the beginning of a process of extensive investigation and courtroom testimony that would reach its conclusion many months later. Crawford, who had been asleep at home that night, was called in on active duty and told to head to the scene, something he had done hundreds of times over the years.

"It was an extremely cold night," remembers Crawford, "so cold that the ink in my pen that I used to make notes with closed, and I had to revert to a lead pencil at one stage to continue with my notes." Braving the biting cold, both Crawford and Alexander stayed at the scene for several hours, taking down details that would later be used at trial. Once they were finished, the two drove to East General Hospital to interview Turpin, arriving at precisely 4:30 a.m. They had interviewed many murder suspects before, but weren't quite prepared for Ronald Turpin. Crawford, like nurse Zolopa earlier that night, found the cop killer's attitude to be less than caring and devoid of regret over what he had done.

"He was very nonchalant, no remorse whatsoever," says Crawford. "A careless attitude, an attitude that much displayed his violent past. He was a character who thought that the taking of a police officer's life was an everyday occurrence, and made a comment to the effect that 'Everybody's gotta go sometime,' with just a shrug of the shoulders. That was his response when told that Constable Fred Nash had passed away."

Once a typewriter was brought into the room, Crawford began typing a caution form, which Alexander proceeded to read to Turpin. Caution forms were standard police procedure, and reading them to suspects was something the detectives had done many times before. What made this time unusual was the suspect was being charged with murdering a police officer.

"I wish to caution you that you are arrested on a charge of murder, that you are not obliged to say anything unless you wish to do so, but whatever you say will be taken down in writing and may be given in evidence," read Alexander. When asked if he wished to sign the form, Turpin whined that he couldn't, because of the injuries to his arms.

As part of their investigation, Crawford and Alexander had the difficult task of being present at officer Nash's autopsy, which was held at East General Hospital on the morning of February 12. It was standard procedure for a homicide officer to attend the autopsy of a victim or killer so he could describe details to a jury at a later date, and so he could take possession of evidence, which could include tissue, blood, or bullets. Crawford had attended many autopsies to this point, but Nash's was the first of a fellow police officer, which troubled him and Detective Alexander more than it normally would.

Dr. Stewart Penny, the head pathologist at East General, began the autopsy on Nash at 10:50 a.m. The officer was weighed and measured, and notes were taken on his physical condition and injuries to his body were described in detail. Two .32-calibre bullets recovered from the police officer's body were handed to Crawford; a third had been found earlier on a stretcher and was kept as evidence. Two blood samples from Nash were then given to Alexander. These items, and the autopsy report, would later be used at Turpin's trial. Dr. Penny concluded Nash had been struck several times, and the official cause of death was listed as shock and hemorrhage due to lacerations of his lung and left chest wall.

"It was a morbid situation as far as I was concerned, because I knew Nash," said Crawford. "I knew his brother, I knew the family, and it was the murder of a brother police officer."

No one, however, was more affected by Fred's murder than his wife and children, who were left not only without a father and husband, but with no source of income. The death of Constable Nash also raised a number of pointed questions. Why was Nash alone in the patrol car at the time of his shooting? Should a pension from the City of Toronto — virtually unheard of at that time — be paid to Nash's widow and her daughters, and if so, how much, and for how long? Would a jury recommend mercy at Turpin's trial and send him to prison for the rest of life or let him die on the gallows? These and other questions would have to wait until after Nash's funeral.

Turpin was still in hospital under twenty-four-hour police guard on Thursday, February 15, the day Frederick John Nash was laid to rest. The day before, the *Telegram* ran a photo of Patricia blowing out candles on her eighth birthday cake, along with her sister Judy. The girls' grandparents felt the children should observe the birthday, to distract them from the grief of their father's death.

Snow and drizzle slicked the streets as hundreds of mourners, family, friends, neighbours, and total strangers went to Saint Michael and All Angels Church on St. Clair Avenue in the city's west end to pay their final respects to the slain constable and his family. More than 2,000 people stood outside the church in the cold and sleet that day, while another 650 packed the inside of the church. Seated in the front pews were Chief of Police James Mackey, Police Commission Chairman Charles O. Bick, Lieutenant-Governor Keiller MacKay, Toronto Mayor Nathan Phillips, and Metro Chairman William Allen. Wearing a red coat, black hat, and black dress, Mrs. Nash sat next to her eldest daughter, eleven-year-old Jackie. Of the four girls, Jackie was the only one present at the funeral of her father — it was decided the other girls were too young to attend the service.

All listed attentively as Reverend James M.N. Jackson spoke. Reverend Jackson had been Fred's Scoutmaster when he was a child, prepared him for confirmation, and married him and Dorothy twelve years earlier; he now stood over the purple-draped mahogany casket at his funeral. Jackson made no specific mention of the gun battle that killed Nash; instead, he departed from the usual Anglican tradition of giving no address and paid a powerful tribute to Nash, his voice resonating off the church walls:

> It is not generally our custom to speak at funerals. We feel the funeral service speaks for itself, but today we want to make an exception. When leaving the church you will notice in the west hall a very remarkable stained glass window, which shows Christ dying on the cross, and rising beside him, St. Michael the Archangel. On the other side, Satan is being cast into the pit. The rampant evil which crucified the Son of God is still

rampant in our cities today and the pain which we feel is no less. It is hard to be close to the bitter cross and know its bitter sweetness. But when a man lay down his life for his friends, the love of God rises up ... well done; good and faithful servant.[21]

The church then broke into song, with police officers and detectives leading the singing of "God, That Madest Earth and Heaven." The service over, mourners left the church. Outside, mother and daughter stood in the cold and sleet, little Jackie holding a single red carnation in her hand. It came from a bunch of flowers sent to her family from her schoolmates at Beaumonde Heights Public School. While the youngest daughter, two-month-old Karen, was at home with a babysitter, her sisters — eight-year-old Pat and six-year-old Judy — stood outside the church on the edges of the crowd clutching flowers. One of their cousins had brought them from their nearby grandmother's house, and they waved to their mother as the funeral cortège for their father passed by.

An eighty-two-man police honour guard, led by Mackey, preceded the hearse carrying the body of Constable Nash. Five policemen on horseback were in front, and following them was a contingent of four hundred officers from all over the province, including the Ontario Provincial Police and the Royal Canadian Mounted Police. Drummers, their instruments shrouded in black, slowly marched along in the sombre procession. After two blocks, police entered cars and proceeded to Sanctuary Park Cemetery. At the cemetery, the guard of honour — made up of Mackey, deputy chiefs, and out-of-town chiefs — fanned out to give Dorothy Nash and the immediate family the privacy they desperately needed. The murder of a police officer was always big news, and droves of photographers stood outside the church and along St. Clair Avenue as the hearse went by, snapping away at family and friends with tears trickling down their faces.

At the cemetery, uniformed officers from police departments all over Ontario volunteered to take part in the ceremony. Under a green canvas canopy, Mrs. Nash and her brother-in-law, Harold, received hugs and words of condolence from hundreds of mourners. Nash's parents were at the funeral, as were Dorothy's mother and father and Nash's eighty-six-year-old grandfather.

One of the greatest reminders of the family's loss that day was seen in messages placed among the flowers. On top of the casket were red roses and white mums, along with a nosegay that read simply "Daddy — in Loving memory," with the names of the four young daughters of the slain officer. Another arrangement of white chrysanthemums and pink rosebuds was marked "Husband." Nearby, a bunch of yellow daisies had just "Brother."

When the funeral was over and everyone left , Dorothy Nash went home, where they had a reception for her late husband. At least one hundred friends and family were in and out of the house paying their respects, while a police officer named John Kryskow volunteered to drive out-of-town guests back and forth to the bus station, or wherever they needed to go. The same officer who had emptied Nash's locker at the police station, Kryskow brought the slain officer's personal effects, including his wallet and cigarettes, to Dorothy. Her daughters had met the police officer before, when he occasionally acted as crossing guard at their public school. He was a nice man, they said, and although Dorothy didn't know it at the time, Kryskow would soon become a significant part of her life. In the meantime, she had to face the challenges of raising four young daughters by herself — daughters who had had a father before he met Ronald Turpin.

CHAPTER 4

Things That Go Bump
in the Morning

*I didn't take too good a look at him right at that time. I just saw all this blood
and I said, "Well, let us get out of here and close the door and call the police."*
— Frank McGuire

Like many fall mornings in Toronto, it was wet and chilly on Friday, November 17, 1961. A light drizzle slicked the city streets, and a few scarlet and orange leaves still clung to near-naked branches here and there, blazing bright reminders that winter was only a few weeks away. Located a short distance west of the city's downtown core, the Annex was one of the nicest neighbourhoods to go for an autumn stroll. With its tree-lined streets and magnificent, century-old houses, the area provided a gorgeous feast for the eyes but remained a working-class section of town. Found between the prestigious upper-class houses and luxury apartments of Avenue Road and the more rustic semi-detached homes on Bathurst Street, the Annex was home to everything from the prestigious University of Toronto to world-famous Honest Ed's, a venerable bargain house that sold everything from suitcases to sandals at reasonable prices.

It was on this otherwise unremarkable, pleasant fall morning that a man and a woman were butchered in what would for many years remain one of the city's most shocking double homicides.

Just after 6:30 a.m., a telephone operator for Bell Canada received a nightmarish call, one she would never forget. On the other end of the receiver, she heard fumbling sounds, like someone had dropped the telephone and was frantically struggling to get at it without success. Seconds later, a series of loud, piercing screams came, which sounded like the cries of a baby in distress. It became apparent these were not the terror-filled screeches of a child after the Bell operator plugged in the call to the police operator and kept the line open. More gruesome screams were heard, mixed with the sounds of a struggle and a woman's voice pleading something that sounded like, "Oh, my throat!" or "Not my throat!" The operators were helpless as they listened to the unknown female's final, horrified moments of life.

The call was quickly traced to phone number Walnut 5-9478, whose address was in the heart of the Annex at 116 Kendal Avenue. Police were notified, and they immediately sent a squad car. It is a well-known fact that in an emergency, every second counts, and police sped to what would tragically be the wrong address. Unlike New York and other major American cities, Toronto didn't have a lot of numbered streets. Many roads, avenues, and streets were named after famous people, which resulted in some street names sounding an awful lot like other street names. Instead of going to 116 Kendal Avenue in Toronto — a house just south of Dupont Street — police were dispatched to 116 Kendale Drive in Scarborough, a full half-hour's drive away from the scene of the crime.

A large, three-storey semi-detached building, the Kendal Avenue house was divided into four apartments, and one of the tenants — a postal worker named Frank McGuire — got there before the police. As he returned home from the night shift around 7:00 a.m., McGuire put his key in the lock and was about to open the door when he noticed something peculiar. The light was on in the downstairs hallway, which was odd for that time of day. Peering through the glass panel, but without opening the door, McGuire saw the lower part of a man's body lying in the hallway. Sensing something was terribly wrong, McGuire went to the landlord's house two doors down at 112 Kendal and caught him in the middle of shaving. By sensibly not entering the house, McGuire allowed the crime scene to be preserved intact. As he later told police, "I didn't go in because I've seen enough on television to know not to disturb anything."[22]

Polish-born Zygmunt Turlinski, the owner and landlord, had bought the rooming house only a year and a half previously with his wife, Maria. Each floor was rented, and there was never a shortage of prospective tenants. The basement was occupied by a couple, Harold King and his wife, who went by her maiden name, Margaret Ladd. Postal employee McGuire rented most of the ground floor. Another couple, the Craters, lived on the second floor and also used the large front room on the main floor. The third-storey apartment had recently become vacant, having previously been rented by a young woman named Joan Meadows.

The Craters hadn't lived at the house very long, just since mid-September, when Turlinski and his wife placed a sign in the window of their own house advertising a room for rent at 116 Kendal. Soon after the sign went up, a black couple calling themselves Mr. and Mrs. Crater knocked at the door, said they were interested, and put down a $5 deposit. The first week's rent for the Craters was $32. To Turlinski, the Craters seemed nice enough, and they paid by cheque or sometimes gave him cash. They always handed over the rent on time, something the Polish immigrant and his family appreciated.

When Turlinski and McGuire hurried back to the house, they saw a little square card with the name "Jean Rochelle" printed on it tucked above the doorbell. It had been there for weeks already, put up around the same time the Craters moved into the house. McGuire peered through the glass in the outside door; the legs were still there in the hallway. Unlocking the door, they went inside, where they saw something they would never forget behind the second inside door.

Lying face up on the hardwood floor was the still-warm body of Therland Crater, eyes wide open, staring lifelessly at the ceiling. He was dressed only in white boxer shorts, as if he had come downstairs to open the door for someone and been slaughtered on the spot. A lone house shoe was just out of reach of the enormous pool of blackish red blood that was forming around his upper body and slowly seeping into the floor. Crater's right arm was raised above his head, his left arm down by his side, a position that suggested he'd defensively tried to ward off his attacker. A coroner would later determine Crater bled to death after having his throat slashed, leaving his left internal jugular vein and left common carotid artery severed. Whoever wanted to kill Crater was a professional; to make sure the job was done right and he was truly dead, four bullets were pumped into his body before his throat was cut. "They were taking no chances of his staying alive,"[23] deputy chief of police George Elliott told the *Toronto Star* following the murders.

Without touching Crater's body to see if he might still be alive, the two men decided to phone the police. Turlinski wanted to use the house phone, but McGuire said it was better to leave it alone and to call the police from Turlinski's house. They waited on Turlinski's porch until the officers arrived a few minutes later, then went back to the murder house, where the police told them to stay in McGuire's apartment while they investigated. The questioned remained: if Therland Crater was dead, where was his wife? Police investigating the scene soon had their answer.

Upstairs in the bedroom, officers discovered the body of Carolyn Ann Newman, also known by her working name, Jean Rochelle. Police quickly determined that Crater and Newman were living common-law. He was her pimp, she was his prostitute, and the main floor room of the house was where she turned her tricks. Newman's lifeless corpse was found sprawled on a double bed, on her back. Illuminated by the glow of a single bedside lamp, police saw what seemed at first glance like a woman getting up to go to work in the morning. All she wore was a short, salmon pink nightie and no underwear. Newman's naked legs were slung over the bed, touching the floor, while her upper body was on the mattress. A telephone was on the floor near her legs, while the receiver was tucked underneath her right knee. It soon became obvious this was the same woman whose screams had been heard by telephone operators earlier.

A police report made at the time recorded the bloody tableau exactly as officers found it: "The deceased Newman was found lying on her back on the bed in the second floor bedroom located in the north-west corner of the house. She was wearing night attire and her throat had also been horribly cut."[24]

Like Crater, Newman's throat was slashed from ear to ear. Her major blood vessels were severed, and she bled to death. Unlike Crater,

Newman had not been shot. Whoever killed her probably thought bullets were unnecessary: the wounds to her neck were so deep she was almost decapitated. A police officer checked her pulse, and found nothing. She was warm the touch, almost the temperature of the living. The injuries to her neck and Crater's were similar and brutally effective, leading police to believe Crater was the intended target and Newman was a witness, someone tragically trapped in the wrong place at the wrong time.

Sheets were piled on her upper body, leaving Newman's naked legs, neck, head, and shoulders exposed. The crime scene was sealed, and homicide detectives John Bassett and John "Jack" Webster arrived and immediately took charge of the investigation, along with members of the Criminal Identification Bureau, who took photos and checked for fingerprints.

"It was easily determined from normal observation that her throat had also been horribly cut and that she was dead," wrote Webster in his synopsis of the case. Searching the second floor of the house, police found it to be "quite clean and orderly." A partially eaten birthday cake sat on the kitchen table — Crater had turned forty-four less than a week earlier — and an empty whisky bottle sat on the living room floor, along with a woman's purse, its contents strewn all over. On the second-hand dresser, police discovered a marijuana cigarette; a further search uncovered heroin and empty capsules in the house. The scene painted a picture of the killer or killers searching for something — but what? For the past few years, Toronto had been in the midst of theft, prostitution, and drug-related crimes involving Americans coming to the city to set up drug dens and whorehouses. Canadian police suspected whoever committed the brutal murders might have come from south of the border.

On the bed just inches from Newman's right leg, police found a men's yellow gold ring. Badly bloodstained, it was set with what looked like eight diamonds. String was wrapped around the base of the ring, probably to make it smaller. The ring, along with dozens of other pieces of evidence, would become crucial elements for police in creating a sequence of events leading up to the double homicides. In an impressive display of police teamwork, homicide detectives, narcotics officers, and members of the morality squad from Toronto and Detroit — along with the Royal Canadian Mounted Police and the Federal Bureau of Investigation — were able to piece together who Crater and Newman were, and why they were killed.

On the unoccupied third floor of the murder house, detectives quickly set up a temporary police station and called all border points from different telephone lines, so word of the double murder spread quickly. Within hours, police created a timeline of the crime.

They believed the killer (or killers) rang the doorbell at 116 Kendal Avenue that morning sometime between 6:30 and 7:00. Crater went downstairs in his underwear to see who was there, opened the door — most likely to someone he knew — panicked, tried to run away, and was shot in the back. To make certain he was dead, the killer slashed his throat with a razor or a sharp knife. Newman, seeing what was happening, must have screamed from the top of the stairs, and the killer raced upstairs to the bedroom, probably grabbed her from behind, and slashed her throat from ear to ear. Her body, like Crater's, was still warm, suggesting they were killed within moments of each other.

Although no one actually saw the killings take place, someone heard them. The couple who lived in the basement apartment heard unfamiliar voices around 6:20 a.m., then "scuffling and wrestling" and someone saying, "You don't have to hold me like that; let me go." This was followed by noises that sounded like a car backfiring, a heavy thud, female screams, running footsteps, and finally silence until the police arrived.

Working with officers from Toronto's morality squad, police determined Crater and Newman initially came to Toronto from Detroit, Michigan, in August. They first took up residence at another Annex area house before moving to 116 Kendal Avenue in September. Crater was unemployed, passing the time taking a course in locksmithing, while Newman was working as a hooker under the alias Jean Rochelle. At just 5' 3" tall and 120 pounds, Newman was attractive, and anything but shy about advertising her line of work. Operating out of numerous downtown hotels like the Waverley, the King Edward, and the Barclay, she let men buy her drinks at the bar, slipping business cards with her name, address, and phone number to prospective clients. The name on the cards was Jean Rochelle, and the address was 116 Kendal Avenue.

Crater and Newman were criminals, and involved in much more than just prostitution. Jim Majury, a police detective at the time, remembered a rash of fur thefts in Toronto led by black gangs that went on for several years. The daytime thefts took place more frequently in the spring and fall than during the summer months. It was a bold act that saw women walking into high-end furriers, picking out an expensive piece or two, then making a dash for the front door, where men were waiting outside in cars with the engines running. Once the women were outside, the cars, and the expensive furs, disappeared. Police suspected Crater and Newman were part of the fur-stealing ring. About a week after investigating the two, Majury heard about the killings at Kendal Avenue.

Newman's death was a sad example of someone who got involved with all the wrong people at an impressionable, early age. Born in Pittsburgh, Pennsylvania, she was only twenty years old at the time of her murder. In high school, she started associating with a bad crowd, and picked up habits from other teens, which led to conflicts at home. When her family had enough of her behaviour, Newman was placed in a series of foster homes, and ran away when she didn't like the rules of the house. Soon, she gave birth to a child, and put it up for adoption.

After an arrest for shoplifting, she tried to turn her life around, completing a course in cosmetology. Although she finished her studies and passed the required state exam, Newman wasn't able to find work as a beautician after leaving school, and soon turned to prostitution. Arrested and convicted in Detroit on five occasions for prostitution and receiving, she met Therland Crater — the man who would soon become her pimp — around March of 1961. By August, the pair were residing in Toronto, living common-law as husband and wife.

Like Newman, Therland Crater picked the wrong people to associate with, and it would eventually cost him his life. Born in Little Rock, Arkansas, he was an extremely small man — just 5' 2" and 145 pounds — but gifted with an exceptionally good physique: lean, wiry, and muscular. Dropping out of high school in Grade 11, he worked as a factory labourer, got married, and had three children, Felix, Ferland, and Wilhelamina, all of them teens at the time of his murder. The daily routine of honest work, kids, and married life wasn't for him, and his wife, Mary, divorced him in 1954 on the grounds of repeated acts of extreme cruelty, non-support, and repeated imprisonment. Arrested a staggering twenty-two times and with five grand felony convictions to his name, Crater served prison terms for a variety of offences, ranging from burglary to larceny, and was on probation from the Detroit House of Correction when he was killed.

To Canadian police, it wasn't Crater's past criminal activities that interested them as much as the reasons why he came to Toronto in the first place. Through cooperation with fellow officers in the United States, they soon learned Crater was being investigated by members of the Federal Bureau of Narcotics and the Detroit Police Department in November 1960 on charges of violating the State Narcotics Law. Instead of being prosecuted, he struck a deal and became an informant, a "special employee" of the U.S. Treasury Department's Federal Narcotics Bureau. To do his job as a police snitch, Crater continued his close association with a man named Gus Saunders, a well-known Detroit drug dealer and a player in the American underworld. Like many people in the drug trade, Saunders was fearless, and not a man to be taken lightly. The Saunders case was part of a sting operation, and Therland Crater was their special informant, the man whose testimony would put an end to a major drug dealer.

After being searched to make sure he wasn't carrying any drugs, Crater was given $110 in marked bills and dropped off in front of a Detroit drugstore, where he stood around waiting while agents and officers watched from a distance. Soon he met Saunders's wife, Eloise, and the two disappeared into an alley. They were picked up in a white Dodge by Freddie Saunders, Gus and Eloise's son. The drug buy was successful, and Crater had an envelope full of heroin. Apart from narcotics agents and police officers who witnessed the operation, Therland Crater was the only witness in the case. By becoming part of the police sting, Crater made himself a marked man.

Word spread quickly in the Detroit underworld about a reward of an estimated $5,000 for anyone who would kill Crater, who was to be the key witness in the case against Saunders the following Monday. Police believed Crater also double-crossed the wrong people when he was supposed to ship thousands of dollars' worth of heroin from his Toronto hideout to Chicago. The shipment never arrived, and it was revealed that the RCMP — based on information from agents in Detroit's Federal Narcotics Bureau — warned Crater a month before his death that the U.S. underworld wanted to find him.

Toronto newspapers immediately latched onto the story, and ran front-page headlines like "Double Murder Victims Executed By Hired Killers." The day after the murders, the *Telegram* wrote, "Besides silencing a dangerous witness, police believe the garish way the killings were carried out was to serve as a warning to others who might have thoughts of 'squealing' on their friends."[25]

On November 12, just days before they were killed, Crater and Newman were arrested by Toronto morality officers on bawdy house charges. Specifically, Crater was nailed for a "keep bawdy house" charge, and Newman was held for "being a common prostitute." Both were photographed by police at the Don Jail the same day. In his mug shot, Crater stares straight ahead, the wide gap between his upper teeth visible. Having had his picture taken by police many times before, he is almost without expression. Carolyn Newman, blouse buttoned to the top, four strands of simulated pearls around her throat, smirks slightly for the camera in her profile shot. Neither knew these would be the last photos taken of them while they were still alive.

The pair made bail of $1,000, which was arranged by their counsel, Mannis Frankel, who was given Crater's car as security after he drove them home. Following their appearance in court, both were remanded to the Don Jail for a medical examination, and released around 4:00 p.m. on Thursday, the day before they were killed. Police believed Saunders and his underworld cronies did not know where Crater was hiding until he was recognized either at the Don Jail or in magistrate's court by some criminal who tipped off Saunders that Crater was in Toronto. Detroit police doubted Crater feared for his life, since he could have sat and waited in the safety of Toronto's Don Jail instead of posting bail and making himself a target out on the streets.

In his report, Detective-Sergeant Jack Webster — one of the key homicide officers on the case — wrote:

It was obvious to the investigating officers that from start to finish, the people involved in these most brutal murders were actively engaged in "the illicit drug traffic" and "prostitution." It would appear that these two illegal activities go hand in hand and are controlled by individuals so cunning and ruthless that police officers everywhere must ever be on the alert, to use every means at their disposal to stamp out their growth within their jurisdictions.[26]

It was the belief that the killer or killers came from the United States that set off alarm bells not only with the police, but with politicians and the media. Toronto, like Vancouver, Montreal, and other major Canadian cities, had its share of murders. However, this did not have the makings of a murder committed out of passion, jealousy, or rage. The killing of Crater and Newman was the first double homicide in Toronto in at least eight years, and proved to be the first gangland killing in Toronto by hired American killers. For the past few years, U.S.-based gangs had been moving into Toronto, committing thefts and peddling drugs and sex, and the city was getting fed up with it.

Newspaper editorials were quick to criticize politicians and rally the public about the need to investigate American gangsters, pimps, prostitutes, and crooks coming to Canada to commit crime; they called for the formation of a royal commission to investigate organized crime. One paper wrote of the murders as "irrefutable proof that the long arm of American gangsterism reaches right into Ontario, right into the province's capital city, right to the very fringes of Queen's Park." The editorial continued:

It's not just the murder of two Americans, by Americans, in Toronto. It's the mounting evidence — of which this murder is simply a part — that U.S. crime syndicates are getting themselves well and profitably established in Ontario; with drugs, with prostitution and with gambling. (Metro police report a growing influx of prosti-

tutes from Buffalo, Detroit and New York. Are they coming here as individuals — or being sent by a U.S. organization?)[27]

The media had a free-for-all when it came to the motive behind
the gruesome killings. Some suggested international gambling. Others
said it had to do with white slavery. Still others believed narcotics peddling was the real reason for the slaughter. While Toronto Chief of
Police James Mackey would not give a definite reason for the murders,
he said, "the killings might be linked to marijuana peddling between
U.S. and Canada or the control of Negro prostitution, in which
Detroit thugs are reported to be active here."[28]

The head of the RCMP, Clifford W. Harvison, called the influx of
American gangs into Canada "a matter of increasing concern." These
undesirable groups were in the country to take direct control over
existing criminal organizations and to expand their criminal activities
from cities like Detroit and Chicago to Toronto.

Immediately after the bodies of Crater and Newman were discovered, police fanned out looking for specific cars with U.S. license plates
and quickly rounded up fifteen individuals — mainly dope addicts,
pimps, and prostitutes — by 3:00 p.m. the day of the murders.
Detectives from homicide and morality checked out all the known
underground haunts, and charged a number of Americans for prostitution and vagrancy. In all, two hundred Toronto police were sent out to
find clues; in Detroit, police questioned dozens of persons over several
sleepless days and nights. Their tactics paid off. A 1958 two-tone
salmon and beige Buick with a Michigan licence plate kept coming up
in their investigation as the car the suspect drove to Toronto to commit the murders. And one name was mentioned over and over again
in connection with the case, a known associate of both Therland
Crater and Gus Saunders. That someone was Arthur Lucas.

Toronto police soon determined Lucas made several long-distance
phone calls to Crater and Newman's apartment the week they were in
the Don Jail on bawdy house and prostitution charges. Earlier calls
were registered between the two men, and police established Lucas
was no stranger to Toronto, having made several recent trips by car

from Detroit. The next step was to trace Lucas's recent whereabouts and track him down.

Arthur Lucas had acquired a lengthy criminal record in the United States going back to the 1920s for benign offences like vagrancy. By 1927, he was convicted of robbery and grand larceny, soon adding forgery, "picking up numbers" (better known as gambling), and armed robbery to the list. By the time of the murders of Crater and Newman in 1961, Lucas has spent many of his fifty-four years in the State Prison of Southern Michigan, Jackson Prison, and the infamous Leavenworth Penitentiary in Kansas.

Lucas was probably having a joke at the state's expense when he stated on his official employment record that he was a "painter and decorator." To others, the burly black man from Detroit was a salesman. In reality, Lucas made his living from drugs and "pandering," an antiquated term used for someone living off the avails of prostitution. Although Lucas never liked to use the word, he was a pimp, plain and simple. He would place girls in brothels, pay their bail if they got arrested, and buy them the clothes they wore when walking the streets, looking for their next client.

Over six feet tall, with massive shoulders and dark, penetrating eyes — everything about Arthur Lucas was larger than life. Although his prison weight was officially recorded at 190 pounds, anyone who ever met Lucas — "Luke" to his friends and underworld associates — would disagree. Some, including seasoned homicide officers who walked next to him, claimed he weighted well over 250 pounds, and was at least 6' 3" tall. Despite his size, Lucas would pack his body into an appropriately tailored suit, always leaving the jacket unbuttoned. He rarely wore a tie, preferring instead to put on casual striped shirts buttoned to the top of his neck. To complement his image, Lucas often wore a snappy black fedora. At other times, he'd put on one of his many grey porkpie hats, which were invariably too small for his huge head, giving him a slightly awkward, comical look. Of course, no one with any sense would ever tell Lucas he looked anything but handsome.

It was Lucas's eyes that people remembered, and feared, the most. "He had very large eyes," remembers former Toronto detective Jim Majury, "but they were dead, they had no expression."

Since Lucas wasn't prone to smiling, the gold crown covering his two centre, upper front teeth was rarely seen. He had moles above both eyebrows, and one on his forehead. His hair, black and close-cropped to his skull, did nothing to soften a stare that said, *I've seen more and done more in my life than you can ever imagine, so back off.* Physically, he wasn't athletic; Lucas was just plain big and thick and lumbering, a consequence of his size, bad knees, swollen feet, and operations for varicose veins.

"He was slow-moving, methodical," said Majury. "Everything he did was just kind of mechanical. He didn't have any emotion at all. When you got to understand what he was in fact, and what he appeared to be, it was kind of scary, to see a man like that, who was capable of what he was capable of."

Somehow, Lucas managed to look much younger than a man fast approaching his mid-fifties. His words, like his movements, were painstakingly measured, and he spoke only when absolutely necessary, like when police tracked him down in Detroit. To their astonishment, he freely admitted being in Toronto. Although an all-points bulletin issued for Lucas described him as "extremely dangerous," he offered absolutely no resistance when police found him at home.

In a statement made by Lucas at Detroit police headquarters on Saturday, November 18, 1961, he said he was in Toronto on the previous Thursday, the evening before the killings. He checked into the Waverley — a nondescript hotel just over a mile from 116 Kendal Avenue — at 4:00 p.m. An hour later, he drove to the house and saw Crater's car, a white Ford Galaxie, parked on the street. He tried the doorbell, found that nobody was home, and returned to the Waverley.

While drinking beer in the hotel's taproom, Lucas struck up a conversation with a slight black man who said his name was Willie White. White said he needed a place to stay, but didn't have the $4 necessary to get a hotel room of his own. Lucas, feeling charitable, bought his new pal a few rounds of whisky and told Willie he would get a room with twin beds for the two of them, and he could share the hotel room free of charge. The two checked into Room 311 under the names Arthur Lucas and Willie White, and Lucas paid $8 for the night. The two men had no luggage, but one of them carried a briefcase.

The two men were readily remembered by hotel staff for a number of reasons. Physically, they couldn't have been more dissimilar, very much like a black version of Stan Laurel and Oliver Hardy. Lucas was massive, and White was scrawny, thin-faced, and about 5' 6", but looked less than half Lucas's size. Lucas also did all the talking, and joked about the colour of the Canadian two-dollar bill he received in change after paying for the room with ten dollars in American money. The general manager thought Lucas was "pleasant" and the two shared a few comments about horse racing. He also remembered seeing a heavy gold ring on Lucas's hand.

To hotel staff, the little man seemed nervous as he stood silently next to Lucas. The manager couldn't even make out his face clearly under his grey fedora, and thought he might have a small moustache or goatee — it was hard to see his face clearly in the shadows. One man later described the pair in colourful terms: Lucas was a big "strong arm type like you see in a murder movie," and White was "a dapper dandy type." The *Toronto Star* newspaper would later describe White as a "sullen-faced negro."

At the time Crater and Newman were killed, police believed more than one murderer was responsible for the double execution. When police questioned forty-four-year-old Gus Saunders, he admitted to knowing Crater and Newman, and said he had been friends with Arthur Lucas for over twenty years. Further investigation revealed that Lucas turned over a reported $5,000 to Crater for a shipment of drugs. After repeated delays, Crater made the shipment, and Lucas packaged it and sent it to drug pushers.

The evidence was mounting against Lucas as police searched for Willie White, the man who could provide an alibi for Lucas. Unfortunately for Lucas, White's description didn't match any known Detroit gangster, and police in Toronto and Detroit made searches of all criminals with the surname White, with no luck. Then there was the gold ring found on the bed just six inches from the dead body of Carolyn Newman. Police tied the ring to Lucas, who had bought it the previous September from a Detroit pawnshop for around $54. Lucas established another connection to Therland Crater when he said he left the ring as a pawn to him for a loan of $15.

Other pieces of evidence soon came to light. It became known that Lucas and Gus Saunders sometimes exchanged cars, with Lucas trading his Buick for Saunders's 1962 Chevrolet. When police found Lucas's Buick, there was blood in the car's front seat, and on a handkerchief found in the vehicle. Others came forward and said Lucas also had a gun, an old .38 Ivor Johnson revolver, which had been used by his associates. The weapon happened to be the same calibre of gun Crater's killer used to pump four bullets into his body before slashing his throat.

On the Sunday after the murders, the frame from a bloodstained Ivor Johnson revolver was found on the Burlington Skyway Bridge, which happened to be one of the fastest routes between Niagara Falls and Toronto. That the gun was missing its cylinder led police to believe that it was thrown out of a moving car, but ended up hitting the guard rail and landing on a narrow concrete path on the side of the bridge instead of going over the edge. Anyone who knew the bridge would realize it crossed not water but land, and police searching the Omaha Street area underneath quickly found the gun's missing five-shot cylinder, sitting upright in a puddle of mud. They hoped to have the same luck tracking down the other murder weapon, a knife.

Using army mine detectors, twenty police from Toronto, Hamilton, and Waterdown lined up and searched the area under the bridge for the knife, with no success. Forensic experts were able to narrow down the type of weapon used to kill Crater and Newman, and believed it was a "banana" — a type of folding knife — or, more likely, a linoleum knife. With short wooden handles and blades that curved like an eagle's talon, linoleum knives were often used by prostitutes as protection against tricks gone bad. Small, easily concealable, and razor sharp, a linoleum knife was the ideal killing tool, and one Lucas would have been familiar with from his extensive dealings with hookers.

Although police quickly identified Arthur Lucas as a key suspect in the murders, getting him back to Toronto would not be so simple. When told of the capital murder charges, Lucas said he would fight extradition to Canada. One of the newspaper reporters sent to cover the story was Gwyn "Jocko" Thomas, whose breaking story on Crater was featured on the cover of the *Toronto Star* on November 19, 1961, with the headline, "Double Murder Victim 'Secret Police Agent.'" Thomas was flown to Detroit to cover the extradition hearing in federal court in Detroit, along with Toronto homicide detectives Jack

Webster and John Bassett. Word was out that the Detroit mob wanted to have Lucas killed before he could tell his story in court, and he'd have a greater chance of surviving in Canada than in the U.S.

"The Detroit police had to offer him a bodyguard, and they spirited them out of Detroit, and put them in a hotel in Windsor, because the drug mob in Detroit were very powerful," says Thomas. "They were mafia: if they wanted to get rid of you, they could get rid of you very quickly, just the same as they were trying to get rid of Therland Crater, because he was going to be evidence in a big prosecution there in Detroit. He was an informer, but he was also mixed up with Lucas in running drugs from here to there."

Although Thomas — along with the rest of the press — wasn't allowed to talk to Lucas, he remembers him vividly. "He appeared to me to be a man who was very, very ignorant of what was going on, and he had a hangdog look about him, a sad-looking face on him. And I think he realized from the very beginning that he was in really deep."

For a time, it looked as though government bureaucracy was on Lucas's side. Ordered extradited to Canada by U.S. District Judge Theodore Levin on January 12, 1962, Lucas was deemed "undesirable" by Canadian immigration officers at the Windsor border, who did not want to allow him entry into Canada. Although the warrant was signed and stamped, Toronto detectives had to call senior immigration officers in Ottawa to get clearance to bring Lucas into the country. It would be the last time Lucas would see the United States.

CHAPTER 5
The Trial of Arthur Lucas

I'd be a madman if I did what they say I did.
— Arthur Lucas

Without exhibiting their customary restraint, Toronto newspapers covered every salacious detail of the trial of *Regina vs. Lucas* when it began in Courtroom 33 of Toronto's City Hall[29] on April 30, 1962. The gruesome nature of the killings, along with the tantalizing elements of gangsterism, drugs, prostitution, gambling, and theft imported from the United States, proved irresistible and made the case front-page news from the start.

The fate of Arthur Lucas was in the hands of a young, inexperienced, but immensely gifted twenty-nine-year-old. With his movie star good looks, undeniable charisma, and taste for finely tailored suits, lawyer Ross MacKay was a larger-than-life figure who sometimes seemed more like an invention of Agatha Christie or Raymond Chandler than genuine flesh and blood. With his dark hair swept off his forehead and eyes that didn't miss a beat, MacKay was reminiscent of lantern-jawed Austrian actor Maximilian Schell, who had recently starred as a lead defence attorney in the motion picture *Judgment at Nuremberg*.

The child of divorced parents, MacKay was an only child who was raised by his mother in the Annex area of the city, not far from the house where Crater and Newman were murdered.

Graduating in the top forty out of two hundred students from Toronto's Osgoode Hall Law School, MacKay was bright and outgoing but without pretension, preferring to meet clients at one of the city's many downtown bars instead of the confines of a stuffy office. Skilled at pool and poker, MacKay was a devotee of jazz, especially bebop, and loved listening to the fast and furious uptempo music of saxophone wizard Charlie Parker and trumpeter Dizzy Gillespie.

In 1956, MacKay married his sweetheart, Joyce, and was soon attracting the attention of several prestigious Toronto law firms. He was hand-picked to article with G. Arthur Martin, a tremendous honour, since Martin was widely regarded as one of Canada's top criminal lawyers. MacKay soon earned a reputation as an expert at cross-examination, a man who could anticipate what witnesses would say next.

He was popular with the ladies and chummy with the guys; things were looking up for the young MacKay, but close friends knew his one weakness: alcohol. MacKay developed a taste for the stuff when he was still in his early teens, and he was drinking a 26-ounce bottle of rye every day when he took on Arthur Lucas as his client. It was the neophyte lawyer's first murder trial; it would not be his last.

Although MacKay was not one to back away from a challenge, nobody could dispute that the odds were already against him and his big, black, menacing-looking American client. Even though no one actually saw Arthur Lucas shoot or slash the throats of Crater or Newman — or caught a glimpse him in the house, or even on the street — the Crown's case was formidable, as was the Crown prosecutor himself.

A brusque and intimidating man, Henry Herbert Bull lived up to his surname. During the Lucas trial, he boldly presented a voluminous amount of circumstantial evidence, supported by a parade of witnesses ranging from respected police officers and forensic examiners to persons of less than honest repute. Bull was articulate and confident to the point of fearlessness, and he didn't particularly care if he offended someone in or out of court. The son of an Anglican choirmaster, Bull had already been an assistant solicitor with the provincial treasury department, an assistant Crown attorney, and a major in the Second World War. By November of 1961 — the same month Crater and Newman were murdered — Bull was made chief of thirty assistant Crown attorneys.

Unwilling to lose in any situation, Henry Bull was passionate about the law; he was the archetype of what would become known as the Type A personality, which is associated with aggressive, impatient, and competitive behaviour, as well as a greatly increased risk of hypertension and coronary heart disease. Curiously, his sensitive side came out in the form of drawing. While following even the most tedious details of day-to-day court proceedings, Bull could be seen sketching cartoons of other lawyers, defendants, witnesses, policemen, even judges, all the time absorbing spoken testimony in exacting detail. As he was fond of telling others, "I hear everything that goes on while I draw."[30]

By the time Ross MacKay met the man who would present the case against his client, Henry Bull was already in his early fifties, a seasoned lawyer with decades of courtroom experience. Compared with the Government of Ontario's abundance of legal, investigative, and financial resources, MacKay was seriously handicapped. Not only did he have inadequate time to prepare and insufficient manpower necessary for a case of this magnitude, MacKay would also be burdened by the admission of evidence that would remain controversial for decades to come.

Even before the trial began, American witnesses scheduled to appear in court told Canadian authorities they feared for their lives, a number of them requesting police protection. "Some of the witnesses are worried, and we feel these worries are justified,"[31] said an unnamed Detroit narcotics detective. One such witness was Morris Thomas, a friend to Lucas, Crater, and Saunders. Thomas occasionally ran drugs for Lucas and was himself a known heroin user. Voluntarily arrested in Detroit, Thomas was held as a material witness to the double murder. American narcotics detectives told Toronto police Thomas's life was in danger after he was threatened and had to go into hiding following Lucas's arrest.

Taking no chances of losing one of their key witnesses, police had Thomas — flanked by homicide officers and a member of the Royal Canadian Mounted Police — escorted from Detroit to Toronto. The court would hear from him and others at Lucas's preliminary hearing in late March 1962. Earlier that month, newspapers covered Lucas's return to Toronto. The *Globe and Mail* ran a stark flash photo of Lucas soon after the plane carrying him and Toronto detectives John Bassett and Jack Webster landed on Canadian soil. Above the caption "Charged in Throat Cutting" was the towering black man, centred between the two detectives, glowering at the cameraman. It remains one of the most intimidating photos of Lucas, and it did little to change public opinion of him as anything but a heartless, cold-blooded killer.

Appearing before Magistrate Thomas Elmore, Lucas's lawyer attempted to have the preliminary hearing against his client postponed. It was a case that had already "attracted notoriety" and "international ramifications," according to local newspapers, who couldn't get enough of the gory murders. Ross MacKay gave Elmore a number of reasons for a delay. He had only been brought into the case a week earlier, he said, and an ongoing Royal Commission on Crime constituted an unhealthy climate for his client's trial. Unfortunately for MacKay, Elmore said there were no merits in his objections, and flatly turned down his request for any further adjournment. The trial would go ahead on schedule, whether MacKay was ready or not.

One of the first witnesses at the preliminary hearing was Harold King, who lived in the basement of 116 Kendal Avenue along with his wife. He claimed he didn't know Crater and had only seen him once during the time he lived in the house. On November 17, the morning of the murders, King's wife woke him up and told him to listen to some noises she heard coming from upstairs. "It sounded like two or more people struggling," he testified. "I heard a male voice say: 'OK, you don't have to hold me like this.'" The voice was followed by scuffling, and what sounded to King like three shots being fired. "I heard a female voice scream, and then the pounding of footsteps on the stairs. I couldn't tell whether they were going up or down,"[32] testified King. The house then became very quiet, and only when police officers arrived at the scene did the couple suspect something was terribly wrong. They heard, but did not see, the terrifying final moments of two people being murdered just a few feet above their heads.

Many others gave testimony at the preliminary hearing that helped built a strong but circumstantial case against Lucas. Detective Bassett said he saw Lucas in Detroit following the shooting, and fingernail scrapings from the accused man tested positive for blood. Another Toronto detective, Norman Hobson, discussed the discovery of the blood-caked .38-calibre revolver on the Burlington Skyway Bridge. The first person at the murder scene, postal worker Frank McGuire, remembered peering through the outside door of the house and seeing legs through the pane, while landlord Zygmunt Turlinski said that he was upstairs in the house the night before the murders and saw Crater making a long-distance phone call. Michael Lundy, manager of the Waverley Hotel, said Lucas was pleasant and calm when he checked into the establishment with his newfound friend, the mysterious Willie White. Although police in the United States and Canada made extensive searches for White — the man who could have provided an alibi for Lucas — no trace of him was ever found.

The most damaging testimony at the preliminary hearing came from Morris Thomas, who said he had known Lucas since 1958. He remembered Lucas telling him about being in Toronto on November 12 — less than a week before the murders — and being run out of the city, along with a woman. Thomas testified Lucas called him the morning of November 17 and said the person he went to see in Toronto was not there, but his car was on the street and maybe he had been "busted" by the police. He also said that Lucas owned a .38-calibre revolver, and that he, Thomas, acted as a messenger boy for Lucas, delivering heroin for him around Detroit.

Compounding the challenges of the trial for defence attorney Ross MacKay was the judge who would preside over Lucas's fate. A legendary figure in Canadian law, James Chalmers McRuer had the nickname "Hanging Jim," a moniker that rarely, if ever, gave him any grief. While others were able to leave their day's work in the courtroom, McRuer rarely spoke about anything else, even at the family dinner table. To this day, some consider McRuer Canada's greatest law reformer, while others say he was the nastiest person they ever met. Few knew what he was really like, including his own children, who would later claim to have learned more about their father from reading a biography about him than from McRuer himself. One thing was for certain: McRuer was someone who never left anyone with feelings of indifference.

McRuer's humble origins began with his birth in the family farmhouse on August 23, 1890, to Scottish parents near Ayr, Ontario. An eager student and quick learner, McRuer attended the University of Toronto and Laval University and then graduated from Osgoode Hall before commencing his long legal career in 1913. Soon after becoming a lawyer, McRuer was made a lieutenant in the First World War. As early as 1935, he served on several royal commissions for textiles, the penal system, criminal sexual psychopaths, and insanity as a defence in capital cases. Over the years, he presided over some of the most memorable cases in Canadian legal history, such as the spy trial of Igor Gouzenko, the Evelyn Dick "torso" murder case, and the trial of Boyd Gang members Steve Suchan and Lennie Jackson, who were hanged in 1952 for the shooting death of Toronto Sergeant of Detectives Edmund Tong. By the time of the trial of Arthur Lucas, James Chalmers McRuer was a man in his early seventies and had sent many others to the gallows.

From April 30 to May 10, 1962, the trial of Arthur Lucas saw the all-white, all-male jury presented with an overwhelming amount of information from Toronto homicide detectives, morality officers, members of the Detroit narcotics bureau, ballistics experts, customs officers, and people who knew Lucas, Saunders, Crater, and Newman. A staggering 54 witnesses and 105 exhibits were introduced by the Crown, ranging from scale floor plans of the murder house to the sensational, blood-encrusted men's ring found on the bed just inches from Carolyn Newman's dead body. For the defence, lawyer Ross MacKay would call only three witnesses: Lucas's older sister, Lizzie Fisher; his girlfriend, Lillian Boykin; and Lucas himself. The pieces of evidence against Lucas were circumstantial, but combined, they proved to be utterly compelling, painting a bloody portrait of a murder for hire and of a woman who was tragically trapped in the wrong place at the wrong time.

Knowing the amount of testimony the jury was about to face — a total of 1,571 pages — Justice McRuer cautioned them the trial would be a long one. "It may last a week or it may last two weeks, and during that time you will be required to be kept apart. You will not be permitted to go home or to communicate with anyone."[33] The Sheriff's office was at the jury's disposal for getting their belongings. To keep their minds focused on matters relating to the trial only, members of the jury were cautioned not to use the phone, watch television, listen to the radio, or read newspapers.

On the first day of the trial, Crown attorney Henry Bull relentlessly summarized the precise details of the case, urging jurors not to take notes but to listen carefully to all the evidence. Although the killings of Therland Crater and his common-law wife, Carolyn Newman, were connected, the Crown made the decision to proceed only on the Crater murder charge against Lucas. This determination would soon prove to be controversial.

"The allegations in this case, of course, are allegations of fact," said Bull to the jury. "They only become fact when you say they are." The murder of Crater was accepted as a fact, said Bull, proceeding to explain how drugs tied Crater, Lucas, and Saunders to one another, and why Crater's decision to turn police informant cost him his life. He spoke about how it was common for Saunders and Lucas to trade cars, Lucas's two-tone Buick for Saunders's Chevrolet. Bull then introduced another friend of Lucas's, Morris Thomas, a man who often shared his $75-a-month Burns Avenue apartment in Detroit. It was Thomas's testimony that would ultimately cause the most damage to Lucas's defence, and it was at the Burns Avenue apartment that police later found men's shoes splattered with blood, bloody handkerchiefs, and ammunition.

After Bull had called his first witness — a Toronto police officer who made scale floor plans of 116 Kendal Avenue — the next witness, Ian MacDiarmid, took the stand. A Toronto detective with the Criminal Identification Bureau, MacDiarmid took numerous photos of the upstairs and downstairs murder scenes, then of the remains of Newman and Crater at the city morgue, before returning to the house to take more photos of bullet holes in the walls, the living room, the empty stairway leading upstairs, and the exterior of the structure. Inside, the house was dim, and MacDiarmid had to use a flash with his Crown Graphic 45 camera. The gruesome images, captured in stark black and white, remain disturbing to this day. There was no doubt the sight of Crater and Newman, drenched in their own blood, eyes open and staring and dead, would unfairly influence the jury. Ross MacKay objected to the admission of these photos and, with the jury absent, argued his point with Justice McRuer and Prosecutor Henry Bull, who was adamant about allowing the images to be seen.

"I do intend to object to the admission of those particular photographs, that is photographs of the deceased persons, in evidence," an impassioned MacKay told Justice McRuer. "In my respectful submission, they have no real probative value in this case at all, and, as such, should not be admitted into evidence by your lordship, exercising your discretion."[34] MacKay singled out one photograph in particular, an image revealing Carolyn Ann Newman on the bed, photographed only from her waist to her knees. In the picture, the dead woman's naked legs are spread apart, thighs daubed with her own blood. Just inches away from her exposed pubic area, a men's gold ring lays in plain view on the edge of an expanding blood-black area that, on closer inspection, resembles the profile of a man — or a demon.

"I do not think I am overstating it when I say that I think the photographs are gruesome, and in my respectful submission they can only tend to inflame the jury's minds," said MacKay. Bull immediately countered with the argument that it was crucial for the jury to see the crime scene photos.

"I submit that all murder is gruesome," said Bull, "and that the pictures, if dealt with in the same dispassionate way that all other evidence is dealt with in a murder trial, can no more inflame their minds than the lurid description by word, but they are a much more accurate and clear description of what occurred at the time than any words could possibly convey. They have probative value to that extent." Citing other Canadian trials that allowed the use of crime scene photos, Bull then turned his attention to photos of Crater and Newman taken at the city morgue. His argument was that these photos needed to be presented to the jury "to show the nature and the location of the wounds." Bull was unwilling to withdraw the morgue photos of Carolyn Newman.

To MacKay's dismay, Justice McRuer ruled the photos admissible on the grounds that they established certain facts about the case. "I feel quite sure that this jury will not have their minds inflamed, and that the photographs will not bring about any injustice," said McRuer. MacKay rightfully objected further about the relevancy of showing the jury crime scene photos of Carolyn Newman, since Lucas was charged only with the murder of Therland Crater. Justice McRuer still wasn't persuaded by the young defence lawyer's arguments, and allowed the images to be displayed.

MacKay watched as crime scene photos, each with detailed descriptions underneath, were passed around to the jury. Although Justice McRuer previously cautioned the jury against allowing their minds "to be in any way inflamed by the gruesome nature of the photographs," it was impossible to look at the photos and not be influenced by them to the point of tears. Among the many pictures in the stack of 8" x 10" glossies were ones of Crater lying in the hallway of 116 Kendal Avenue in a pool of his own blood and a close-up of Crater in the morgue, eyes and mouth yawning open, the enormous gash on his neck clearly visible.

To emphasize the horrific nature of the crimes, Bull opened the trial with the throat-slitting of Carolyn Newman: "Although the murder charge before the jury involves only Crater, ... the facts surrounding Miss Newman's death are important as they relate to the murder of Crater."[35] Jurors were told details of Newman's pitiful cries for help, and the desperate steps she took to try to save her life, phoning the operator for help, which arrived too late.

Bull established how the body of Crater was discovered when postal employee Frank McGuire and landlord Zygmunt Turlinski took the stand. Turlinski recalled seeing Crater the night before the murders, making a long-distance phone call to someone in Detroit. He also remembered the next time he saw Crater, lying dead in a puddle of blood in his front hallway.

Although Turlinski still owned the house at the house at the time of the trial, former tenant McGuire had long since moved to another apartment. On the morning of the murders, he recalled for the jury how, upon returning home from the night shift at the post office he put his key in the front lock and saw a pair of legs on the other side of the door. At first, he thought there had been a fight or someone had fallen down drunk — either way, he knew something was wrong. Stricken with polio at a young age, McGuire realized he couldn't get away quickly if there was trouble in the house, "and I didn't want to get mixed up in anything if there wasn't anything going on." He then walked as quickly as possible to get Turlinski, and when they returned and opened the door, they saw "a chap on the floor."

"Did you recognize who it was?" asked Bull.

"Well, I didn't take too good a look at him right at that time," replied McGuire. "I just saw all this blood and I said, 'Well, let us get out of here and close the door and call the police.'" The two men then went back to Turlinski's to call the police, and waited on the front verandah until the accident squad came a few minutes later.

The couple that lived in the basement, Harold King and Margaret Ladd, also remembered hearing the scuffle going on above them through their acoustic tile ceiling that morning. Ladd remembered waking up her husband.

"I heard someone say, 'You don't have to hold me like that; let me go,'" said Ladd. The voice sounded male, and "it had terror in it. You could tell that the man was frightened." She then heard something hit the floor, and a female scream. This was followed by the sound of feet running on stairs. "I heard light feet and then heavier feet," she told the court. When it was her turn to be cross-examined by Ross MacKay, Ladd became puzzled, then irritated, by his line of questioning. During her examination Ladd felt like MacKay was treating her more like a suspect than a witness.

MacKay:	Have you ever been in any trouble with the police?
Ladd:	No, I was not. Could I ask a question?
MacKay:	Yes.
Ladd:	What does that have to do with my testifying here today?
His Lordship:	Well, do not worry about that.
MacKay:	Why? Do you have something to hide?
Ladd:	No, I have nothing to hide, but I just don't see how it has any bearing on what is going on here today.[36]

When King took the stand, MacKay immediately asked him if he knew anyone in Detroit or if he was acquainted with Morris Thomas, drug-runner, heroin addict, and Lucas's occasional housemate. As with Ladd's testimony, it looked like MacKay was trying to shed doubt on King's strength as a witness and to suggest that somehow he and his wife were directly involved in the murders. When King denied knowing Morris Thomas, MacKay confronted him, saying he saw the two men chatting outside the court room. At that point, Justice McRuer told King he could not give evidence and again cautioned the jury not to communicate with anyone outside the courtroom unless they did so through Sheriff's officers. Beyond the danger of information leaking to the jury from the media and vice versa, there were other reasons for concern, namely the death threats made against Lucas.

"The word that was circulating in the sixties was that the high-profile drug dealers in Detroit were about to make a run at Lucas, and murder him while he was in the hands of the Toronto police," says retired homicide detective Jim Crawford, who often chaperoned Lucas back and forth from Toronto's City Hall courtroom to the Don Jail during the trial. "Needless to say, the security to and from court throughout all his days of court appearances was heavily policed with homicide officers and other senior backup officers, to thwart this threat of killers coming in from Detroit."

Well over six feet tall and about the same weight as Lucas, Crawford was handcuffed to the burly black man while escorting him to and from court, but Lucas never made any attempts to run. At the time of the trial, Crawford felt Lucas was likely going to be executed. "A homicide officer in those days was pretty much obligated to babysit the killer who was facing the hangman's noose," says Crawford, who himself was accompanied by heavily armed members of the Emergency Task Force. If Arthur Lucas was going to die, police on both sides of the border wanted to make sure it was at the end of the hangman's noose, and not because some gangsters wanted him dead before he could turn police informant and name names.

Bull's next move was to examine the telephone operators who took the frenzied call from Carolyn Newman as she was about to die. The court heard from both Elizabeth Williams and Jemima McCabe, telephone operators for Bell Canada and the Toronto Police Department respectively. Williams received the fateful call from Newman on the

day of the murder and recorded the time it came through: 6:35 a.m.
The jury listened attentively as she recounted the call.

Bull:	When you plugged in where that light was on your board, what did you hear?
Williams:	I heard a woman screaming.
Bull:	Yes, and did you hear any words?
Williams:	No, I did not.
Bull:	Did you hear any other sounds?
Williams:	Well, there was a series of really loud screams and then a few moments later there was like a fumbling sound, like as if somebody was perhaps trying to get the receiver, and kind of like baby cries.[37]

When she received no response on the other end of the phone, Williams called the police operator and kept the line open. Bell employee Robert Diamond then received an urgent request from the switchboard operator to trace an emergency call from the Walnut exchange. "There was a woman screaming on the line and that was all I heard," police operator Jemima McCabe told Henry Bull. After connecting the call to the radio line and the police dispatcher, McCabe stayed on the open line. She heard screams and scuffling in the background. Most of the words were unclear, expect for "Oh, my throat" or "Not my throat." She heard nothing after that. McCabe then received a call back from the Bell operator, who gave the wrong address, 116 Kendale Drive instead of 116 Kendal Avenue. This incorrect location was passed on to the police dispatcher. Minutes later, McCabe took a call from Turlinski and McGuire, with the right address this time. Her time-stamped card was presented in court as evidence, a graphic reminder of how a slip-up may have cost Carolyn Newman her life.

"Location 116 Kendale Drive, Woman screaming — Bell operator traced line." On the back of the card, the later time was recorded, with the revised address and the notation, "Party reporting someone murdered at 116 Kendal Avenue." To compound the tragedy, the court learned that Kendal Avenue in Toronto was in 11 Police Division, while Kendale Drive was located in Scarborough's 20 Police Division, miles away in the east end. Unfortunately, the two addresses were located beside each other on the dispatch list, which was ultimately the reason police were sent to the wrong address and lost precious minutes.

The first police officer to respond was John McMaster, who was on patrol the morning of the Annex-area murders, arriving at 116 Kendal just two minutes after receiving a radio call. The first thing he saw entering the house was Crater lying in the hallway, and since there was a slim chance Crater was alive, the police officer checked him for pulse and respiration.

"At that time I observed a large gaping wound in the left side of his neck," McMaster told the court. "The body was quite warm, I would say almost normal temperature. The blood around the body was just beginning to congeal at the edges. It was still quite liquid in the main flow, although there did not appear to be any more blood flowing from the wound."[38] Crater was definitely dead, and McMaster went upstairs with another police officer to search the house, while several other officers who arrived stayed on the ground floor.

In the upstairs bedroom, police found Carolyn Newman naked on the bed, illuminated only by the light from a small bedside lamp. McMaster saw the blood pooling around her neck and checked for a pulse. There wasn't any, and, like the body of Therland Crater, Newman's temperature was warm, almost normal. It was then that the officer saw the telephone and the gold ring on the bed. The upstairs of the house was silent, except for the sound of water running in the bathroom. Someone, possibly the killer, left the tap on in the sink.

By 8:16 that morning, Toronto homicide detectives Jack Webster and John Bassett arrived at the house, which was being guarded by a uniformed police officer. Once photos were taken of Crater, the two officers turned the body over. It was then they saw that Crater not only had his throat slashed but also had bullet holes in his back. Proceeding upstairs to view Newman's body, both detectives noticed the men's yellow gold ring on the bed near her leg. Rectangular in shape and set with eight stones that appeared to be diamonds, the ring itself wasn't particularly unusual, except for strands of string wrapped around the base.

After Newman's corpse was photographed on the bed, they gently set her on the floor. The bodies were then taken to the city morgue, where Newman was positively identified by Ronald Battersby. A Toronto morality detective, Battersby knew the young woman from her arrest for prostitution just days before she was murdered. She was using at least three different names at the time: Carolyn Crater, Carolyn Ann Newman, and Jean Rochelle, the alias printed on business cards she handed out to potential clients.

Under cross-examination by defence attorney MacKay, Battersby said he did not identify himself as a police officer when he went to the house to see Newman but posed as a prospective customer by the name of Johnny. When Newman answered the door after 2:00 a.m. on November 12 — the day of her arrest — she wore a short housecoat over baby doll pyjamas, and she led the detective to the upstairs bedroom, where she was promptly arrested.

The trial of Arthur Lucas had been underway only for a few days when Justice McRuer chastised defence attorney Ross MacKay for showing up late to court. Although it might have seemed relatively inconsequential then, it would not be the only time Lucas's lawyer was tardy during the trial. He gave no explanation to the judge, but close friends and family knew the enormous pressure he was under and suspected he was starting to exceed his bottle-a-day limit of alcohol. In court, Lucas appeared respectful to his lawyer and grateful to him for his help, calling MacKay "Mistah Ross." Sitting in his dank, cramped cell in the Don Jail between court appearances, even the condemned man with the IQ of 63 was doubting his lawyer's abilities, and later shared his opinion with a psychiatrist at the Don Jail.

"The lawyer wasn't fighting the case — he had no experience of murder cases and he drank," complained Lucas. "Well, you could smell it and not one time did he visit me in jail — only before the preliminary. Yes, that was in the jail — he came up before the meal but never did he visit me during the trial, which lasted 10 days. Well, I think he should have been telling me something and planning the defence."[39]

Others who witnessed the Lucas trial disagree, and commend MacKay for his abilities. A law student at Osgoode Hall at the time, Nancy Morrison followed the Lucas trial whenever possible, sitting in the courtroom and studying MacKay as he fought for his client's life.

"Those trials changed my life," says Morrison, today a respected judge in British Columbia. "I fell in love with the courtroom." MacKay already had a reputation as a rising star, and Morrison wanted to see him in action. "He had a presence that was absolutely undeniable. He took very few notes. He sat back, and he watched, and in my view, the best lawyers do that," she says. "He didn't have his little head down writing notes furiously — he'd write the odd note to himself. But he watched like a hawk. And when he got up to cross-examine, he did it effortlessly, conversationally — never bullied, never theatrical, quiet. Really, really talented."

What impressed Morrison the most was MacKay's innate ability to make his clients sympathetic to the jury, even Arthur Lucas, who had the face and build of a B movie tough guy. "MacKay had that innate ability that the really good lawyers have to steer your questioning of any witness, to bring out all the good parts," she says. "At the end of each trial, I knew a lot more about his clients than you would normally know. He was able to bring out bits and pieces, so at the end of the trial, this wasn't a nameless, faceless monster sitting there who just committed murder: it was somebody who had many aspects."

Homicide detective Jim Crawford, who escorted Lucas to and from court, says no one could have provided a better defence for Lucas than MacKay. "I spent many hours with Ross while he was defending Lucas, and I felt sorry for him, because he didn't have much to work with, because we didn't leave him much to work with," says Crawford. "Our function was to see this killer hang."

Although Ross MacKay might have won the respect of some people, persuading the all-white jury that Arthur Lucas wasn't a cold-blooded man who killed a friend for money was his biggest obstacle. The pathologist who performed the autopsies on Newman and Crater testified how each of them died, creating a graphic image for the jury of the couple's terrified final moments. Dr. Chester McLean autopsied Newman first and concluded that her right internal jugular vein and common carotid artery were completely severed. The deep gashes to Crater's neck were the same, but found on the left side of his throat. Unlike Newman, Crater was also shot four times. Both bled to death. Newman's throat was slashed four times, and Crater's at least twice, resulting in the heart pumping a shower of blood that would have spurted at least seven feet.

"Apart from the transposition from left to right, these were strikingly similar and effective wounds," said McLean, when asked if the wounds were alike. "In my opinion, it was not an amateurish job."

Although the weapon used to slash the throats of Crater and Newman — believed to be a folding or linoleum knife — was never found, a bloodstained gun of the same calibre used to kill Crater was discovered on the Burlington Skyway Bridge after the murders. When it was turned over to Toronto police, the grip was removed by examiners, and more blood was found underneath. When Detroit police, armed with sawed-off shotguns and .38-calibre revolvers, went to Lucas's Burns Avenue apartment, they discovered a shotgun shell and ammunition for a number of weapons, including .38-, .22-, and .25-calibre guns. The circumstantial evidence against Lucas kept mounting as the car he swapped with Gus Saunders, a 1962 Chevrolet, was seized and examined by police. Inside, they discovered a stained handkerchief, a stained shirt, a raincoat with suspected bloodstains, and fresh fingernail clippings. At the Detroit apartment belonging to Lucas's wife, Delores, police uncovered a pair of men's underwear and a small red plastic red pail containing pinkish water that looked like it was mixed with blood.

When Lucas returned to the apartment he shared with his girlfriend, Lillian Boykin, his sister, Lizzie, his friend Wesley Knox, and, occasionally, his seven-year-old son, Detroit police took no chances. Heavily armed, they were inside waiting for Lucas when he opened the door. In his typical cool as ice fashion, he showed no surprise whatsoever when he saw the cops waiting for him. "Oh, you were here, eh?" said Lucas, who was handcuffed and placed under arrest for investigation of murder. Lucas would not be the only one arrested in the days following the Kendal Avenue killings, as Detroit police quickly rounded up and questioned a number of people connected to the case: Gus and Eloise Saunders, Lester Ramsey, Tommy Peterson, Cynthia Griggs, Lillian Boykin, Jaban Massey, Wesley Knox, and Morris Thomas, whose testimony would cause the most damage to Lucas.

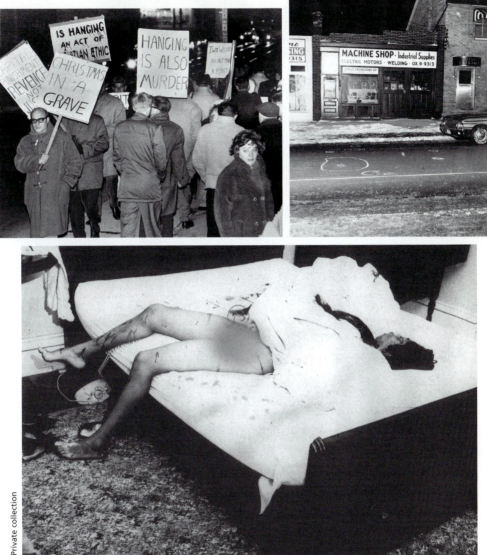

Top left: Outside the Don Jail, dozens of protestors braved the 22-degree cold to oppose the hangings. Many were university students. **Top right:** Photo taken after 3:00 a.m. on February 12, 1962, where Frederick Nash was shot by Ronald Turpin. Areas outlined in chalk included where Nash fell and where empty cartridges were found by police. Icy streetcar tracks are visible in the foreground. **Bottom:** A gruesome scene awaited Toronto police in the upstairs bedroom at 116 Kendal Avenue. Carolyn Ann Newman, just twenty years old, was on the telephone with the emergency operator when her throat was slashed. Less than six inches from her right leg lay a men's gold ring (circled).

Top: Rare photo of Ronald Turpin in one of Toronto's City Hall courtrooms in May 1962. Taken three and a half months after Constable Nash was killed, the photo shows the scar on Turpin's left cheek, the result of his gun battle with Nash. **Centre:** For years, many suspected Constable Nash pulled over Turpin's 1954 Pontiac Sedan delivery truck because of its terrible condition: the vehicle was rusted and the right front headlight was held to the body with electrical tape. **Bottom:** Photo taken March 23, 1962, from the roof of the Danforth Hotel on the southwest corner of Dawes Road and Danforth Avenue, looking east from Dawes Road.

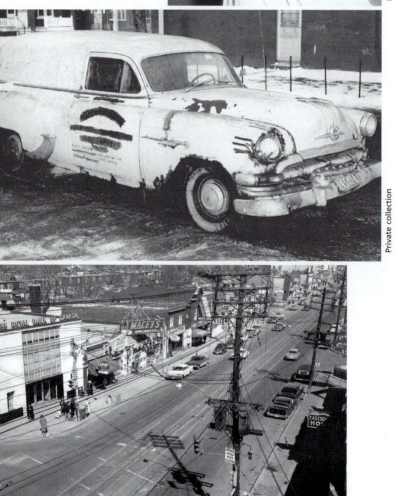

December-10-1962   4043

I. Arthur Lucas.

I am Given mrs. Lizzie Fisher promise to get the following articels.
From one. miss. Lillian Baykin. address
4403 mc cellen street. Ditroit. michigan.
one. Bar with four stoals.
Two Bed room suits
one. dinnering room. set. with 6 cheiars
one. Breakfast. set with 4 cheiars.
one. Foor madel. t.v. Riada h.i.f con-
one. Foor madel. h.i.f
one. Table madel h.i.f
one. Tape recorder. poarble.
Two. porable. t.v.
and my clothes 15 suits or more.
Four sport coats
one white leather sport coat
Two overcoats
Two tap coats.
all my points an shurts an under clothes
Five pairs of shoes
six. hats
one. cook stove.
one. Fragadair

        Signe. arthur. Lucas.

                    A

This is the segnature of said arthur Lucas.

One of the last letters written by Arthur Lucas on the eve of his execution. A man who prided himself on his snappy appearance, Lucas willed most of his clothing to his older sister.

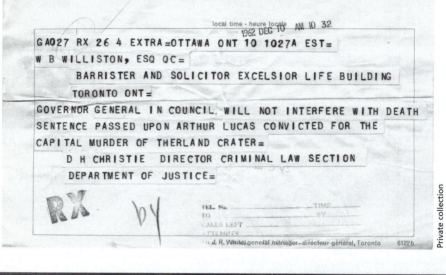

CN Telecommunications

local time · heure locale AM 10 32
1962 DEC 10

GA027 RX 26 4 EXTRA=OTTAWA ONT 10 1027A EST=

W B WILLISTON, ESQ QC=

BARRISTER AND SOLICITOR EXCELSIOR LIFE BUILDING

TORONTO ONT=

GOVERNOR GENERAL IN COUNCIL WILL NOT INTERFERE WITH DEATH

SENTENCE PASSED UPON ARTHUR LUCAS CONVICTED FOR THE

CAPITAL MURDER OF THERLAND CRATER=

D H CHRISTIE DIRECTOR CRIMINAL LAW SECTION

DEPARTMENT OF JUSTICE=

RX by

TEL. No. .... TIME ....
TO .... BY ....
CALLS LEFT ....
ATTEMPTS ....
J. R. White, general manager · directeur général, Toronto   6122b

Top: December 10, 1962, telegram sent to Lucas's appeal lawyer Walter Williston, saying that the government would not interfere with the condemned man's sentence of death.
Bottom: Echoes from a night of violence: the scene of the gunfight between Nash and Turpin. Turpin's dilapidated truck is on the far left, and Nash's squad car blocks the street-car tracks. To the far right is the Hallowell Funeral Home, which also operated a private ambulance service that drove the fatally injured officer to East General Hospital.

METRO TORONTO   3891/61 NOV 12/61

METRO TORONTO   3840/61 NOV 12/61

Top: The last known photos of Therland Crater, taken at Toronto's Don Jail on November 12, 1961, just four days before his brutal murder. **Bottom:** Carolyn Ann Newman's mug shot. Neither she nor her pimp/boyfriend Therland Crater could have known they would be dead just a few days later.

"WOW, IS THAT THE SAME OUTFIT THAT GAVE US FIVE THOUSAND DOLLARS ?"

Top: The murder of Constable Nash left his wife and four young daughters without a pension. Toronto's City Council was divided on the issue of pensions for police widows and their families, which was captured by *Toronto Star* editorial cartoonist Duncan Macpherson. **Bottom:** Don Jail death row looking south, 1952. The area was nicknamed "Hospital Nine," due to its proximity to the prison dispensary.

METROPOLITAN TORONTO POLICE

To-day's Most Wanted Persons

███████ MTP 1141/49
28 yrs. 5'5½, 153 lbs., medium build,
brown hair, blue eyes, medium complexion, scar on forehead.
        Occ. Teletype 25 Jan.18/62
        Charge: Armed Robbery

John BLANCHE: MTP 2132/57 @ Ronald
TURPIN: 27 yrs., 5'9", 160 lbs.,
medium build, blue eyes, dark brown
curly hair. Scar over right eye -
Scar right eyebrow near nose.
        Occ. 56463/61
        Charge: Shoot with Intent.

███████████ MTP 608/47
                        30 yrs,
5'11½", 165 lbs., medium build,
black hair, brown eyes, medium complexion.
        Occ. 65677/61
        Charge: Bench Warrant
        Theft and Possession

███████████████ FPS871807
26 yrs., 5'9", 170 lbs., dark complexion,
brown eyes, dark brown hair. Believed in
Toronto Area.
        Occ. Teletype71 Jan. 24/62
        Charge: Escapee Joyceville
                Penitentiary.

One of the rare surviving copies of the Metropolitan Toronto Police "To-day's Most Wanted Persons" posters. Ronald Turpin is second from the top. He appeared on the poster six times, from October 26, 1961, to January 25, 1962. Along with Turpin's age, height, and weight, the poster gives his alias: John Blanche.

Bram Everitt

Karen E. Davis

The Salvation Army Archives, Toronto

Top: Cyril Everitt conducting a Sunday sermon for inmates inside the chapel at the Don Jail, while his wife, Olive, accompanies him on the piano. Circa 1960. **Bottom left:** Toronto police officer Frederick Nash in uniform, in 1955 or 1956. Nash joined the Toronto Police Department on August 13, 1951, and served in Number One Division, Number Nine Division, the Morality Division, and, at the time of his death, Number 25 Division. **Bottom right:** Cyril Everitt.

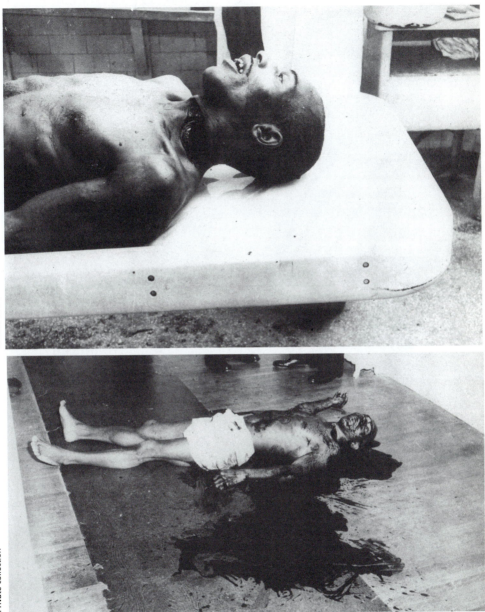

Top: Murder most foul: Therland Crater at Toronto's Lombard Street morgue, the brutal slashes to the left side of his neck clearly visible. **Bottom:** Therland Crater, dead in the downstairs hallway at 116 Kendal Avenue.

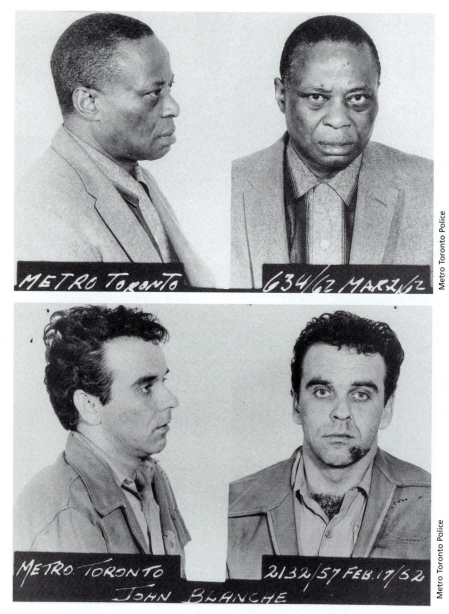

Top: Arthur Lucas's mug shot. Bottom: Ronald Turpin's mug shot.

Metro Toronto Police

```
D  INION OF CANADA      )      AN INQUISITION, indented for Our Sovereign
                        )    Lady, the Queen, at the COMMON GAOL OF THE
PROVINCE OF ONTARIO     )    COUNTY OF YORK, situate in the City of Toronto,
                        )    in the County of York, on the Eleventh day
COUNTY OF YORK          )    of December, 1962,                      and in
                        )    the Eleventh Year of the reign of Our Sovereign
TO WIT:                 )    Lady the Queen, before  Dr. Harold Cotnam

                             of the City of Toronto, one of the Coroners of
                             our said Lady the Queen, for the said County, on
                             view of the body of:

                        ARTHUR LUCAS

                                     then and there lying dead upon the
oath of
```

good and lawful men of the said County, duly chosen and who being then
and there duly sworn and charged to enquire for our said Lady the Queen
when, where, how and by what means the said Arthur Lucas came to his
death, do upon their oaths, say that Arthur Lucas came to his death at
the Common Gaol of the County of York, on the Eleventh day of
December, 1962,
from being hanged by the neck until he was dead, in accordance with
the sentence under which he lay in the said Gaol.

IN WITNESS WHEREOF as well as the said Coroner, as the Jurors aforesaid
have hereunto set and subscribed their hands and seals on the day and
year first above written.

BBCotnam M.d. Coroner   *Toronto.*

William J. Allan   208 Riverdale Ave

Maxwell R. Hackett 1095 Dundas St W.

Fred L. Gourlie 439 Kingswood Rd

George E. Atkinson 380 Shuter St.

Roland F. Blackburn 3 Claudius Gate Scarboro.

A little-known piece of paperwork: immediately following the hangings of Turpin and Lucas, a coroner's jury composed of public citizens was required to view the bodies of both men and determine how they died. Attendance at the coroner's jury was mandatory, although one member of Turpin's jury eluded his responsibility by showing up drunk.

Department of Health

File No. ....

Date .... May 24, 1962.

MEMORANDUM TO

Dr. C. H. Lewis,
Assistant Director,
Hospitals Division,
Mental Health Branch,
Department of Health,
Parliament Buildings, Toronto, Ont.

FROM

Doctor J. Grodsinski,

Ontario Hospital.

RE Psychiatric examination of Ronald
Turpin born April 23, 1932, charged
with capital murder, at present at Don Jail,
Toronto.

On May 23, 1932, I examined this man. The family history discloses a morbid, alcoholic mother, sexually promiscuous. She did not take care of him and he has been placed in a number of foster homes. Many of them he resented and was not able to adjust. School claimed to be interrupted, but he supposedly achieved Grade 8 education. The work record is obviously very unsatisfactory, interrupted by numerous committments to Reformatories and Penitentiaries. The medical history is non-contributory and there are no signs of abnormal sexual adjustments as well.

During this examination the patient co-operated freely. He was able to present a coherent, fairly well organised story. His vocabulary and organization of thought were adequate considering his educational and social background. He was showing rather poor ability for abstract thinking and his stock of information and interests outside of his activities was very limited. I judge his intelligence being somewhere in the dull normal range, therefore, not being of sufficient deficiency of intellect to prevent him to understand the nature and the consequences of his actions. There is a definite paranoidal attitude in his thinking, especially about the Police in regard to him. During this examination I could not detect sufficient disorganization in his thought processes or emotions which would imply legal and psychiatric irresponsibility for his actions. He is suffering from a personality disorder but in my mind not amounting to a degree of certifiable insanity.

Dr. Psych,
Medical Specialist
Group 2.

JG/rd

Top group: On June 9, 1962, Arthur Lucas was asked to make four pencil drawings — a girl, a house, a tree, and a person — for psychiatrist J.P.S. Cathcart. In the doctor's opinion, Lucas was not the criminal mastermind he had been portrayed as. When the drawings were later shown to the head of psychology at Ottawa General Hospital, he believed Lucas was mentally defective: "He's just a tool but there is lots of anxiety showing in this item — he's scared of something." **Bottom:** One of several psychiatric evaluations made of Ronald Turpin by Dr. Joseph Grodsinski. It discusses his "morbid" and "sexually promiscuous" alcoholic mother, and Turpin's "definite paranoidal attitude" about the police. Although Grodsinski concluded Turpin suffered from a personality disorder, he did not believe he was certifiably insane.

CERTIFICATE OF SURGEON

I, WILLIAM HENRY HILLS, M. D., SURGEON OF THE COMMON GAOL OF THE COUNTY OF YORK, IN THE PROVINCE OF ONTARIO, HEREBY CERTIFY THAT I THIS DAY EXAMINED THE BODY OF ARTHUR LUCAS, ON WHOM JUDGMENT OF DEATH WAS THIS DAY EXECUTED IN THE SAID PRISON, AND THAT UPON SUCH EXAMINATION I FOUND THE SAID ARTHUR LUCAS WAS DEAD.

Prison Surgeon

Dated this Eleventh day of)
December, A. D., 1962,   )
at the City of Toronto.   )

Top: The signed certificate from Don Jail doctor William Henry Hills following Lucas's death (a similar certificate was issued for Turpin). Nowhere in the certificate or the coroner's jury report does it state Lucas was nearly beheaded. **Centre:** Snake bracket close-up, inside Don Jail. **Bottom:** Rotunda view from main floor, inside Don Jail.

Top: Former gallows area, inside Don Jail. **Bottom:** Don Jail, exterior centre block south view.

Top: Don Jail, front doorway, with the bearded face of Father Time glowering on all who enter. **Bottom:** Present-day photo inside the Don Jail cell range, second floor north door leading to the gallows.

Top: One of several ballistics photos presented during Turpin's trial on May 25, 1962. **Bottom:** Police photograph of the exterior of 116 Kendal Avenue, photographed on Friday, November 17, 1961. When tenant Frank McGuire and landlord Zygmunt Turlinski opened the door, a horror awaited them.

Both a drug dealer and a drug addict, Thomas told the jury how he travelled to Chicago with Therland Crater to buy heroin, which they would then cut into smaller amounts called Bonita and repackage in pink gelatin capsules or pieces of aluminum foil. The heroin then made its way to drug pushers, who sold it on the street to addicts. Thomas gave the money he received to Lucas, who paid him between $20 and $35 for his efforts. In a dramatic attempt to discredit Thomas's testimony as being that of a drug-addled witness, defence attorney MacKay asked Thomas to roll up his sleeves and reveal his needle-scarred arms to the jury. The sight of the Crown witness's pockmarked flesh would have been a powerful image, but Justice McRuer refused to allow it.

In the eyes of the jury, Thomas's testimony was quickly eroding any remaining credibility Lucas had left. He continued to tell the court about his friend's weapons, including two .38-calibre handguns. Thomas freely discussed the gold ring that was found on the bloodied sheets next to Carolyn Crater's naked body. It had thread wound around it, and he remembered seeing it on Lucas's hand. "It was too large for his little finger," Thomas told the court, "so he put — I think it was adhesive tape he put on it." Thomas's words confirmed what another witness, Wesley Knox, had told the jury earlier. A friend of Lucas's for twenty years, Knox remembered buying the ring from some guy on the street for fifty bucks, then pawning it. When he told Lucas about the ring Lucas seemed interested and went downtown to buy it for himself.

Midway through the trial, the court heard testimony from a number of scientific experts. One positively identified fingerprints on the Chevrolet that Lucas drove to Toronto as being his. Another testified he examined Lucas's hands, which were "freshly manicured," and found blood under one of his fingernails, along with blood on the nail clippings found in the Chevrolet, on the car's door handle, and on two handkerchiefs. Some of the samples were Type B, the same blood group as Crater and Newman; other samples proved positive for human blood, but the expert couldn't categorically state the exact blood type. Ballistics experts tested the .38-calibre Ivor Johnson revolver found on the Burlington Skyway Bridge and stated three of the bullets removed from Crater's body were that same make as unfired bullets he also tested.

With the jury absent, MacKay objected to a report prepared by a Detroit firearms expert, "on the ground that it is in the nature of a confession or at least a very damaging admission." As was the case with the crime scene photos of Carolyn Newman, Justice McRuer allowed the report to be admitted into evidence. A detective sergeant with the Detroit police, Earl Leedle examined Lucas's hands for residual gun powder the morning after the murders. A small amount of faint green powder was found on the webbing between the forefinger and the thumb on his right hand, embedded into his skin. It was partially burned and tested positive for nitrate, a component of gunpowder. The Ivor Johnson revolver, said Leedle, was notorious for its cheap quality and would have cost as little as $7 or $8 when it was originally made. This particular .38, he said, was very old and out of timing, meaning the cylinder didn't line up with the barrel, resulting in a lot of blowback. When fired, gasses and debris — like unburned powder — would shoot out the cylinder and get on the hand of whoever pulled the trigger.

It was at this point in the trial that an impassioned MacKay told Justice McRuer, with the jury absent, the Crown's case was completely circumstantial:

MacKay: May it please your lordship, before the jury returns in my respectful submission, on the Crown's case, they have made out no case to answer. In my respectful submission each piece of evidence that they have adduced during some eight days of this trial is completely circumstantial, and, by cross-examination of certain witnesses and indeed on the Crown's own evidence, each piece of the puzzle that the Crown is attempting to put together is completely consistent with innocence.

His lordship: The difficulty is, Mr. MacKay, that you do not regard circumstantial evidence as a

matter of each piece being consistent with
innocence. The question for the jury to
decide is on the collective circumstances,
are they consistent with innocence.[40]

McRuer vehemently disagreed with MacKay's claim that there was
"no case to go to the jury," as Arthur Lucas was about to take the stand.
He would be the first of only three witnesses called for the defence;
the others were Lucas's sister, Lizzie Fisher, and his girlfriend, Lillian
Boykin. At fifty-four years, Lucas was feeling his age. Out of shape,
with aching knees and varicose veins, he asked to sit in court, a request
which Justice McRuer allowed.

Lucas's testimony was compelling, as MacKay allowed his client
to reveal to the jury details from his life of crime, including early
convictions from the 1920s and 1930s for armed robbery and mail
fraud. During the final years of the Great Depression in 1939, Lucas
foolishly cashed someone else's government cheque, a crime that
earned him a three-year sentence of penal servitude. In 1946, he
was given a twelve- to twenty-year sentence for living off the avails
of prostitution.

Women were of little use to Lucas unless they could serve his purposes, namely being sent out on the street to make him money. At the
time of his arrest for the murder of Crater and Newman, police asked
Lucas where his wife, Delores, was, and his flippant reply was, "Out on
the street corner some place. Besides, I have five other women."

Making a living from prostitutes wasn't the only way Arthur Lucas
got money. For two years, Lucas was gambling, or "picking up numbers," to get by and was locked up for this crime. He freely admitted
talking to Therland Crater about opening up a bawdy house, and he
visited him in Toronto in late August or early September. While the
two men discussed their plans, Newman and Boykin were working as
hookers out of the Silver Dollar Room, next door to the Waverley
Hotel. Lucas told the jury he knew Crater for about ten years, and
Carolyn Newman for about a year. Another close friend of his was Gus
Saunders, whom he had met in prison fifteen years earlier. Still, Lucas
denied any connection with Saunders when it came to narcotics or

making his living from drugs. The only time he handled drugs was when he bought some for one of his girls who was an addict.

When it came to the police sting operation against Saunders, with Crater testifying against him in court, Lucas said the Bill of Particulars — which identified Crater as a witness in the upcoming Saunders drug trial — was common knowledge. "If somebody have a squak on you, somebody have got a case against you, the prosecution have to produce him," said Lucas. When MacKay asked him if he killed Crater and Newman, Lucas adamantly denied committing the murders. The last time he saw Crater he was alive, said Lucas, who checked out of the Waverley and left his overnight roommate, Willie White, standing outside on the street corner. Around the time the murders were committed, Lucas claimed to be drinking coffee at Wong's Restaurant on Dundas Street, then he got into his car and driving back to the United States, entering at Niagara Falls.

"I didn't cross no toll bridge," said Lucas when asked about the Burlington Skyway Bridge. Once he entered the U.S., Lucas claimed to have driven to Cleveland to see another man about setting up a brothel, then gone back to Detroit and his estranged wife's apartment on Collingwood Avenue. He relaxed in the apartment, eating dinner and watching a bit of TV, before he called his own home on Burns Avenue, where Wesley Knox answered and said, "Lucas ain't home."

Lucas suspected something was wrong. Knox obviously knew his voice, and Lucas asked his wife to call back fifteen minutes later, when she was also told he wasn't home. Something was definitely up, so Lucas called the home of Fred and Grace Kedzcierski, where he figured Morris Thomas might be staying. As it turned out, Thomas was at the Kedzcierski household, and Lucas told him something was wrong at his house. Lucas gave Thomas the keys to the Chevrolet and told him to get over to the Burns Avenue apartment. Time passed, and he didn't hear a word from his friend. Going outside and hailing down a cab, Lucas then spent the next few hours at a friend's apartment, and in a bar looking for the other woman in his life, girlfriend Lillian Boykin. When that failed, he went back to his apartment and was welcomed by police, who arrested him on the spot. The tale Lucas told the jury was plausible but convoluted.

Next came Lucas's cross-examination by Crown attorney Henry Bull, who wasted no time asking him about his ties to prostitution and the Detroit criminal underworld. In a confusing exchange that frustrated Bull to no end, Lucas said he never ran a bawdy house but "was engaged in prostitution, placing girls in places away." When Bull asked him about Crater being a witness against Gus Saunders in an upcoming drug trial, Lucas was indifferent, saying he never discussed the case with Saunders "in any way, shape, form or fashion."

> Bull: You were not that interested?
> Lucas: It was none of my business.
> Bull: And you were not interested in Gus Saunders'
>   trial?
> Lucas: Not a bit.[41]

Next to testify was Lizzie Fisher, Lucas's sixty-one-year-old sister. A simple woman, she worked as a housekeeper, and she listened patiently as Ross MacKay asked her about her brother. It would prove to be the first and only time Lucas lost his composure during the ten-day trial, when she said her younger brother made his living "through girls," although she didn't know anything about him being connected to narcotics.

The last to testify on Lucas's behalf was his girlfriend, Lillian Boykin. A mere twenty-one years old, Boykin described herself as a "professional prostitute" who lived with Lucas at his Burns Avenue apartment in Detroit. When she was in Toronto, she confirmed working out of various downtown hotels and clubs with Carolyn Newman, picking up strange men at the bar. When MacKay asked her about the .38-calibre found on the Burlington Skyway Bridge, Boykin said she didn't recognize the gun, but testified Lucas had owned a different gun, which she saw about a year and a half previously. "It had a white pearl handle on it, and it looked like a lady's gun. It was real fancy," she said.

Thanking the jurors for their efforts over the past ten days in his closing remarks, MacKay called them the "supreme Judges of the facts" before launching into a brilliant summary of the case, highlighting every conceivable bit of evidence presented at the trial, and telling the jury how it just didn't add up. Calling the Crown's case "almost entirely circumstantial," he said there was no possible way his client could be the killer.

"Arthur Lucas," said MacKay, "doesn't fit the bill."

Many of MacKay's points were valid. He questioned the character, and the testimony, of many of the Crown's witnesses. He summarized how Margaret Ladd — one of the basement tenants — didn't hear any shots, even though the murders were "going on right above her head." The brutal throat-slashing of Crater and Newman would have seen blood spurting at least seven or eight feet, testified the pathologist who performed the autopsies. "Whoever did the killing would have been covered with blood," the pathologist pointed out — and Lucas wasn't. Instead of shying away from the highly questionable bloodied bedclothes that were found on Carolyn Newman's body, MacKay addressed them directly.

"You saw the sheet, that gory mess," said MacKay of the evidence that literally stank up the courtroom earlier in the week. "Wouldn't there be some blood on Arthur Lucas's clothes if he had done this killing? You heard the experts' opinion that washing will not take out the stains or smears of blood. No evidence of any blood on Arthur Lucas's clothing anywhere." Other bloodstains, such as those found in the car, could have been there a month or more before the killings, as the experts could not attach a date to them.

The trial transcripts cannot reveal the degree of nausea experienced by the court when the bloodied sheets found on Carolyn Newman's remains were shown in court, a point MacKay discussed many years later in 1984 on a radio program for the Canadian Broadcasting Corporation, *The Scales of Justice.*

> The Chief Justice [McRuer] had ruled that the trial should be restricted to capital murder of the man Crater only, not the woman [Newman]. The sheets were not relevant, since Lucas was not on trial for Newman's murder. But the Crown sought to introduce the blankets from the woman's bed as evidence. The blood flow had been … unreal. But the objection was overruled. There was no air conditioning, it was hot weather, and

the stench of blood was over-powering. My last objection to his Lordship was that the stink of the blood and the blankets was making everybody in the courtroom sick to their stomachs. There's no doubt in my mind that the stench effectively denied Lucas a fair trial.[42]

As with the blood samples presented during the trial, MacKay attempted to raise serious doubts about the ballistics evidence. "I say this gun is not Arthur Lucas's gun anyway," he remarked about the .38-calibre Ivor Johnson revolver found on the Burlington Skyway Bridge. As for the tiny speck of gunpowder residue on Lucas's hand, MacKay said it might not even have been gunpowder; if it was, the material could have been transferred to his hand when he was in contact with two Detroit police officers. And if the revolver was defective and out of timing, as Detroit Detective Sergeant Earl Leedle testified, wouldn't there have been much more blowback of explosive materials on the hand of whoever pulled the trigger, instead of a tiny speck of unburned green powder?

MacKay was critical of many of the witnesses who testified for the Crown, and questioned their credibility. In his opinion, Morris Thomas — the well-known heroin user who ran drugs for Lucas — was a liar whose testimony simply could not be trusted. "He is a dope addict," MacKay told the jury. "He is not a test pilot for drugs, as he tried to make us believe. There is no such thing, of course. You saw the scars on his arms. He is a dope addict to begin with." Wesley Knox fared no better in MacKay's opinion. A man who knew Lucas for two decades, Knox held no legitimate occupation, instead doing odd jobs around Lucas's apartment, where he lived rent-free. In MacKay's eyes, he was "an unfortunate little man" and "a confirmed drunk."

MacKay saved his comments about his client for last.

"First of all, I want to point out to you that he was not under any obligation whatsoever in law to get in that witness box and testify under oath before you gentlemen," said MacKay. "He did so voluntarily, knowing that doing so would permit his criminal record to be put in." MacKay also commented on Crown attorney Henry Bull's lengthy examination of his client to elicit sympathy from the jury.

"He was in that witness box some four hours approximately — a man of the Negro race in a foreign country, a convicted man, and he was subjected to four hours of very severe examination," said MacKay. If Arthur Lucas was indeed a merciless, hard-hearted murderer, he was one of the worst the world had ever seen. "Does a professional killer visit his intended victim some several times?" asked MacKay of the jury, raising other questions for them to deliberate. Would a real hit man check into a hotel room using his actual name and address? Would a professional killer use an old, inexpensive gun that was notoriously defective? Most of all, would a contract killer be so careless as to leave his ring at the scene of the crime, on the bed just inches away from the body of one of his victims?

"If Arthur Lucas was a professional killer, if the Crown's theory is correct in this case, he was the most careless, foolish, professional killer I think that any of us has ever heard of," said MacKay, whose closing remarks to the jury summed up his client perfectly:

> Gentlemen, Arthur Lucas is no model citizen, as you have heard. I guess the word that we are most familiar with in dealing with him is that he is a pimp, but he is not a murderer. There is a vast, vast difference. Therland Crater on the evidence in this trial was his friend. Carolyn Newman was the friend of Lillian Boykin, who was Arthur Lucas' girl. Arthur Lucas does not fit the bill of a professional killer that you must find him to be to fit the Crown's theory.[43]

After a ten-minute recess, court resumed and Crown attorney Henry Bull presented his closing remarks to the jury. He wasted no time disagreeing with MacKay's belief that the Crown viewed Lucas as a professional killer. Instead, Bull maintained Lucas was not a skilled hit man, but just a murderer who deliberately plotted and killed his so-called friend Therland Crater.

"You do not have to know why Therland Crater was killed," Bull told the jury. "The plan may have formed out of fright, hate, vengeance, for monetary reasons, lust, greed, passion, anger — any one of a number of motives, it does not matter which one it is, but if the motive causes the murderer to form a plan and to deliberate upon it and to pursue that plan and deliberately carry it out and commit the murder, it is capital murder even if you do not know why." The Crown had two things to prove: the identity of the killer, and that the murder was planned and deliberate. The motive for the death of Crater was not necessary, but satisfying the jury beyond a reasonable doubt that Lucas was the killer was crucial.

"Whatever the reason, it is the Crown's case that Lucas came to Toronto looking for Crater, found him, killed him, and then disposed of Miss Newman, the only eyewitness, calling police operators before her throat was cut,"[44] Bull said.

"If it was not the Accused, then your function is through, he is not guilty," Bull continued. "It is a simple question: there are no two ways about that one — not guilty — if you are not satisfied as to the identity of the person who did it."

Bull then launched into a colourful, impassioned speech about the validity of the Crown's evidence. In MacKay's opinion, Bull said, the 105 exhibits presented to the court were "completely circumstantial." Bull used the metaphor of a jigsaw puzzle, something the jurors could relate to, for the wealth of material introduced over the past ten days. The evidence was scattered bits and pieces of colour that, when assembled, took shape and became an image of a house with hills and trees. Circumstantial evidence, said Bull, was strong, "because when all the pieces are put together, when all the threads of help which by themselves can be plucked apart by a child, are woven together, they form a hawser which can haul the *Queen Mary*." Eyewitnesses, said Bull, were notoriously unreliable, since their testimony could be tainted with errors or outright lies. Scientific evidence, normally cold and factual, was described by Bull in rich, stirring prose: "A blood spot is eloquent; the grooves and etching on a piece of lead from the rifling and the scoring of the inside of a revolver barrel speak with more assurance than all the tongues of man."

He then went on to explain the Crown's theory behind Crater's demise, and how Lucas rang the doorbell at 116 Kendal Avenue, muffled his gun to silence the sound, and shot Crater. Being right-handed,

Lucas then dropped the gun, whipped out a knife, and deftly slit Crater's throat from ear to ear. As for the ballistics evidence that the .38-calibre Ivor Johnson was cheap, it was, said Bull, still a gun.

When the court resumed at 9:50 on the morning of May 10, 1962, Justice McRuer gave his lengthy, three-hour charge to the jury, which ran to sixty-five pages in the official transcripts. There were, said McRuer, only three possible verdicts: acquittal, guilty of murder, or guilty of capital murder. The last, capital murder, involved planning and deliberation and called for the death penalty. The standards of proof, said McRuer, were different in criminal cases compared to civil cases.

"Does the evidence establish beyond a reasonable doubt that the Accused killed Crater, and that he meant to kill him?" asked McRuer. "If it does not, you must acquit him, and you have nothing more to consider. If it does, he has committed murder." He then cautioned the jury about not allowing Arthur Lucas's previous history to influence their decision in arriving at a verdict of guilty or not guilty.

The jury deliberated for five hours, and returned to the courtroom at 5:55 that evening with their decision about the fate of Arthur Lucas.

The Clerk of Assize:	Gentlemen of the Jury, have you agreed upon your verdict?
The Foreman of the Jury:	Yes, your Honour.
The Clerk:	What is your verdict, Mr. Foreman?
The Foreman:	The Prisoner, Arthur Lucas, is guilty of capital murder.[45]

Upon hearing the verdict, Lucas showed no emotion whatsoever. The jury was then sent back to their room to deliberate if they wished to make any recommendation of clemency, which would have seen Lucas sentenced to life imprisonment instead of the gallows. When they returned to the courtroom twenty minutes later, the foreman said, "My lord, we make no recommendations." Without any sign of remorse, Justice McRuer passed sentence on Arthur Lucas: "Lucas, stand up. The sentence of the Court is that you be taken to the place from whence you came and there kept until the 25th July next, and then taken to the place of execution and there hanged by the neck until you are dead, and may The Lord have mercy on your soul. Remove the Prisoner."

After thanking the jury for their efforts for the past ten days, Justice McRuer then gave his respects to the many police officers involved in the case. To his credit, Crown attorney Henry Bull then paid tribute to Lucas's young lawyer.

Mr. Bull:	My lord, with respect there is another aspect of the conduct of this case which I think is worthy of publicity, and that is that the defence was conducted under the auspices of Legal Aid. Mr. MacKay has given his services under that without remuneration, and I think that is something that is too seldom realized by the public.
His Lordship:	I just want to add my word to that, Mr. Bull, and say that Mr. MacKay has, in the conduct of the defence of this case, which was a difficult defence, done credit to the profession to which he belongs, and I am quite confident that the profession will feel honoured in Mr. MacKay's services as he renders them to his clients in the future.[46]

Justice McRuer's comments about MacKay's future services could not have been more prophetic, as MacKay would soon find himself back in court fighting to save the life of another of his clients — Ronald Turpin.

CHAPTER 6
The Trial of Ronald Turpin

If you live by the gun, you'll die by the gun.
— Ronald Turpin

Less than three weeks after fighting for the life of Arthur Lucas, twenty-nine-year-old lawyer Ross MacKay found himself back in court defending accused cop killer Ronald Turpin. Although he was widely regarded as an exceptionally talented young lawyer, the pressure on MacKay was overwhelming as he returned to the same courtroom at Toronto's City Hall on May 28, 1962. On May 10, he had listened as Justice James Chalmers McRuer sentenced Lucas to be hanged by the neck until dead. The case of *Regina vs. Lucas* was MacKay's first murder trial; *Regina vs. Turpin* would be his second. Armed with few resources and practically no money to defend Lucas, he found himself in the exact same situation. Defending two death penalty cases back to back in such a short time would affect MacKay for the rest of his life and would forever cement opinions others had of him and of his abilities as a lawyer.

At the preliminary hearing held earlier in mid-April, police officers spoke about what happened that frigid February night on Danforth Avenue when Frederick J. Nash was shot and killed by Ronald Turpin after what appeared to be a routine traffic stop. Toronto Police Constable Frank Byrnes said Turpin had already been captured and handcuffed by the time he arrived at the scene of the shooting, and he spoke about how he put a shot and bleeding Turpin into the police cruiser, accompanied by a cadet. Several officers said Turpin — despite having shot a police officer and being wounded himself in both arms and the face — appeared quite calm after being arrested and seemed to comprehend everything going on around him. On April 17, an Ontario Supreme Court grand jury returned a true bill against Turpin and committed him for a spring trial, which would be delayed for one day when MacKay insisted the head of Toronto's homicide squad be called to give evidence.

"I know there's a rush to get this case on to the spring assizes, but this is a murder case and I'm entitled to call all the witnesses I want,"[47] MacKay said to Magistrate F.C. Hayes. The trial of Ronald Turpin, like the earlier trial of Arthur Lucas, would remain controversial for years to come.

The judge presiding over the Turpin trial was George Alexander Gale. As was the case with James McRuer, the judge in charge of the Lucas case, Gale was committed to judicial efficiency, a man who — as his son would later say — "liked to get on with things." A pioneer when it came to streamlining court schedules and procedures to allow for cases to flow through the courts faster, Gale had been practicing law for fourteen years when he was made a Supreme Court judge in 1946 at the relatively tender age of forty, becoming one of the youngest persons appointed to a superior court in Canadian history. Considered by many lawyers to be tough but fair, the veteran judge had no time or patience for courtroom theatrics.

For the Turpin trial, MacKay faced a talented Crown prosecutor no less skilled than Henry Bull, his opponent on the Lucas case. As deputy Crown attorney for Metro and York county, Arthur Otto Klein was a lawyer with nearly three decades of experience. After graduating from Osgoode Hall Law School in 1933, Klein quickly rose to the position of assistant Crown attorney by 1938. During the Second World War, he served as a pilot and flying instructor with the Royal Canadian Air Force, and on return to civilian life immediately went back to law. His prosecutions included members of the Boyd Gang. By the time of the Turpin trial, Klein was in his early fifties, and well-acquainted with the courtroom and rules of evidence. As was the case with the Lucas trial, the Crown would call a large number of witnesses, sixty-five, compared to just five for the defence.

On the first day of the trial, MacKay attempted get a change of venue for his client by claiming various articles and fundraising drives for Constable Nash's widow and four young daughters as being prejudicial to his case. "It will be impossible for Mr. Turpin to obtain a fair and impartial trial because of newspaper accounts and a wealth of sympathy for the deceased person's family," said MacKay. Some of the charity events at the time included hockey games and a baseball game, with much-needed monies going to help the family of the slain police officer.

Newspaper coverage, said MacKay, was also against his client, as he singled out a headline from the *Telegram* of February 12, 1962, which read, "Dying, He Fires 3 Bullets Into Gunman, Officer Shot Dead On Street." MacKay then cited an editorial from *Hush* to get a different Ontario city, like Ottawa or London, to host the trial of his client. A controversial fifteen-cent Toronto tabloid, *Hush* featured risqué headlines like, "Toronto Call-Girl Stable Run by Detroit Tailor," photos of scantily clad models, the latest gossip on Hollywood movie stars like Elizabeth Taylor and Rock Hudson, and thinly disguised "lonely hearts" ads in the back that hinted at illicit sexual encounters.

MacKay took exception to "He Died a Hero," an editorial that ran in the March 10, 1962, issue of *Hush*. The editorial, he said, used expressions like "a thirst for vengeance" about the shooting, and never referred to Turpin by name, calling him instead a "dangerous gunman," "armed suspect," and "assailant." The editorial stated Nash "was a model police officer" who was "tall, muscular, fearless and devoted to his duty." MacKay reasoned that, given the various newspaper accounts, it would be impossible to find a jury that didn't believe Nash died a hero.

Immediately, Klein opposed any change of venue. "What has happened in this case with regard to the newspaper publicity is no different from what happens in the great majority of criminal cases where there is a crime of any seriousness at all committed."[48] Justice Gale agreed with Klein, saying the case would still have received "enormous publicity" in cities like Ottawa, and there was no need to move Turpin's trial to another location. Of the publication itself, Judge Gale called *Hush* a

"rag" with a very limited circulation "amongst persons who have peculiar tastes," and said that anything printed in it shouldn't be given serious consideration at all. Had a similar inflammatory editorial or article
appeared in reputable newspapers such as the *Toronto Star* or the
Telegram, MacKay might have had a chance getting Turpin's trial moved
to a less hostile location.

As questionable as *Hush* might have been, the editorial raised a
number of valid points, ranging from police understaffing to the issue
of lone officers patrolling the city late at night, without any backup.

> Metro Police Commission is well aware that the city is
> lousy with criminals, actual or potential killers; that a
> policeman risks his life if he goes alone into certain sec-
> tions after dark; that the present 1,500-man to 2,318
> member force is less than adequate for its job, notwith-
> standing its efficiency. Yet, as a measure of economy, and
> possibly with an eye on political consequences, it sends
> men out alone in cruisers. Moreover, if a policeman even
> draws his gun on anyone who does not shoot at him first,
> and more especially if he wounds an opponent, he is sub-
> ject to disciplinary action, treated as a trigger-happy
> bully, and possibly put on trial. In vain the Police
> Association has protested against this injustice. Police
> Commissioners, holding down nice, cushy jobs, still play
> to the political gallery; and even while the blood of
> Constable Nash stained the pavement, their Chairman
> announced that the system would not be changed.
> If there had been two men in Constable Nash's
> cruiser at the time of the tragedy, probably not a shot
> would have been fired, and a dangerous gunman might
> have been captured without a struggle. Most likely,
> too, Constable Nash would now be a living, but soon
> forgotten, hero instead of a glorified dead one.[49]

As was the case with Arthur Lucas, the trial of Ronald Turpin
would see over one hundred exhibits presented in court, including

crime scene and autopsy photos, money from the robbery at the Red Rooster Restaurant, handguns, clothing worn by Nash and Turpin the night of the shooting, blood samples, and six Metropolitan Toronto Police Bulletins circulated in stations between October 26, 1961, and January 25, 1962, which clearly showed Turpin's face and description.

On the second day of the trial, Crown prosecutor Arthur Klein outlined the events of the night of the shooting. Turpin, who had just broken into the closed Red Rooster Restaurant in Scarborough, was driving his broken-down Pontiac truck on Danforth Avenue when he was pulled over by Nash. When asked for identification, Turpin lied, telling Nash his name was Orval Penrose. Witnesses saw the men struggle, heard shots, and saw Nash fall to the road. Turpin attempted to flee in his truck, which would not start, then tried to get away in Nash's patrol car, and was apprehended before he could get the car going. Both the police officer and Turpin were taken to East General Hospital, where Turpin was treated for superficial wounds, while Nash died from his injuries after being shot three times.

One of the first witnesses to testify about Nash's condition when he was rushed into emergency was Claude Davidson, a doctor on call at East General when Nash was brought in at 2:35 a.m. on the morning of February 12. Already on intravenous and oxygen, Nash was "dead white in colour and moaning something like, 'Put me under, put me under.' He had no pulse at the wrist or at the ankles. There was a faint pulse at his neck, indicating he was in grave shock," said Davidson. Although every effort was made to save the officer's life, including blood transfusions and the insertion of a tube into his lungs to help him breathe, he died half an hour later, at 3:05 a.m.

Minutes later, Dr. Davidson went to another emergency room to see Ronald Turpin, who was booked for surgery at seven o'clock that morning. Unlike the fatal wounds suffered by Nash, Turpin was in very good condition, with no evidence of shock. His constant complaining about the pain in his arms from being shot was getting on everyone's nerves, and he was given an anaesthetic and had his wounds cleaned and sutured. After a rubber drain was put in, Turpin was kept at the hospital under police guard for a few days before being transferred to the Don Jail.

About eight hours after Nash was shot and killed, another doctor had the grim task of performing the autopsy on the body of the slain police officer. The head pathologist at East General Hospital, Dr. Stewart Penny, weighed and measured Nash before detailing the bullet wounds that killed him. Although Nash had been shot three times by Turpin's Beretta semi-automatic pistol, he had four puncture wounds — one was a through and through, which pierced Nash's left thigh and exited out the buttock. The fatal wound was to his chest, which caused massive internal bleeding. During the autopsy, Dr. Penny turned over two .32-calibre bullets he removed from Nash's body to Detective Jim Crawford, and two samples of blood to Detective Sergeant Irvine Alexander.

After introducing evidence that revealed the damage made by Turpin during the break-in at the Red Rooster Restaurant, the court heard from a number of his friends and acquaintances. The first was Orval Penrose, whose identification Turpin used when pulled over by Nash on that night on Danforth Avenue. A buddy of Turpin's for about ten years, Penrose said his chauffeur's licence and a passenger motor vehicle permit were re-issued after he reported them lost to the police. During his cross-examination, MacKay asked Penrose about Turpin's anxieties involving the law.

> MacKay: Did he ever tell you that he was in fear of his life from the police hunting him?
> Penrose: He did mention that.[50]

Fear of the police would become a central theme of Ross MacKay's defence, as he attempted to portray his client as a man hounded by the police virtually night and day until he became a twitchy paranoiac. It was a bold strategy that would attempt to make sense of why Turpin shot Nash that fateful night, a tactic that MacKay continued with the next witness, Alexander Stevenson. A procedure clerk at the Dominion Bank, Stevenson lived in the same Toronto apartment building as Turpin's girlfriend, Lillian White, during November and December of 1961.

MacKay: Did the police come to visit your apartment dur-
                     ing that period?
Stevenson: Quite often, sir.
MacKay: Quite often?
Stevenson: Yes.
MacKay: Would they come almost daily?
Stevenson: No. Not daily, sir — on and off.
MacKay: And what were they coming to your apartment for?
Stevenson: Looking for Ronald Turpin.[51]

Although Stevenson did not state that Turpin feared for his life, he did say he was wanted for questioning by police about earlier shootings. One of them was the unsolved murder of a drug dealer named Lorne Gibson, the other an incident at a party at the apartment of Della Burns, another friend of Turpin's. He was at the get-together that night with his girlfriend, Lillian White, who, as soon as she was sworn in, asked Justice Gale for the protection of the Canadian Evidence Act.

White's answers were brief and defensive, as she was quick to assert that she was Miss White, *not* Mrs. White. She had known Turpin for two years and lived common-law with him on and off from February 1960 to just before Christmas 1961. White explained Turpin gave her a gun, which she hid in the basement laundry room of her apartment building. She told the court the reason she retrieved the gun and put it in Turpin's truck on the afternoon of February 10 was because he was leaving town and wanted to get rid of the weapon. Turpin didn't tell her exactly where he was headed, just up north somewhere. And though he wasn't present when White put the gun in the truck, she later told him where it was, and he assured her he'd dispose of it.

Under cross-examination by MacKay, White said Detective Sergeant John Fallis asked her to tell Turpin to bring the gun to police. It was around this time Turpin and White made a trip to Buffalo, and he couldn't be found by Toronto police. On her return to the city, White said, she was "interviewed by police every night" about Turpin's whereabouts. He told her he was in fear for his life from the police.

MacKay:	Did Mr. Turpin indicate to you that his understanding was that if he was apprehended by the police he was going to be killed?
White:	Yes, sir.[52]

MacKay then called Marion Steiner, a woman who had known Turpin for two years. Steiner testified to Turpin's growing paranoia, stating she was visited by police officers "every night, every morning" daily for almost three months when they were looking for Turpin. Steiner was different from many of Turpin's other friends and hangers-on, in that she didn't have a criminal record and had never been in trouble with the law. She recalled one incident when a police officer came to her apartment and made threats against her missing friend. "He said he could wait three months, six months, but he was going to get him, and when he got him he wouldn't have a chance." At that time, Turpin was out of town, and phoning Steiner two to three times a day to find out what was going on. Every conversation was about the police, she said, and how upset Turpin was that they were after him. "He was afraid of being shot on sight,"[53] said Steiner.

Next to testify was another friend of Turpin's, Della Naomi Stonehouse, known to the police by her alias, Della Burns. Although she gave her profession as hairdresser, the reality of her employment was far different. A prostitute, the tall, flaming redhead had a lengthy criminal record, including convictions for forgery, conspiracy to possess narcotics, vagrancy, and possession of a firearm. Like many of Turpin's pals, Burns was never in one place for very long, hopping from one apartment to the next.

She described for the court the shooting at her apartment at 222 Wellesley Street East. She heard a shot outside her apartment, and as she opened the hall door, "a man came in waving a gun." Burns claimed to have never seen the man before. She did remember the gun, describing it as small and black.

Like the testimony of Stevenson and White before her, Della Burns said Turpin actually believed twenty-six police officers were after him, and that if he were apprehended, he would be killed. Police officers scoffed at Turpin's claim, saying they were under no such orders to shoot him on sight. One of the officers referred to him as "Pretty Boy Turpin," a sarcastic reference to Depression-era bank robber Charles Arthur "Pretty Boy" Floyd.

Although it was bone-numbingly cold and already after two in the morning when Constable Nash was shot and killed, a number of people in the immediate area saw and heard — to varying degrees — what happened that night. One of them was Alice Fairney, a young woman who was just returning from a dance with her date, who heard "about six shots" coming from the corner of Dawes Road and Danforth Avenue. To her, they came in "two bursts," a number of bangs followed by a pause, then more gunshots.

One of the witnesses closest to the scene of the shooting was thirty-six-year-old cab driver Leonard Boreham. Sitting behind the wheel eating his sandwich and sipping coffee, Boreham put down the newspaper he was reading when he heard something that sounded like a car backfiring. Looking up, he saw a disturbance going on across the street. Two people were struggling near a parked vehicle, and once they got past the streetcar tracks, "the one in uniform seemed to let go and drop to the pavement," testified Boreham. Moments later, he heard several bangs, and saw flashes from the man's hand. After hearing three or four shots, Boreham made a quick U-turn, called his dispatcher on his radio, and raced to No. 10 police station, about half a mile away. The taxi driver said he may have heard more gunfire, but as he sped off, he never looked back to see where the shorts were coming from.

Another witness was John Ough, who lived above the Hallowell Funeral Home. A partner in the business and an ambulance driver, Ough was preparing to go to sleep after 2:00 a.m. when he also heard bangs that reminded him of a car backfiring. Looking out his window, he saw Constable Nash on the ground and "heard approximately three more shots." From above the funeral home, Ough said another man was standing nearby, about ten to fifteen feet from Nash, but he couldn't say for certain if the man had anything in his hand. "I looked towards the officer lying on the ground and he was struggling to reach for his revolver which was about a foot away from his hand." Running downstairs to offer assistance, Ough said by the time he reached the fallen police officer, he was lying face down on the pavement and another officer had Turpin at gunpoint.

Next to testify was John Wrycraft, a streetcar driver for the Toronto Transit Commission who was forced to stop his empty vehicle on Danforth Avenue where the tracks were blocked by Nash's patrol car. As he stopped, Wrycraft saw Nash stooped over, struggling to get up and falling back down again, a gun in his right hand. When he got out of his streetcar to help, Turpin confronted him with a gun in his hand and said in a very quiet voice, "Get into the car or I'll shoot you." Wrycraft did as the gunman said. He then saw Turpin jump into his truck, which failed to start, then run over to Nash's police cruiser and get behind the wheel.

"The next thing I heard was mashing of gears, sir, as though he was trying to get it going and couldn't get it going, sir," said Wrycraft, who witnessed Turpin struggling to get the police car started until another squad car arrived and placed Turpin under arrest.

At approximately the same time, a woman named Frances McCarthy was wakened by noises, which her husband said sounded like revolver shots. The couple managed the Eastbourne Hotel on Danforth Avenue and were asleep in bed at the time. Looking out the window, McCarthy saw a man talking to the streetcar driver, then trying to start the grey police car. She heard gears grinding when another officer arrived at the scene and handcuffed the man. That officer was John McDonnell, who received a call on his police radio at 2:15 a.m. and drove to Danforth and Dawes Road, where he saw Nash lying on his stomach on the roadway. McDonnell testified:

> At the time I stopped the scout car I observed and heard — first I heard the sound of gears clashing and simultaneously I looked up and I could see I was stopped beside a grey Ford, which was a scout car. The motor was running of the scout car. There was a man sitting behind the wheel. I could tell by the appearance of this man that he was not a policeman and he had no business

being in this car. I jumped out of the scout car that I was in and at this time I had my gun, my revolver, in my hand. I raced across to where the scout car that this other man was sitting in, and when I reached the scout car I pointed the gun at the accused Turpin, who was sitting in the driver's seat of the scout car, scout 610.[54]

McDonnell then placed Turpin under arrest for the shooting and ordered him to put his hands in the air. With his limbs hanging loosely by his sides, he complained, "I can't, I've been shot in both arms." The officer then ordered Turpin to lean against the scout car on his elbows, which he did. When McDonnell started searching Turpin, he said, "I give up. I haven't got the gun. The gun is in the car," then added, "Look after the officer." Placed in the back seat of McDonnell's police cruiser, Turpin incessantly whined, "Get me up to the hospital, I've been hurt bad."

Just as McDonnell was telling the streetcar driver to call an ambulance, Ough came by with his ambulance from the Hallowell Funeral Home and offered his assistance. McDonnell then retrieved the gun from the front seat of Nash's scout car. As fate would have it, Nash's police car wasn't the only thing that wasn't working that night, as McDonnell noticed Turpin's gun had jammed.

Within minutes, other officers arrived at the scene. Nash had already lost a lot of blood. He was drifting in and out of consciousness, and his breathing was shallow. On the ground just three inches from his right hand lay his black Webley police revolver. As a precaution, one officer brushed the gun away from his hand, since he didn't know if it was empty or still loaded with bullets. As Nash was carried into the ambulance, Turpin kept moaning about the bullets lodged in his arms. "Take it easy, I've been shot too."

Once the ambulance left for the hospital, policemen blocked the scene to traffic and began the process of gathering evidence. The spot where Nash crumpled face down to the ground was outlined with white chalk. Other officers searching the ground found .32-calibre shells nearby and a spent bullet, which were also circled with chalk and photographed.

Both Nash and Turpin were rushed to the same hospital, East General, and seen by emergency room staff and other personnel on duty the night of the shooting. They would later testify in court about what they saw and heard. As Nash lay dying in one room, Turpin was in another, constantly grumbling, "My fuckin arms hurt" to anyone who would listen. He stopped whining when nurses gave him four different injections, including penicillin and morphine. Meanwhile, in Emergency Room 2, doctors were struggling to save Nash's life when orderly Harry Hollingsworth heard the clunk of a bullet as it fell out of the officer's clothes; it was saved as evidence.

The first lawyer to see Turpin after the shooting was Donald Bitter, who had represented Turpin on other charges earlier in his criminal career. Bitter remembered being told by another lawyer who shared the same office space, "Your silly client Turpin got himself into a jam — he shot a cop." When he saw Turpin at the East General Hospital, the gunman was conscious long enough to say, "He shot first" before slipping back into unconscious. Believing he was in possession of a possible dying declaration by Turpin, Bitter contacted lawyer Ross MacKay and told him what Turpin said. "I thought it really was a dying declaration, considering Turpin's physical condition at the time, having been shot," says Bitter. "I had every reason to believe Turpin was dying."

Nash soon succumbed to his injuries, and two senior homicide detectives — Irvine Alexander and Jim Crawford — took Turpin's statement in Emergency Room 3. Both officers drove straight from the scene of the shooting to the hospital, and were both surprised and disgusted by Turpin's reaction.

Under examination by Prosecutor Klein, Alexander said he and his partner saw Turpin at 4:30 that morning, and told him officer Nash was dead. Instead of showing any remorse, he looked at the detectives and blurted out, "Is he dead, seriously?"

A typewriter was carried into the emergency room, and detective Alexander read Turpin the standard police caution. "I wish to caution you that you are arrested on a charge of murder, that you are not obliged to say anything unless you wish to do so, but whatever you say will be taken down in writing and may be given in evidence."[55] Turpin agreed to this, and his statement was taken down. His age at the time:

twenty-eight. Where did he live? "No fixed address," he replied. Who was Orval Penrose? "A guy I knew years ago."

Turpin then proceeded to tell the two detectives that Nash pulled his gun on him after he stopped his truck. "I can't tell you why, I know he did," said Turpin. "He told me to put my hands on the trunk. I turned swiftly and he fired. He hit me in the left arm. Everything happened so fast I couldn't tell you after that."

When asked what he knew about the 7.65-mm Beretta semi-automatic pistol found underneath the seat of his truck, Turpin simply replied, "Nothing." He explained that he was just driving downtown and didn't know why Constable Nash stopped him. "If he hadn't shot me I wouldn't shoot him," he told Alexander and Crawford. "The cop came across the street because he couldn't get the car started. He was near me and made a grab for my gun. I let him have a couple of shots and he reached with his gun. Then I said, 'Fuck it,' and said to myself, 'I can get him again.' I threw my gun down and he fired at me from the ground."[56]

Turpin's arrogant, tough-guy attitude came across loud and clear when it came to the subject of police. On trial for the murder of one Toronto police officer, he bragged to Detective Crawford he could have easily taken the life of more than one cop that night. "The second guy [I] could have got him too but I said, 'Fuck it,' and threw the gun down," he said about officer John McDonnell. Once his statement was over and it came time to him to sign the police caution form, all he said was, "I can't, my arms."

Years later, lawyer Donald Bitter remembers the many sides of Ronald Turpin, a twenty-eight-year-old who had spent virtually his entire life in and out of foster homes, reformatories, and jails. On the surface, Turpin often appeared reasonable and outgoing, but he could never escape his past, no matter how hard he tried.

"Turpin was good company, but he may have been a sociopath," says Bitter. "I knew he was a bad apple." Bitter also believes it is likely Nash, having served on the morality squad and frequently dealing with individuals like Turpin and his associates, recognized him from one of the many Metropolitan Toronto Police "To-day's Most Wanted Persons" posters.

As a young second-year law student, Stephen Posen volunteered to assist Ross MacKay during the trial to gain valuable experience, and remembers Turpin as a petty criminal, but not a violent man.

During the Turpin trial, MacKay started to slip, showing up late to court several times. As Justice McRuer had reprimanded him a few weeks earlier during the Lucas trial, so did Justice Gale, who didn't particularly care to hear any explanations why the defence attorney was late. The courtroom was an institution demanding respect and there were, in Gale's court, no excuses.

"This trial is going to take long enough without having it extended by any unreasonable delay on the part of counsel in attending when we are supposed to start,"[57] said Gale. Although MacKay was articulate during the trial of his client, some doubted the defence. MacKay's drinking had been steadily increasing since Arthur Lucas was sentenced to death on May 10, and he was now up to two bottles a day. While MacKay did not come to court visibly intoxicated, some days were better than others.

"It was unfortunate," says Posen. "There were a couple of mornings when Ross came into court, and had apparently been drinking, and showed the effects of having been drinking. And at least on one occasion that I can recall, the judge commented about that." In praising MacKay's outstanding presence in court, Posen coincidentally drew a comparison between MacKay and actor Maximilian Schell in *Judgment at Nuremberg*.

Another issue of the defence strategy that concerned the young law student was that it seemed less focused that it could have been. MacKay tried to use every possible defence to murder, instead of concentrating on a specific, effective defence, says Posen. At one point, he remembers, he overheard MacKay telling Turpin something along the lines of, "I don't want to know your story yet. I want to test everything they say, and use all potential defences." As a result, MacKay didn't actually get Turpin's version of what happened the night of the shooting "until well on into the trial," when it may have been too late to focus on the best defence, which may have been self-defence.

There were other stories as well that MacKay wanted to introduce to the jury, but they were not about his client but rather Constable Nash. The police officer, recently advanced to the morality squad, had allegedly been drinking off-duty one night at the Town Tavern. A now long-defunct downtown Toronto jazz club, the Town Tavern was a great place to catch the likes of the Oscar Peterson Trio, or to meet people and do business. There was purported to be a scuffle, with some-one getting pushed around, but no real violence. Since any records of this incident are sealed or missing, exact details of the skirmish are unknown, but in any event, Nash was sent back to being a beat cop from the morality division three months before he was shot and killed.

Since there were no direct eyewitnesses to the shooting, it was dif-ficult to say with any degree of certainty who shot first. The jury would have to make their determination based mainly on the testimony of witnesses who saw or heard part of the incident, including Ronald Turpin himself when he took the stand.

MacKay was straightforward with the jury about Turpin and his lengthy criminal past. In 1949, when he was just fifteen or sixteen years old, Turpin was convicted in Ottawa for shopbreaking with intent and theft. Numerous other offences followed, including posses-sion of housebreaking instruments, auto theft, attempting to utter a forged document, theft from the mails, and three counts of escaping lawful custody. None of his convictions involved violence or guns.

When it came time for MacKay to ask Turpin about his childhood, the response he received was that it was virtually non-existent. Between the ages of eleven and sixteen, Turpin was in and out of Bowmanville Training School, Children's Aid, and foster homes. When asked the number of homes, he simply couldn't remember.

> The only actual — I'd be put in a foster home for a matter of maybe six months and for some reason, maybe the people didn't care for me or because maybe I didn't care for the people, or they complained to the foster supervisor, or they would take you and put you in a new home. You may get frequently a different home — three or four a year for that matter. I couldn't exactly

state why I was moved all the time, but sometimes I
did run away from the homes.[58]

Restless and bored, Turpin was unable to keep legitimate jobs for
any length of time. He would either get fed up with the low pay or
working conditions and quit or get fired. One of his longest terms of
employment was working for Union Furniture from April to October
1961. But over the years, he'd largely earned his living from stealing.

"But that you weren't caught; is that it?" asked Justice Gale.

"That's about it," replied Turpin.

MacKay then asked Turpin about the night of October 26, 1961,
when there was a shot fired at a party he was attending downtown
with girlfriend Lillian White. He couldn't say for certain what time he
arrived at Della Burns's apartment, but he remembered he had been
drinking before he showed up. Although he claimed he wasn't drunk
by the time he got there, Turpin admitted he was tossing back two,
sometimes three, 26-ounce bottles of whisky every day.

Once they were inside the apartment, the two sat in a corner of the
room and made themselves comfortable. "Della was running around and
being host, I imagine, and I heard a shot from the hall, so I went to the
hall myself." Pushing past other guests, Turpin was the first to reach the
door. Opening it, he saw four guys and a girl, whom he had seen around
before but didn't know by name. They came into the apartment, and
when Turpin asked them about the noise, one of the men told him,
"Don't worry about [it]. Everything is taken care of. It's okay." Poking his
head out the door into the hallway and seeing it empty, Turpin went
back inside the apartment. Minutes later, the door burst open and in
came somebody hollering about the four men who'd entered the apartment. There was a struggle, during which a revolver fell out of the hand
of the man who'd just entered the apartment. Turpin grabbed the gun.
A shot was fired, and the gun fell. People were yelling "Police!" and
bolting out of the apartment, Turpin and White along with them.

When they reached White's apartment, Turpin shoved the gun
into the pocket of his overcoat. "I took it with full intentions of getting rid of it the next day," he told MacKay. The next morning, Turpin
was hungover in bed when White handed him the phone. A friend of

his, Lois Fry, was on the other end, and told Turpin a detective was at her apartment and wanted to talk to him. The detective said he wanted the gun, which Turpin said he had no intention of bringing in, since he was "not going to take any bum beat." Although the detective told Turpin any fine would be minimal, Turpin again refused to surrender the weapon, which upset the detective.

"He was mad, you know, because I wouldn't see things his way," said Turpin. "He was hot, so I told him I didn't care what he considered or what charge he put out, that I was having no part of it, and that's all there was to it." According to Turpin, the detective threatened to put out a warrant reading "attempted murder." Turpin said if that was the way he wanted it, there was nothing he could do, and he'd have to take his chances. The reason he didn't hand the gun over, he said, was because someone advised him against surrendering the weapon.

> Turpin: I spoke to an attorney-at-law about this, and he informed me that if I did give the gun to [the detective] I might just as well give the body.
> MacKay: Might as well give the what?
> Turpin: Give the body. More or less, so to speak, to hang yourself.[59]

The gun was then hidden in the laundry room of Lillian White's apartment building. The reason he kept the gun — instead of burying it or throwing it in the river — was to have something to bargain with. Fearing a few "rotten apples" on the police force might beat him up if he couldn't produce the weapon, Turpin kept it as insurance. He claimed not only were police showing up at his friends' apartments looking for him, but some members of the force allegedly had a personal grudge against him, which came across in threats.

"If you see that curly-haired bastard, he'll find out — he'll wind up with a bullet in his head. You tell him that" and "You'll find him in Lake Ontario with a brick tied to his leg" were a few of the threats he claimed to hear from police through his friends. Although Turpin said the threats were childish — "It didn't seem logical that a police officer would have to use that [sic] tactics" — he believed the threats were real.

To avoid confronting the authorities, Turpin got out of the city. On one trip, he stayed at a lodge in the Haliburton Mountains, about 150 miles from Toronto. The only visitor he had was Lois Fry; he told his girlfriend, Lillian White, to keep away, fearing that she would be followed. Whenever he phoned friends in the city, he claimed the police made more threats, "that I would get mine when they put their hands on me." Another time he went to Buffalo with White, only returning to Canada when he ran out of money. All the while, he kept calling people he knew in Toronto from a pay phone, checking up on the alleged police manhunt for him.

Just before Christmas 1961, Turpin and White were back in Toronto, staying at places like the Metropole Hotel, the Isabella, the Seahorse, and apartments here and there. Still fearing reprisals from the police, the couple stayed in cheap hotels and motels, with Turpin only sneaking out at night to walk his German shepherd or grab a drink with friends. One of the places he stayed was the Andrews Motel, near the Red Rooster Restaurant, which he later robbed. Since Turpin rarely held down a real job, money was always a problem.

"When I was in Buffalo I felt I was a little out of reach," Turpin said of the police. "I was right in their back yard here."

After a while, Turpin's friends told him the police were onto him and knew he was back in Toronto. Once he heard the police knew he was back in the city, Turpin rarely spent more than a few days at any one location before packing up his few belongings and heading off to another hideout. MacKay asked his client about his fear of being at the receiving end of a "severe shellacking" by police.

MacKay: Well, after moving out of the Andrews Motel, did the belief that you have described before about those threats being real — did that belief continue in your mind?

Turpin: Yes, it did. I was still quite afraid to be apprehended and taken to Headquarters.

MacKay: Do you mean you were afraid of being arrested?

Turpin: I wasn't so much afraid of being arrested as I was to who would arrest me.

MacKay: What do you mean by that?

Turpin: As I stated earlier there's certain officers that I know of who wouldn't hesitate about the fact of handing out physical violence.[60]

It was then Turpin recounted the infamous 1952 riot at the Guelph reformatory, where he was sent in his late teens. Although there were no fatalities, the place was out of control, and police had to be called in to help the guards. Windows were smashed, fires were set, and the institution was left in ruins. Turpin was stripped, forced to run naked down a corridor full of broken shards of glass, beaten with wooden bats, then left in a cell for two days.

Continuing his examination, MacKay asked Turpin for his memories of the night of the shooting. He had been drinking with Della Burns and left her place in the panel truck given to him by Lillian White. On his way to the Andrews Motel where he was staying, he parked the truck, broke into the Red Rooster Restaurant, and stole all the cash in the basement office, $632.84. His plans were to leave up north the next morning and trade in the truck for a car later that day.

Once he finished his break-in at the restaurant, Turpin got back into his truck and drove from Scarborough in the east end towards the city core. Out of the darkness, a car appeared in the rear-view mirror. As it pulled up alongside his vehicle, he recognized it as a police cruiser. "The car drew up beside me," Turpin told the court. "I then looked sideways and I seen the officer sitting in it. Only the outline, I didn't see no face or what the case may be, and he at that same moment flashed a light inside my vehicle, and then — I imagine it was only an instant — I was ready to pull out and he flicked the light off and on, indicating for me to, as I took it, the indication, to stay, so I stayed there."

Officer Nash got out of his squad car and walked to the driver's side of the Pontiac. Turpin rolled down his window, and Nash then went to the passenger side. Shining his Radar-Lite flashlight in Turpin's face, he asked him for identification. Nothing was said about the break-in Turpin had just committed at the restaurant as Turpin handed Nash the ID he stole from his old friend Orval Penrose. Nash then told Turpin to get out of the truck. As he did, Nash reached across and took the key out of the truck's ignition and asked if Turpin had any other forms of identification on him.

Turpin claimed Nash then looked under the seat of the truck, "and he came out and he picked up the Radar-Lite, and as he did, he pulled out his own revolver. He pulled his revolver on me." He claimed Nash then ordered him to walk to the back of the truck, holding Turpin's gun and the flashlight in his left hand and his own service revolver in his right.

"Your name isn't Penrose," Turpin testified Nash said as he pushed Turpin face first onto the fender. According to Turpin, Nash was about to strike Turpin with his gun when Turpin instinctively brought his arms up and the gun went off, a bullet tearing through his left forearm. Stunned, Turpin grabbed his arm, and while staggering back from the car, the gun went off right in his face.

Turpin:	There was a flash of flame come out of the gun. It was that long [indicating]. It got me right dead in the face. I didn't know if I was dead; I didn't know where I was.
MacKay:	Did you know you had been shot?
Turpin:	I know I been shot, of course. I know I was shot, but I didn't know — I don't know — it's hard to explain this. I've never had the experience before in my life. What I am trying to say is if anyone has ever had a gun fired right in their face they know the feeling — I am talking about. It's point blank, and you can't describe it. It's just — it's just there, I mean. It's the only thing you can have in your mind. The way I felt right then, I was dead, the man was going to kill me.[61]

When MacKay asked what happened next, Turpin was vague, and he couldn't remember if he'd tried to grab the officer's gun or turned around and ran. He remembered firing just one shot from his Beretta as he stood next to something, "and I was looking across the road, and I see a man on his elbows." Turpin was then shot again, in the right arm this time: "[T]he man fired at me. He fired, and I can remember seeing the flame come out of the gun, and I was standing in the road. I was looking like this [indicating] to see where I was going to get hit, and I raised my arm, and I fired." The next memories Turpin' had were of being arrested, taken to hospital, and told the officer he shot was dead.

"Did you mean to kill or have any thought of killing P.C. Nash?" asked MacKay.

"I had no thought of killing the man. I didn't even know the man," replied Turpin.

It was then Prosecutor Klein's turn to cross-examine Turpin, and he wasted no time challenging Turpin's claims of police persecution and of shooting officer Nash in self-defence.

Klein:	You say police constable Nash was shot accidentally?
Turpin:	I can't say to you that the man was shot accidentally. The only thing I could say is if I did shoot the man in the way that it is trying to be said, it had to be for self-defence.
Klein:	Self-defence?
Turpin:	Yes.
Klein:	Did you say that you did not know what you were doing at the time of the shooting?
Turpin:	After I was shot in the face, I can't recollect anything until you have just heard what I have said.
Klein:	What did you say — you can't recollect?
Turpin:	Well, I didn't remember anything till until I was looking up and seeing the officer.
Klein:	That is as far as you go, is it, just that you don't recollect?

Turpin: (Pause) My meaning by "recollect" is that I
            had no memory of it. That's what I meant
            by it.[62]

In court, Turpin conceded there were three reasons the police would want him under arrest: the gun under the seat in the truck, the brown paper bag full of money from the Red Rooster Restaurant break-in, and the warrant out against him for the shooting at Della Burns's apartment the previous October. As he drove along the Danforth the night of the murder, he kept looking in the rear-view mirror, nervous about being caught following the robbery he just committed.

"So you were trying to avoid police officers?" asked Klein.

"I was trying to avoid police officers for four months, to be truthful," said Turpin, who told Klein the reason he gave the name of his friend Orval Penrose instead of his own was to avoid arrest by prompting Nash's memory, since he was wanted under the name of Ronald Turpin.

Recounting for Klein his version of how Nash was going to strike him with the gun, Turpin began contradicting the story he'd just finished telling the jury. Did the police officer hit him? He couldn't say for certain if Nash accidentally missed hitting him or intended to miss. When he raised his arms, Turpin said his intention was to avoid the blow, not to run, grab the weapon, or take hold of Nash's arm. As soon as he heard an explosion and felt pain, he staggered back to the left rear fender of the scout car.

Turpin's recollections were vague, and he claimed he couldn't even remember if Nash's police car was running when he was hauled out of it and arrested by Constable McDonnell. At East General Hospital, he remembered being treated for five bullet wounds when he arrived, "One on my face, one in each arm, and one in each hand." Turpin was floundering under Klein's cross-examination. He said he had "no idea" how the gun got into his hand. He said he fired just a single shot. "How can you remember that?" asked Klein. "Because I remember the officer looking me right in the face. He was looking right up at me," said Turpin. When asked if he was trying to hit Nash, Turpin admitted he was. "In the chest?" asked Klein. Turpin couldn't say for certain, just that he was returning fire, "I guess, for self-preservation."

When Klein asked him about the gun under his seat, Turpin told the court he only became aware the Beretta semi-automatic pistol was in the truck when Lillian told him she put it there. Klein challenged him about what, precisely, he was going to do with the weapon: discard it or keep it? At first he said he wanted to dump it up north somewhere, then he told Klein he planned to hide the gun.

After Klein was done with Turpin, the police inspector in charge of the morality division was called to the stand by MacKay. Herbert Thurston knew Constable Nash, who was part of the morality division for a brief time. It was an attempt on MacKay's part to introduce information about the incident at the Town Tavern, and to portray Nash as a renegade cop.

MacKay:	Inspector, in the late fall of 1961, whilst there was a commission going on in this city regarding police violence, did any incident come to your attention involving Mr. Perry and P.C. Nash?
Thurston:	There was an incident involving the both of them, yes.
Mr. Klein:	My lord —
The Witness:	But not in relation to part of your question.
His lordship:	Well, why do you tie the two in? Were they related at all?
MacKay:	Why do I tie the commission —
His lordship:	Yes.
MacKay:	— in with the incident?
His lordship:	Yes.
MacKay:	Well, my lord — and with respect, this is perhaps something for argument — my reason for asking the question is that I feel it is open for an inference to be drawn

The Witness:	It had nothing whatsoever to do with it.
Mr. Klein:	With police violence?
The Witness:	That is correct.
MacKay:	I am asking. This is my witness.
Mr. Klein:	Well, I am objecting from here on. It is not admissible, in any event.
His lordship:	Wait a minute (To the jury): You had better leave, gentlemen, while we hear about this.[63]

that the demotion was made because there was some aggravation at the time about police violence.

The heated discussion then continued in private, and they discussed the question of how the commission investigating allegations of police violence was relevant to the trial.

"My submission is that, in view of the defences that I have raised, it is readily apparent — and it will be put to the jury — that Mr. Nash's propensity or non-propensity for violence would have the greatest relevance," MacKay told Justice Gale. "Surely if the defence is going to be one of self-delusion or delusion about self-defence —"

"You are seeking to show that Nash was a violent man, putting it simply?" asked Gale of MacKay.

"Yes, it comes down to that, my lord," replied MacKay.

The reason for Nash's demotion from the morality division, said Thurston, was because the off-duty officer was found drinking in a bar called the Town Tavern in the fall of 1961. He was a probationary detective at the time. And although there was an allegation of force, it did not involve Nash, who had already left the tavern when the incident took place. Still, Thurston recommended Nash be transferred back to the beat.

If that was all MacKay had to offer to show Nash was prone to violence, he was on a "fishing expedition," said Justice Gale, "and I think you have been told already that the pond has been fished out." Prosecutor Klein then asked the judge to keep this incident out of the trial, on the grounds that it was privileged. He agreed, and ruled MacKay could not introduce certain documents to the jury. The judge agreed. MacKay was not willing to give up without a fight.

His lordship:	I think it would be quite improper and against public interest to allow counsel in a case of this kind to try and glean something without any foundation whatever. I mean, it would not stop here if I ruled you could proceed in this way. You could bring down the Chief of the Toronto Police Department and get him to bring all the records with him.
MacKay:	That is exactly what I intend to do.
His lordship:	Well, we will stop now, because it is entirely without any foundation that you propose to do that.[64]

With the jury still absent, Gale went on to say that any documents sought by MacKay would amount to releasing private and confidential communications between members of the Metropolitan Toronto Police Force, material not meant to be viewed by the public "in any sense of the word." Inspector Thurston then qualified that Nash had not been demoted, but as he was still on probation he was simply moved back to the position he'd held before coming to the morality division.

Following the Judge's ruling, next to testify were two psychiatrists who separately saw Ronald Turpin to determine his mental state. Dr. Norman Easton, a staff physician at the Ontario Hospital and an experienced court examiner, spoke to Turpin in the Don Jail on April 18, 1962. Their first meeting was brief, lasting only five minutes. Easton met Turpin again at the jail on May 24, and the two talked for an hour and a half.

"I would say that he was not insane at the time [of the shooting]," recalled Easton, who'd attended the entire trial since it began on May 28 and heard all the evidence. "I concluded that the man was not insane because he did not show any of the usual signs and symptoms which are characteristic of that condition."

An unpublished document dated April 26, 1962, reveals that MacKay initially advised his client against submitting to a psychiatric evaluation. Crown attorney Klein suspected an insanity defence might be raised and, since it was a capital case involving the death penalty, he requested two psychiatrists examine Turpin. In court, Dr. Easton stated he did not believe Turpin's claims he would be killed by police, nor in his opinion did Turpin suffer any "hysteria" following the gun blast in his face. The doctor's reports make unusual reading, and portray Turpin as variously arrogant, reclusive, friendly, reserved, and defensive. The report of his brief initial meeting with Turpin on April 18 is less than one page in length, yet it speaks volumes about the many strange sides of the man on trial:

> He [Turpin] entered the room with great bravado. He was not wearing an undershirt and his shirt was open to the waist exposing his chest which was covered with a heavy growth of black hair, of which he appeared to be very proud.
>
> I introduced myself by name, told him I was a physician and not a lawyer, and that I was not interested in whether or not he was guilty but had been asked to report on him as an individual. His reply was "I am sorry but I refuse to talk because I have been advised by my attorney, Mr. Ross McKay [sic], (whom he said was staying at the Barclay Hotel) to say nothing to anyone when he is not present."[65]

Over a month later, on May 24, Dr. Easton re-examined Turpin at the Don Jail, after receiving word from MacKay that Turpin "was now prepared to talk." To Dr. Easton, the individual now sitting in front of him was an entirely different man. This time, Turpin was friendly, cooperative, and willing to discuss his past life. To the doctor, Turpin revealed his early life leading up to the night of the murder.

His father was still alive, or so he thought, Turpin told the doctor. His half-brother was serving a stretch at Kingston Penitentiary. His parents separated when he was young, and his childhood was spent with relatives, with the Children's Aid Society, and in foster homes. He went to the Bowmanville Training School at age thirteen because of "incorrigibility," and it was at this time, Grade 8, that his formal education came to a halt. "From then on until about one year ago his life was one of repeated crimes and he never supported himself by lawful means," stated Dr. Easton in his report. Within months of leaving Bowmanville, the teenaged Turpin racked up numerous convictions for shoplifting, burglary, car theft, forgery, and escaping from custody.

During the psychiatric examination, Turpin spoke about one of the few legitimate jobs he ever held: working for Union Furniture and Showrooms Company, selling furniture and placing tenants in furnished apartments. It was one of the rare times that Turpin kept himself out of trouble, but it came to an end after about seven months, and he blamed police surveillance. This was one of several claims of police persecution Turpin made during the examination, using expressions like "threatening violence" and "sadistic attacks." The only positive thing to happen to him during this time, he said, was falling in love with a girl whom he planned to marry (probably Lillian White).

Although Turpin was receptive to his questions, Dr. Easton wasn't accepting his claims of police violence. He found no evidence of serious mental disorder. "His mood was one of mild elation and not in keeping with the seriousness of the situation in which he found himself," stated the doctor in his report, determining there was no evidence of hallucinations or delusions. If anything, wrote the doctor, Turpin was guilty of faulty judgment, but he showed no signs of insanity. To MacKay, the doctor stated: "I don't believe that Turpin believed that he would be killed at the hands of the police."

The other doctor to examine Turpin was Joseph Grodsinski. A psychiatrist for the Ontario Department of Health, he also spent an hour and a half with Turpin, and found him to be open and cooperative. As he had with Dr. Easton, Turpin recounted his childhood, and life in and out of foster homes. His ability for abstract thinking and outside interests was very limited, with intelligence in the "dull normal range," meaning Turpin was able to understand the nature and consequences of his actions. However, Dr. Grodsinski's evaluation was very different from the earlier report when it came to Turpin's attitude about the police:

> There is a definite paranoidal attitude in his thinking, especially about the police in regard to him. During this examination I could not detect sufficient disorganization in his thought processes or emotions which would imply legal and psychiatric irresponsibility for his actions. He is suffering from a personality disorder but in my mind not amounting to a degree of certifiable insanity.[66]

Despite Turpin's paranoid attitude about the police, Grodsinski told the court he came to the conclusion that Turpin was not mentally ill at the time of the shooting and was not a paranoiac. It was not what defence attorney Ross MacKay wanted to hear, and in his closing remarks to the jury, MacKay again brought up Turpin's miserable, displaced childhood. Although his client had been a thief all his life, one thing was constant: he wasn't a man who settled disputes with violence.

"Nowhere there is there any indication of violence or any offence connected with firearms or anything of that sort at all," MacKay told the packed courtroom. His client was not someone who normally carried a gun, and there remained some doubt about who fired first on the night of the shooting. "I say the combination of Mr. Ough's evidence and Mr. Boreham's evidence and Dr. Penny's evidence and Ronald Turpin's own evidence leads almost inescapably to the conclusion that P.C. Nash fired first," said MacKay.

In his charge to the jury, prosecutor Klein called Turpin's evidence "completely worthless" and said his words were those of "an outright criminal, a man who does not know the meaning of the word 'honesty.'" Turpin was, said Klein, someone who would not hesitate to commit perjury to save himself. His words were cutting as he summarily dismissed the testimony of everyone who could possibly aid in Turpin's defence, such as Della Burns, whom Klein called a "paragon of virtue." Stephen Posen, the young law student who assisted MacKay during the trial, was sometimes surprised by Klein's attitude.

"Klein appeared to be articulate, capable, but extremely, extremely biased in terms of wanting to win this case. He was very, very tough on any aspect of the case that might have been beneficial to Turpin, as I recall," says Posen. "And that was disappointing to me, because my understanding was that a Crown Prosecutor was to bring out the truth, rather than to have a point of view about winning a case, in particular a capital murder case such as this. I think he was tough on Turpin because of the fact that the victim was a police officer. It's understandable, but I think it was wrong."

Constable Nash was an easygoing type, Klein told the court, and "not the sort of man who would push Turpin against the fender of the police car and who, when Turpin turned around, according to Turpin's evidence, would then have his arm upraised with the gun pointing upwards about, as Turpin would have you believe, to bring it down on him and hit him." As for the issue of Turpin being out of his mind at the time, Klein pointedly told the jury "the defence of insanity falls to the ground completely." Turpin's inexplicable memory loss was "absolutely groundless." He was resisting arrest, and nothing more, said Klein.

On the last day of the trial, Wednesday, June 13, 1962, Justice Gale spoke to the court. Although he reminded the jury of the need to impartial, his comments were anything but, especially when it came to the calibre of many of the witnesses for Turpin's defence. Some of them, said Justice Gale, "seem to have had somewhat lower moral standards than others." One was, in his estimation, "almost a confessed perjurer," while another, Della Burns, did not strike him "as being one who should be held up as an example of fine Canadian womanhood." Lillian White, Turpin's girlfriend, was described by Justice Gale as "a person who seemed to have lived rather promiscuously and precariously." Others who spoke on Turpin's behalf were nothing more than people who protected the fugitive and were "prejudicial in favour of the accused." On the other side, many of the witnesses favourable to the prosecution, such as funeral home owner John Ough and streetcar drive John Wrycraft, were "decent people," in Gale's opinion.

After reviewing what happened the night of February 12, Gale asked the jury to consider the issue of Turpin's overall trustworthiness and to decide if this was a factor in him resisting being arrested by Constable Nash.

"You heard of his way of life," said Gale. "Is he likely to tell a falsehood to protect himself at this trial? Was he guilty of some contradictions in his own evidence?" The main issue for the judge remained who shot first, Turpin or Nash. If Turpin initially pulled the trigger, surmised Gale, he was resisting arrest or was insane; if he shot at the officer first, it must have been that he was resisting arrest.

Although Justice Gale was entitled to tell the jury what he thought of the evidence, it seemed to Stephen Posen as though he had formed his own opinion during the trial, which he freely shared with the twelve jurors.

"I just had a feeling that Justice Gale had a view of this case, and I don't know when he formed the view," says Posen. "It may have only been at the end, because of the fact that he is entitled to tell the jury what he thinks about the evidence. I don't think he was unfair particularly, but his viewpoint became known to me, and as it became known to me, I'm going to guess it became known to the jury." Posen, who didn't support the death penalty then or today, didn't believe all the evidence against Turpin proved murder beyond a reasonable doubt.

"I may have been biased, because I was assisting on the defence. But I believe that the evidence wasn't strong enough evidence to convict of capital murder. And given that, I would have hoped for better from the judge. But a police officer was killed, and I sort of had the feeling that the circumstances in totality — not the evidence, but the attitude of Arthur Klein and Justice Gale — were leading in the same direction, which was a conviction of capital murder," says Posen. "That's the perception I had. And I had the perception of this underdog accused with this most unfortunate life, and an underdog lawyer with a considerable innate talent, not having done the most focused of jobs. And it just felt to me that there were overwhelming odds against any decision other than a conviction of capital murder."

The odds were decidedly against Turpin, as they had been his entire life. The paranoia he felt towards the police was questioned by Gale, who said the "threats" relayed to the cop killer seemed to "fluctuate in quality and content considerably." As for Turpin's alleged insanity, the judge said there simply was no case to support this as a defence for murder. Turpin's claim of self-defence, said Justice Gale, should be used only as last resort, not "as a mere cloak for retaliation or revenge."

As the jury was about to deliberate, Justice Gale presented them with five alternative verdicts. Turpin could be found not guilty, not guilty by reason of insanity, guilty of manslaughter, guilty of non-capital murder, or guilty as charged of capital murder. The verdict had to be unanimous among all twelve jurors, who retired to consider their verdict at 1:52 p.m., June 13, 1962.

Immediately after the judge finished delivering his charge to the jury, Ross MacKay objected, telling him, "I felt you left that impression with the jury, that there was nothing favourable to say about Turpin in this case." It made no difference. Returning to the courtroom about three hours later, the jury delivered their verdict: guilty as charged. Unlike the previous murder trial of Arthur Lucas, MacKay asked the judge to poll the jury. One by one, the names of the jurors were spoken out loud, and each one in turn repeated the same phrase to the Registrar: "Guilty as charged."

Once the jury was polled, Justice Gale spoke to them about recent provisions to the Criminal Code, and asked if they believed Turpin should be granted clemency. As was the proviso with capital cases, any recommendation to spare Turpin's life and have him serve out the rest of his days in jail instead of being executed had to be unanimous. The jury was not required to make a recommendation, and if they did, it would be included in Gale's report to the Minister of Justice. It took only sixteen minutes for the jury to decide if they should save Turpin from the noose. Their verdict: no recommendation for clemency.

Thanking the jury for their services, Gale discharged them, then spoke directly to Turpin, who silently bit his lower lip and clenched his right hand when he heard the verdict. The silence was broken when Turpin's female friends — one of them described by newspapers as "an attractive brunette" — started sobbing and had to be helped out of the courtroom.

> His Lordship: Turpin, kindly stand up. Have you anything to say before sentence is passed upon you?

The prisoner: Nothing, my lord.

His Lordship: Well, all I wish to say, and I certainly do not wish to add to the torment which must be yours right now, is this. You have had a very fair trial. Everything has been done for you that could possibly be done for you. You have been brilliantly defended. The jury, in my opinion, have reached the only possible verdict upon the evidence. On that evidence they have found that you were guilty upon the charge of capital murder. All I propose to do now is to impose the sentence of the Court. The sentence of the Court upon you, Ronald Turpin, for the crime of which you have been found guilty is that you be taken from the place where you are now to the place whence you came, there to be kept in close custody until the 25th day of September, 1962, when you will be taken to the place of execution and hanged by the neck until you are dead. And may God have mercy upon your soul. Remove the prisoner.[67]

The trial of Ronald Turpin was a long and challenging one for the jurors and the family of Constable Nash. For the officer's widow, Dorothy, the weeks and months following her husband's death were almost unendurable. She purposely did not follow the case of his killer, and was sent by her mother on a three-week tour of England and Scotland around the same time as Turpin's trial to take her mind off her husband's murder.

The moment Constable Nash succumbed to his bullet wounds following the shooting, Dorothy and her children not only lost their husband and father but their entire means of financial support. Toronto city council was waffling about paying Mrs. Nash a pension, and Torontonians did what they could to help the family of the slain police officer. The outstanding money owing for a washer and dryer the couple bought on credit was cancelled by the store owner. A Toronto businessman and developer, Louis Mayzel, started $1,000 university endowment funds for each of the four girls,[68] having taken out similar policies for the son of Edmund Tong, another police officer murdered in the line of duty ten years earlier.

To help with their financial obligations, the Nash Fund was created to help support the family of the slain police officer. Across the city, charity drives helped raise much-needed cash. Proceeds from Toronto Argonaut football players game were collected, along with charity baseball games and an NHL Oldtimers hockey game. Actors staged a benefit play at Theatre Sixty, and there was a two-hour-long B'nai Brith phone campaign, which aimed to raise $16,000 to aid the families of Frederick Nash and Edmund Tong.

In a strange, sad twist of fate, the matter of a pension for Nash's family came up at the same time when the pension for the widow of Sergeant of Detectives Tong was inexplicably slashed by the city from $2,700 to $1,700. No review was made before the $1,000-a-year reduction was applied. Her two children were still living at home — one of them an epileptic dependant on her mother — and every penny was crucial. Having to fight for a pension was just one of a number of eerie coincidences the two widows would share.

Both Nash and Tong were shot on the streets of Toronto; while Nash died within hours of his injuries, Tong lived in agony for seventeen days until his death. Constable Nash was the first Toronto police officer to die since forty-eight-year-old Tong was shot by Steve Suchan, who was sentenced to hang along with fellow Boyd Gang member Lennie Jackson. Both men were hung back to back at the Don Jail almost ten years to the day before Turpin and Lucas would meet the same fate.

The notion of a pension for police widows left the city scrambling for a solution. Until the Nash shooting, there was never an actual policy under which Toronto paid a pension to the families of policemen killed in the line of duty, and it was left to Metro Council to decide how much if anything Dorothy Nash should be awarded.

"Local government is just as responsible for supporting the family of a police casualty as the nation is for a dead soldier's widow and children,"[69] wrote *Telegram* columnist Andrew MacFarlane, who was particularly outspoken on the issue of awarding police pensions. The process of pleading for a pension was demeaning to Mrs. Nash, said MacFarlane, and was the equivalent of "passing around her dead husband's hat for money."

Not to be outdone, the *Toronto Star* printed a poignant editorial cartoon on the subject of pensions for police widows and their families. In the illustration, a bunch of faceless bureaucrats jump around shouting, "No pension for police widows!" "Wot if a garbageman fell on his head?" and "Dangerous precedent!" while two Shriners scurry out of council chambers, one turning to the other and saying, "Wow, is that the same outfit that gave us five thousand dollars?"[70] Both newspapers typified the view of the general public: widows of policemen killed in the line of duty should receive a pension.

Mrs. Nash would have to go through hardship similar to Mrs. Tong's, with months of indecision on the part of Toronto's city council, which drew vast amounts of criticism from local papers, saying the reluctance of Metro Executive Committee to grant Mrs. Nash a pension "embarrasses the community." An editorial in the *Toronto Star* said, "Constable Nash lost his life in protecting the community, and it is surely the duty of the community to see that his widow and children do not suffer unduly because of his sacrifice."

For the city, however, a number of issues were at stake. At the time of his death, Nash earned $5,100 a year. His family would get $2,100 a year from the Workmen's Compensation Board, along with monies from other sources, some of them Nash's retirement fund, which he would have received in any case since he'd paid into it during his time as a working police officer. A $3,000 annual pension was proposed for the Nash family, which would raise Mrs. Nash's pension to the salary of a first-class constable in 1962.

While Toronto Mayor Nathan Phillips recommended approving the entire $3,000 pension for Mrs. Nash, others at Metro Council balked at the amount, feeling the monies she would receive from other sources would be enough for her and four young daughters. Norman C.

Goodhead, a district official for North York, delayed the pension from being awarded even further, asking "How can you differentiate between a police officer killed on duty and a garbage man killed falling off a truck?" and telling council members to rule with their heads, not their hearts.

For widows Nash and Tong, it was a drawn-out and unnecessary ordeal; the decision to pay Mrs. Nash a pension to make her income equivalent to the salary of a first-class police constable was only made in July, and she wouldn't receive any funds until September 1962, after months of uncertainty. The issue of police pensions concerned the mayor and Metro Council enough to seriously consider taking out insurance policies from famed insurers Lloyd's of London for the families of police officers slain while on duty, and it again raised the issue of two-man patrol cars.

When Nash was shot and killed in February 1962, he tragically became the first officer killed since Metro initiated its controversial one man to a cruiser system a year earlier. His death sparked demands for a return to the two-man, or partner, system of patrolling the city in squad cars. At the time, many other major Canadian cities were using two-man patrols. Montreal tried one-man patrols, then soon returned to two police officers per car. In Vancouver, officers travelled in pairs at night, sometimes alone during the day. In large American cities like Detroit, New York, Boston, and Buffalo, officers were never sent out in a car alone.

Like any other issue involving city hall and bureaucracy, some were in favour of the plan, while others said it was not financially feasible. One of the first questions raised was the safety and security of Toronto's police officers. While there is no guarantee Turpin would not have shot Nash that freezing February night if he hadn't been alone, it is likely the presence of another officer at the scene would have reduced the odds. Instead of a second officer, two-way wrist radios were proposed, which seemed more suited to Dick Tracy comic books than serious police work. The idea was ruled impractical and too expensive when the police commission learned the radios would cost $210 apiece. In either case, extra costs to the city remained the key factor.

"I don't see why we should make a change just because an officer has died," said chairman C.O. Bick. "Any check of the records would show that even when we had two men in a car, officers were shot. There is no guarantee this wouldn't have happened if Constable Nash had not been alone." Bick argued that Toronto police already travelled in pairs in potentially dangerous downtown areas, and one-man patrols were sufficient for other areas of Toronto, to get better coverage of the city. Unfortunately, it would be another twelve years following Nash's death before two-man cruisers would be ordered for the city of Toronto.[71]

CHAPTER 7

Spare Their Lives

When you think you have been tricked out of your life, it is very hard.
— Arthur Lucas

He has little if any understanding of himself.
— Dr. W. Arthur Blair on Ronald Turpin

Appeals to save the lives of Arthur Lucas and Ronald Turpin began soon after the death sentences were handed down by Justices McRuer and Gale on May 10 and June 13, 1962. The two were initially scheduled to be hanged in September and October of that year. What followed were months of letter-writing campaigns, television programs, and newspaper editorials led by lawyers, the media, university professors, and Salvation Army Chaplain Cyril Everitt, who vigorously petitioned the Prime Minister and the Minister of Justice to save the lives of the two men.

Ross MacKay may have represented them at their back-to-back trials, but it would be a team of other lawyers championing their appeals all the way to the Supreme Court of Canada. Exceptionally skilled and armed with years of trial experience, the attorneys for Turpin and Lucas nonetheless found themselves stymied by the same obstacles that had dogged MacKay, from a lack of funds to new evidence being ruled inadmissible.

Turpin's appeal to the Supreme Court of Canada would be handled by a lawyer named Patrick Hartt. An avowed abolitionist, Hartt's appeal was lengthy, detailed, and critical. He cited trial judge George Gale for erring in instructing the jury in a number of respects, from the degree of force Constable Fred Nash used to arrest Turpin to his client allegedly shooting a gun at the party of his friend Della Burns in October 1961. Justice Gale, wrote Hartt, also erred by instructing the jury that they were entitled to consider Turpin's "previous criminal and anti-social activities" to determine if he was the type of person likely to shoot a police officer, and that Justice Gale should not have allowed evidence showing that Nash was a man of good character and unlikely to resort to violence, as stated in court by Herbert Thurston, his former superior and head of the morality division.

One of Hartt's handwritten notes recorded that Turpin cleared up one of the many mysteries surrounding February 12, 1962, the night of the fateful shooting on Danforth Avenue. He admitted to his appeal lawyer the real reason he was pulled over by Constable Nash that frigid night was because the officer recognized him from one of the half-dozen "To-day's Most Wanted Persons" posters pinned on Metropolitan Toronto Police bulletin boards across the city.[72] However, Turpin's admission to his appeal lawyer didn't make it into the appeal, or into the public record. For many years, it was believed Turpin was stopped because of the dangerously unsafe condition of his vehicle, especially the battered right front headlight on his Pontiac truck, held to the vehicle by electrical tape. It is not known if Turpin told Ross MacKay about Nash recognizing him as a wanted man. In his appeal, he maintained the same stories about feeling persecuted by police officers, which resulted in him shooting and killing Nash in self-defence.

> Turpin had been told by his friends and believed that he would be subjected to a severe beating and "possibly worse" by certain members of the Toronto police when he was apprehended. It was his intention to leave Toronto and go up north. He knew that Nash was arresting him and he was submitting but he was

subjected to unnecessary violence, shot in the face and the arm before he fired any shot. He testified that he did not intend to kill Nash but he fired as protection from and motivated by the use of violence by Nash.[73]

During his trial, those involved with the case — including Justice Gale, prosecutor Arthur Klein, and the deputy chief of police — simply did not believe Turpin's claims of self-defence, finding it unlikely, if not impossible, that a seasoned officer like Nash would strike a suspect with his revolver. At the time, judges presiding over capital cases were required to submit reports to the Minister of Justice following the outcome of the trial, and in his letter of June 18, 1962, to Edmund Davie Fulton, Gale made his opinion of Ronald Turpin abundantly clear. The trial was a lengthy one, fifteen days in total, and after deliberating for three and a half hours, the jury found Turpin guilty of capital murder and made no recommendation for mercy as he was sentenced to hang on September 25, 1962. Gale agreed wholeheartedly with the verdict.

"I find it quite impossible to recommend executive clemency," wrote Gale in his detailed, thirteen-page memorandum. "The accused is a thoroughly bad and vicious man." Gale concurred with Klein's estimation of the twenty-eight-year-old being a hardened criminal and a soul beyond redemption.

> I believe that he is a man who has come to think that he could live by his wits and a gun and that had he not encountered P.C. Nash he would have killed some other person sooner or later. Perhaps I may be permitted to say, too, that in my opinion the morale of law enforcement agencies in this area will undoubtedly suffer if any leniency is extended to this desperado. Surely juries will seldom decline to recommend clemency. This jury did and I concur in its decision in that respect.[74]

Others shared a similar view of Turpin, who would later be described in the pages of *Maclean's* magazine as "a slick little ferret of a man," the word "slick" somehow being replaced by "sick" over the years. Few in law enforcement disagreed with this opinion of the career criminal.

In a letter written by Deputy Chief of Police George Elliott to officials at the Department of Justice, Elliott summed up the opinion of investigating officers, many of them familiar with Nash personally and professionally. To them, Turpin was nothing but a menace, a cold-blooded, callous killer who felt no remorse whatsoever after shooting Nash, a man with a wife and four young daughters. They were incensed by his flippant comment, "Well, that's the way it goes. You've got to go sometime," made after detectives told him Nash had died moments earlier from his gunshot injuries. Likewise, the deputy chief of police dismissed Turpin's claim about discarding the Beretta semi-automatic pistol somewhere up north, saying the reason Turpin kept the weapon was so he could use it "if he was apprehended in the commission of a crime."

Crown attorney Klein, who successfully prosecuted Turpin, enclosed psychiatric evaluations along with his opinions in his letter to the Minister of Justice. The psychiatrists, wrote Klein, were both of the belief the accused man "was the most callous and cold blooded criminal psychopath that they had ever encountered,"[75] an opinion that was substantiated by evidence given at the trial.

As part of his appeal process, Turpin underwent yet another psychiatric exam, this time by a third doctor, W. Arthur Blair. As with his earlier evaluations, Turpin was seen at the Don Jail, and was extremely reluctant to talk until his lawyer Patrick Hartt placed a call to Cyril Everitt. Once Turpin's spiritual advisor gave his permission, Turpin's mood changed immediately, and he sat down and freely discussed his life with Dr. Blair. In the psychiatrist's opinion, the young man appeared comfortable, but still on edge and highly controlled.

The examination with Dr. Blair was different from the earlier ones conducted by Doctors Easton and Grodsinski. Blair spent two hours with Turpin, and his twelve-page report focused more on Turpin's parents and his childhood than earlier psychiatric evaluations. He painted a picture of a toddler living in a violent, unstable world, with a father who was frequently absent and a mother upon whom he was entirely dependant. Through the examination, Turpin's feelings for his mother fluctuated wildly, from indifference one minute to rage the next.

One of Turpin's earliest memories of his mother's mental instability was when he saw her attempt to commit suicide, or so he thought. Entering her room, he found her sitting there pale-faced, surrounded by wads of blood-soaked gauze and bottles of iodine. If Edith Turpin was trying to kill herself, she either had second thoughts or stopped partway while cutting her flesh, sickened by the sight of her own blood. In his young mind, Turpin could forgive his mother for almost anything but abandonment. Any strong bond he had with her was broken when he was sent to live with Children's Aid, foster homes, and relatives, none of whom seemed to care to have him around except to do chores or act as a sexual plaything.

"He feels that his whole childhood was coloured by sexual incidents," wrote Dr. Blair, describing an incident when two of Turpin's aunts attempted to have sex with him when he was still just a little boy. Any attitudes Turpin had about love and commitment were carried over into his adult relationships with women. Just as his mother refused to commit to him — if she had, she wouldn't have surrendered her child to the authorities — Turpin rarely gave himself to any woman in any way but sexual. He kept his emotions to himself, while "avoiding any permanent, lasting relationships."

In Dr. Blair's opinion, Turpin's early exposure to sexual activity — ranging from heterosexual sex to lesbianism to bestiality — contributed to him essentially bypassing normal early teenage development. "Society has found him difficult only in that he has indulged himself in antisocial behaviour such as stealing, forgery and so forth," wrote Dr. Blair. "He certainly did not inherit a wealth of traits, that if fulfilled would lead him to becoming a useful citizen. Over and above this, his early formative years were chaotic with lack of guidance, lack of love and affection, and rife with unstable, argumentative and physically-violent parents."

Turpin had many other problems, ranging from anti-social behaviour to alcoholism, Blair noted. Still, the doctor determined Turpin was not, nor had he ever been, psychotic. His biggest problem was his complete inability to accept responsibility for his own actions, and this pitiless nature came across in his feelings about Constable Nash's family. "The latter is probably brought out by his attitude towards the death of the officer, in that he says he felt badly about it to begin with because his wife would not have the comforts and material things of life," Blair recorded. "Now he doesn't feel at all badly, since he has come to know that a fund was set up which is providing fairly adequate and secondly, she's got another boyfriend."[76]

Although Dr. Blair did not actually consider Turpin to be a psychopath, his final comments on the man are puzzling and contradictory. "It has been said that psychopaths such as he are notably successful in avoiding long-term incarcerations and he has been a good example of this." For Turpin, the results of the examination proved to create a Catch-22 situation. Superficially charming, manipulative, callous, egocentric, incapable of forming lasting relationships, with poor impulse control and little if any empathy for others, Turpin exhibited many of the characteristics of a psychopath. Still, Dr. Blair did not consider Turpin to be mentally ill, and consequently he could not be placed in a mental hospital. "With the present extent of our knowledge, modern-day psychiatry can offer little to people such as he," wrote the doctor in his concluding remarks.

As part of his appeal process, Arthur Lucas was also the subject of additional psychiatric evaluations. In June 1962, he was asked to make four pencil sketches for a psychiatrist. The subjects were fairly standard, as Lucas drew a girl, a house, a tree, and a person. Under the section on the drawing form marked "Occupation," Lucas wrote "Painter + Pimp." Based on the drawings and a lengthy session, J.P.S. Cathcart was perplexed by the mind behind Lucas's words and sketches. In Cathcart's opinion, the big black man sitting in front of him was anything but the criminal mastermind who snuck into the semi-detached house on Kendal Avenue that brisk November morning, brutally taking the lives of two people and leaving undetected.

"It occurred to me immediately, that for some reason this man had seemingly taken no precautions to cover up his tracks,"[77] wrote Cathcart, who showed the drawings to Dr. Kevan Mooney, head of the psychology department at Ottawa General Hospital. Cathcart did not inform Mooney of Lucas's personal history or the crime he was convicted of committing. Based on the information at hand, Mooney believed the subject of the psychiatric examination possibly suffered from some "organic damage" to the brain. "This man is mentally defective — he hasn't brains enough to plan anything — he's just a tool but there is lots of anxiety showing in this item — he's scared of something," wrote Mooney.

During his session with Cathcart, Lucas adamantly denied killing Crater and being involved with drug trafficking. He praised Everitt to the psychiatrist, calling him his "special advisor," and was critical of defence attorney Ross MacKay. "I think he should have been telling me something and planning the defence," grumbled Lucas, who also commented on his lawyer's drinking. It was one of the rare times Lucas criticized MacKay, who fought for his client with passion but very few resources.

As was the case with Turpin, Deputy Chief of Police George Elliott sent a letter with his opinions of Lucas to the Department of Justice. He considered Turpin "a cold-blooded, callous killer"; Lucas, "a man addicted to violence," fared no better than his fellow death row inmate.

"The drug trafficking, numbers and prostitution rackets (the latter two he freely admits being actively engaged in) are ruled by the underworld under threats of violence. Lucas was ruthless on girls 'working' for him and kept close watch on those connected with him and trusted nobody," wrote Elliott, who said Lucas had no moral obligations and was incapable of showing emotion. There was no doubt, wrote the deputy police chief, that he was the killer, although he stopped short of calling Lucas "mentally deranged," as Deputy Chief of Police George Elliott had.

During his many years in and out of prison, Arthur Lucas was the subject of countless examinations by psychiatrists and psychologists. Labelled as "feeble-minded" and a moron, Lucas was considered a custodial problem early on in life, but no known psychiatric report determined he was violent or aggressive toward others. The legal appeals to save Lucas's life certainly suggested he was a dupe and a man of questionable character, but not mentally capable of planning and executing a double homicide.

Acting on Lucas's behalf was top-notch trial lawyer Walter Williston from the firm of Fasken, Calvin, MacKenzie, Williston & Swackhamer. Cyril Everitt contacted Williston on Lucas's behalf, and he agreed to handle the condemned man's appeal. The material prepared by Williston's team summarized the facts of the case, arguing once again that the evidence presented during the trial, persuasive as though it might have been, was still entirely circumstantial. Lucas's defence was simply that he was not the murderer and had nothing to do with the deaths of Therland Crater and Carolyn Newman.

In Williston's opinion, the evidence against his client was insufficient and tainted, especially the words of Crown witness Morris Thomas, an admitted perjurer whose testimony was the lone source of information about Lucas's dealings in the drug trade. It was also Thomas who positively identified the broken .38-calibre Ivor Johnson revolver found on the Burlington Skyway as belonging to Lucas, and who stated Lucas asked him to bring clean clothes to his Collingwood Avenue apartment in Detroit after the murder. No upstanding citizen himself, Thomas spent considerable time in and out of jail, where he met Lucas for the first time in 1958.

In Williston's words, the man who prosecuted his client — the headstrong and formidable Crown attorney Henry Bull — drew "terrible inferences" from Thomas's testimony and other uncorroborated evidence. With his extensive criminal record for everything from forgery to armed robbery, Arthur Lucas was no role model for righteousness, but Williston argued in his appeal that the man's entire life was fodder for the prosecution. During the trial, the jury heard Bull offering up as hard evidence numerous details of Lucas's life, including his involvement in drug trafficking and pimping, and stating his wife was "a harlot" and that the pair were kicked out of Toronto by morality officers. In Williston's eyes, this information was not only out of proportion, it was damaging to Lucas's credibility.

"The effect of this evidence was to rip up the man's whole life to the extent that he was overwhelmed by prejudice and there was no possibility of him obtaining an unprejudiced verdict from the jury,"[78] stated the appeal.

Justice James McRuer, who presided over the Lucas trial, was not exempt from Williston's criticism. The appeal objected to a number of the comments he made in court, particularly, "The evidence is all relevant and important or it would not be admitted," a sweeping statement that included Morris Thomas's dubious testimony. The judge should instead have cautioned the jury "that it would be dangerous to make any finding of fact in reliance upon the evidence of Thomas alone," wrote Williston.

Filed along with the appeal was forensic information favourable to Lucas. An affidavit from Dr. Harold Fields stated he took a blood sample from Lucas in the presence of two witnesses and, after testing the blood, concluded there was no possibility Group AB could be Lucas's blood. The blood type of both Therland Crater and Carolyn Newman was B, but type AB blood was found on articles in the Kendal Avenue apartment, and in the car, suggesting someone else with AB type blood was the murderer.

A law student at the time, Julian Porter assisted Williston with Lucas's appeal. In a memorandum to Williston, Porter detailed his visit to Dr. Chester McLean, who performed the autopsies on Crater and Newman. "He said that the murder was the most skillful that he had ever seen committed and that both Carolyn Crater and Therland Crater were killed in an identical fashion in a scientific manner," wrote Porter in his memo, who went on to raise disturbing details about the murders. "He said the Police Department were very well aware that there was a second person in the room at the time of the murder, but they have no way of tracing him. He said that a body would not pick up fingerprints, and that hair is very often a neutral factor."[79]

Other valid issues in the appeal included the curious absence of Lucas's fingerprints in evidence, except those found on the car. At no point during the trial did Crown prosecutor Henry Bull suggest the killer, or killers, wore gloves. The most controversial piece of evidence remained the heavy men's gold ring found on the bloodstained bed next to Carolyn Newman's corpse. Wouldn't fingerprints be the surest way to identity it as belonging to Arthur Lucas? And, suggested Porter, wasn't it possible that since police found Newman's purse open on the living room floor, her lipstick, compact, and other contents strewn around, that the killings were motivated by some other factors, such as robbery or drugs?

In Williston's notes, he reveals Lucas told him that human hair was found underneath Newman's fingernails, and that a sample of his hair had been taken and tested, but nothing was mentioned about the test afterwards. Lucas also believed Harold King and Margaret Ladd were somehow involved in the double homicide. The couple renting the basement apartment of 116 Kendal Avenue had testified they heard strange voices and sounds coming from upstairs at the time of the murder. Lucas stated he believed the couple, also black, were part of the Detroit drug connection.

A quarter of a century after the trials, in 1987, when a motion was debated in the House of Commons to reintroduce capital punishment to Canada, the controversy surrounding evidence introduced during the Lucas trial was re-examined. In the appeal, Williston stated that not only were prosecutor Henry Bull's statements to the jury unsupported by the evidence, but when he wrote to Bull regarding information fingerprint and hair sampling, "Bull wrote back that he would oblige when a new trial was ordered or application was made to the minister of justice."[80] Since there was no new trial, the missing information never materialized.

In 1962, signs were emerging that capital punishment in Canada would someday become a thing of the past. Not wanting to miss out on what could possibly be the last executions in the country, newspapers extensively covered the trials and appeals of both Lucas and Turpin, and were not reticent about making their views known to readers. The *Telegram* was in favour of capital punishment, while the *Toronto Star* and the *Globe and Mail* were against it, citing the risks of executing the wrong person for the a crime, while the real killer went free.

A group of Toronto lawyers campaigned on behalf of the two condemned men, including Osgoode Hall Law School professor Desmond Morton, who wrote a piece that appeared on the editorial page of the *Globe and Mail*. Asking the question "Must Ronald Turpin Die?" Morton stated retribution for Turpin's crime didn't have to take the form of hanging him, and that society could instead have him locked up for the rest of his life.

> I believe that the taking of life is only justifiable where the necessity can be demonstrated. The case of Turpin, I submit, provides a clear demonstration of the absence of proof of such necessity. If necessity

there be to hang anyone, surely it would be most likely to be manifest in this case where a professional criminal, with a long career in crime, has been found to have murdered a police officer acting in the execution of his duty.[81]

Morton goes on to suggest that Turpin, if spared, could live out the remainder of his natural life in prison, and possibly become rehabilitated.

If Turpin is hanged we shall all have hanged him, having told him of the time and place of his death and left him hopeless. We shall have employed our agents to do it for us and required decent and humane men to attend to an event which we insist must be hidden from us. It must not be forgotten either that no judicial process has ever been demonstrated to be certain: a possibility, however slim, of error is always present.

Not everyone reading Morton's piece was moved to save Turpin, as the newspaper was inundated by letters, many of them in favour of hanging the troublesome cop killer. "It is necessary to purge our race of such people, and to save the taxpayer thousands of dollars in having Ronald Turpin as a permanent guest of the Government," wrote one irate *Globe* reader, adding that Professor Morton should be more concerned with the plight of Constable Nash's wife and four little girls than saving the life of one of society's "vilest and poorest specimens" who killed a police officer in the line of duty.

Others who fought to save the lives of both men included Frank McGee, the member of Parliament for York-Scarborough, who promised to make recommendations to the federal cabinet to have their death sentences commuted. Since the Conservative government was elected in 1957, the cabinet had commuted forty-eight of sixty capital murder cases, with the death sentence being carried out in twelve cases. By 1960, a new law distinguishing between capital and non-capital murder was passed by the federal government: capital murder carried the death sentence, and non-capital a mandatory sentence of life imprisonment. The executions of Turpin and Lucas were the first since the law was changed, and some, like Everitt, held out hope that the lives of the two men could still be saved.

To lift the spirits of both men, the chaplain visited them regularly at the Don Jail, often several times a day. Separate logbooks were kept, one to record visits from family and friends, including Everitt, and another for lawyers. In addition to these records, inmates on death row — euphemistically called "Hospital Nine" by the inmates because of its close proximity to the jail dispensary — had detailed in brief but descriptive sentences the minute-by-minute goings-on of their daily lives. Guard shift changes were noted, along with the names of visitors and the duration of their stay.

Hospital Nine was no less grim than the rest of the Don Jail. The area was screened off and had two sets of barred gates, so other prisoners couldn't see down the corridor. Guards sat on hard wooden chairs, while above them, three bare electric lights remained on twenty-four hours a day. The walls were a sickly yellow, while off to the side silver-painted radiators hissed and burped as they struggled to keep the area heated. Turpin and Lucas had little privacy in their cells, where they spent the majority of their time. They were permitted two showers per week, but shower curtains were forbidden. When and how often they decided to shower was also noted by guards, along with the other details of their daily existence.

What the prisoner ate that day — if he ate at all — and any health complaints he might have were meticulously taken down. Even the most mundane details, such as how much the prisoner smoked that day, or if he made his bed after getting up in the morning, were written down in black ledger books. On one day at 1:15 p.m., the notation in Lucas's book read, "Visited by Brig. Everitt, gave Lucas pair of glasses, and played checkers." On another day at 9:05 a.m., the guard on duty wrote, "Lucas in bed, reading." A third day at 1:30 p.m. saw "Lucas talking, seems depressed."

Everitt's only son, Bram, was in his late teens in 1962, and he remembers how often his father visited the two men at the Don Jail and how many letters and telephone calls he made to government officials, including the Minister of the Justice and even the Prime Minister.

On Saturday, December 1, 1962, Cyril Everitt was at home watching day one of the now-infamous Grey Cup at Toronto's CNE Stadium on television. Dubbed "The Fog Bowl," the game between the Winnipeg Blue Bombers and the Hamilton Tiger Cats started well, but when a thick fog rolled in from Lake Ontario in the fourth quarter, players were running into each other, and the conclusion of the game had to be postponed. Then came one of the first breaks the chaplain had in many months. The telephone began ringing in another room, and Bram picked it up. He recognized the familiar voice on the other end.

"Diefenbaker here."

As soon as his son told him it was the Prime Minister of Canada on the line, Everitt bolted off the couch to the phone. Their call was a lengthy one, lasting about twenty-five minutes, and Bram remembers his father saying "Yes, sir" and "No, sir" to the Prime Minister, himself an outspoken opponent of capital punishment. Sympathetic and understanding, Diefenbaker said he would present Everitt's views to the cabinet when it considered the two cases. He was shocked when Everitt told him that the same man, the bright but inexperienced Ross MacKay, had defended both Turpin and Lucas. Diefenbaker told him he would try his best, but reminded him that since neither jury recommended mercy, he was handicapped: "Cy, if you can find one shred of evidence why it shouldn't happen, I'll go to bat for you. But right now, all the deal's done, Turpin's a cop killer. But of you can find something about Lucas, I'll be glad to look at it."

Once the call ended, the chaplain told his son the news.

"Arthur Lucas always maintained his innocence, right up until he looked at the end of the rope," Bram Everitt remembers. "But Lucas was also resigned to the fact that he was going to go, because they got him for this one, which he didn't do — according to him — but there was other stuff that he did do. That was how he resigned himself to the fact that he was going to pay for it."

Cyril Everitt wasn't alone in his efforts to save the lives of the two men. Julian Porter, who was assisting with Lucas's appeal, made a trip to Ottawa to see Minister of Justice Donald Fleming on Lucas's behalf and present a final appeal. His father, Dana Harris Porter, had been appointed chief justice of Ontario by Diefenbaker in 1958 and knew Fleming, who was a longtime Progressive Conservative. A former finance minister, Fleming was often criticized for being humourless to the point of being robotic. In a *Maclean's* magazine profile, author Peter C. Newman wrote that other politicians respected Fleming, "but they also regard him as having a personality as warm as the blade of a snowplow."[82]

A small, mustachioed man, Fleming (intentionally or otherwise) bore a resemblance to Mickey Mouse creator Walt Disney. Porter went through whatever arguments he had with the minister of justice and asked him to commute the sentence to life imprisonment. When Fleming asked Porter if he had any other arguments than those that were advanced to the Supreme Court of Canada, the young man had to admit he didn't.

"Well, Julian, I can't help you," said Fleming, and their meeting was over. Downhearted, Porter made a long-distance call to Walter Williston and said nothing more could be done. Fleming soon sent a letter to Williston outlining his position on the Lucas case. The letter was of no comfort to Williston, and was dated December 10, 1962, one day before the scheduled executions. He wrote, "Notwithstanding your most earnest presentation on behalf of the accused, and exhaustive consideration of the case by the Cabinet, we simply could not find grounds for commuting the sentence. I doubt if any capital case has received such thorough and meticulous study by the Cabinet."[83]

Like Porter before him, Turpin's appeal lawyer, Patrick Hartt, also met with the justice minister to try to save his client's life. His appeal to Fleming was also denied. Both Turpin and Lucas were granted two stays of execution, and appeals to higher courts failed in both cases. They were going to die. Realizing there were no other avenues open to his client, Williston wrote a letter to Prime Minister Diefenbaker less than a week before the execution date. In it, he thanks him for his kindness and sympathy. Years later, the pain Williston felt is still palpable. "There is nothing else I can do or say for Lucas," Williston wrote. "Against capital punishment I will always have this indictment: that even when tried by a Judge of great experience, and an appeal is heard by Jurists of great learning, it is still possible that a man can be put to death for a crime which he did not commit. I know that you have suffered the same pang."[84]

The letter undoubtedly struck a chord with the Prime Minister. As a young lawyer, Diefenbaker believed capital punishment to be a dangerous thing, since there was always the risk of an innocent man being put to death. Diefenbaker experienced this first-hand when one of his clients in Saskatchewan was executed. Six months later, the star witness for the Crown admitted to the offence.

Since their arrests and all through the period of their trials and appeals, Turpin and Lucas had spent all their time in the same building where they would soon hang, an imposing structure that had been in operation for almost a century by the time the two condemned men entered its doors. The subject of numerous grand juries over the years, Toronto's Don Jail was a disease-ridden hell-hole that has been variously described as "an overcrowded dungeon," "an insult to humanity," "a black cesspool unfit for human habitation," and, simply, "the Black Hole of Calcutta." The jail's reputation would forever linger in the minds of the guards who worked and the inmates who stayed in its cramped, crowded cells.

If ever a building was cursed from the very beginning, before even the first stone was set in place, it was the Don Jail, so named because of its close proximity to the Don River. Located at 550 Gerrard Street East, a slight distance from the downtown core in Toronto's east end, it is one of the city's few intact structures that predates Canada's Confederation. The jail was the vision of renowned British emigrant architect William Thomas, whose other, more venerated projects include the grand St. Lawrence Hall and St. Michael's Cathedral. In a brief seventeen-year span, from 1843 to 1860, Thomas produced more than one hundred buildings — the Don Jail would be his last, and he would not live to see it completed.

With the explosive population growth in Toronto in the 1850s came an increase in crime and criminals, and the need for a new jail to replaced the outdated structure at Front and Parliament streets. Thomas's jail was based on the panopticon design of the Pentonville England Reformatory Prison, a jail with a central observation post from which guards could look down corridors and keep a watchful eye on inmates at all times. Although the intention of the Don Jail was to create a facility that was more "humane" with respect to the treatment and housing of inmates, the reality would prove to be far different for the troubled project, and for anyone unlucky enough to be incarcerated there.

When work began on the Don Jail in 1858, it was immediately complicated by cost overruns and last-minute demands and changes to the plans from the police board. Amid much pomp and circumstance, the cornerstone of the new jail was set in place on October 25, 1859, and was laid with Masonic honours. A host of Toronto dignitaries were in attendance, including politicians, firefighters, the deputy chief of police, Toronto Mayor Adam Wilson, and numerous masons, including the grand master of the Masonic Order in Canada. Some of the assembled masons, garbed in full dress, carried swords, plumbs, levels, and squares; others wore jewellery that shone brightly in the sunshine, as candles were lit around the stones and prayers given.

Despite the grandiose event, the anonymous reporter who covered the story for the *Globe* noted just how far behind the project had already become. "Not much progress has been made with the Gaol. The ground has been dug out where the foundation is to be laid, but little stonework is yet to be seen." A wooden fence had also been erected around the construction site by this time.

Few at the time could have known just how challenging the building of the jail would become in such a short time — not the mayor, who used an ornate silver trowel during the laying of the corner stone with great honour, not those whose chests burst with pride at the singing of the national anthem, and not the men who strew corn, wine, and oil upon the stone. It was a day for celebration, and once three cheers were given for Her Majesty Queen Victoria, four hundred guests went for a lavish lunch at another of architect Thomas's creations, the magnificent St. Lawrence Hall. No one could have predicted just how despised the Don would become over the decades.

Back at the jail construction site, things were far less glamorous. Numerous delays caused by politicians, different levels of government, and changes in contractors hampered the project. Early on, the foundation needed to be redone, adding unnecessarily to the cost of the jail, which kept escalating as the weeks and months went by.

In their book on William Thomas and his work, authors McArthur and Szamosi wrote about the final days of the renowned architect, as his health declined rapidly. Instead of a gentle death, Thomas was irascible, physically and mentally exhausted from his final project, his health worsening from the effects of diabetes.

> As a good Victorian man with few vices, he was assured of going to heaven, but hell would have been preferable to the bureaucratic nightmare in which he found himself at the end of the year. Thomas never lived to see the way out. At the time of his death, in the winter of 1860, the Don Jail was just a big hole in the ground. Into it the city had poured thousands of dollars, with little more to show for its efforts than a fence and pile of rubble on a windswept embankment.[85]

Following Thomas's death, work was carried on by his son, William Tutin, who found the Don Jail project to be no less of a nightmare than had his father. Even before the structure could be completed, a fire broke out in the winter of 1862, destroying the central building but sparing the wings. To add to the misery of all involved, insurance did not cover the entire cost of rebuilding.

By the time the jail finally opened in 1864, it had taken seven years from drawing to completion, and was thousands of dollars over budget. And yet, the Don Jail remains an impressive, imposing structure, haunted by the memories of the many men and women who died there.

Inspired by classical Italian and English Renaissance architecture, the main entrance is flanked by two enormous columns and vermiculated stonework, carved to look like masses of worms. The centerpiece remains the massive, iron-studded oak door, topped by a keystone featuring the carved stone countenance of Father Time, a bearded man whose face and stern expression were intended to strike terror into the hearts of those who entered. The architectural intention was to make anyone entering the jail feel small, with Father Time above their heads, as if to say, *You've done the crime, now do the time.*

Inside, the jail is no less imposing. The rotunda features an eighty-foot-high ceiling punctuated with skylights. Looking up, Turpin and Lucas and other inmates saw double balconies made of iron, which clanged loudly whenever anyone walked on them. The sound bounced off the stone walls, which were between one and a half and two and a half feet thick, making escape through them virtually impossible.

The cells were the only feature of the jail that was small. All were cramped, and some measured just three by ten feet. Although the jail was meant to contain 550 inmates, it was always overcrowded, often packed with 600 or more. Even before it welcomed Arthur Lucas and Ronald Turpin into its halls, the Don Jail was infamous for diseases like tuberculosis and vermin like rats and cockroaches, and it was freezing in the winter and sweltering in the summer. It was not uncommon for inmates to become violently ill or to choose a different means of escape, namely suicide.

Many inmates of the Don Jail were put to work, doing tasks like mopping or sweeping the floors. John Costello was a seventeen-year-old in the jail, serving thirty days for a traffic offence, in 1962 when he had a visitor. As he sat waiting on the bench, someone to his right turned and started talking to him.

"What are you in for?" asked the stranger.

"Driving offences," replied Costello.

"Do you want to trade places with me?"

"No," Costello said.

Being a teenager, Costello didn't want to pursue the conversation any further. Observing the man next to him, the first thing Costello noticed was his thick, very wavy dark hair, and a pinkish scar on his left cheek. A guard called out Costello's name and summoned him to the visiting area. When his visitor left, the guard that had brought him down from his cell asked him if he knew whom he'd sat next to on the bench. He was shocked when the guard told him it was Ronald Turpin. He had heard about the murder of Constable Nash, and the comments about Turpin being "a little ferret of a man." While watching Turpin, it wasn't his appearance that seemed ferret-like to Costello, but his mind.

"He was very straightforward, so I didn't take him to be a shy person," says Costello. "When they refer to him as 'a ferret of a man,' you can think of a ferret as being a busy little creature — he appeared to be that mentally — kind of busy, a speedy kind of individual. I never had any more meetings with Turpin; as a matter of fact, I'd never even seen him again."

Another time, Costello and other teenagers were mopping the area around Hospital Nine. He saw a guard playing checkers with one of the men in the cells; his muscular, shiny black arms were sticking through the bars. It became obvious that the individual playing checkers with the guard was Arthur Lucas, the other man on death row.

Turpin and Lucas would not be the only men awaiting execution; they were soon joined by a third man as they awaited the outcome of their appeals. Just nineteen years old at the time, Gary Alexander McCorkell, a lanky, average-looking teenager with a baby face topped by thick curls of black hair, was housed in a cell separate from the two older men on Hospital Nine. Mentally unstable and a sickly child, McCorkell suffered from epilepsy and nephritis, a kidney infection that caused him to wet the bed constantly. He was the product of a broken marriage; his mother was reduced to accepting welfare, her court orders for support for her and her troubled son stalled in their tracks. At age four, McCorkell was sexually assaulted in a washroom by an older boy so severely that he required medical attention and screamed for days afterwards.

The victim of a sexual predator, McCorkell soon became the aggressor. At age twelve, he molested a boy four years his junior. His mother's attempts to get him psychiatric treatment were dismissed when a hospital intern assured her everything would work out just fine, telling Blanche McCorkell, "He'll be all right. He has high morals."[86]

The intern was dead wrong. Despite McCorkell's efforts to do well in school, keeping busy with part-time jobs like caddying at a local golf course and setting up pins in a bowling alley, the teenager could not deny his urges. At sixteen, he molested two boys half his age, and was put on two years' probation and began receiving psychiatric treatment. Diagnosed as a homosexual pedophile, he was interested not in young women his own age but in boys much younger.

When he was nineteen, McCorkell's unnatural preoccupation with children reached a low point when he lured two toddlers — two-and-a-half-year-old Michael Atkinson and three-year-old Ronald MacLeod — through a side door in the warehouse of Robert's Furniture Ltd. on Lake Shore Boulevard West in Toronto. McCorkell, who worked as a $55-a-week shipper in the warehouse, tied up the boys with twine, sexually molested them, and suffocated them with his own hands when they wouldn't stop sobbing. In a pathetic attempt to revive them, he carried the children to the second floor from the basement, placed wet cloths over their foreheads, and looked for smelling salts in a first aid kit. When this failed, he calmly walked next door to a private hospital for a doctor and returned with an attendant who knew the youngsters were dead just by looking at them.

When police arrived at the warehouse that cold April day in 1962, they found the two children lying side by side, fully dressed in their winter clothes, eyes partly open and lifeless. One of the homicide detectives on the case, Jack Webster, stated that the clothing the boys were wearing reeked of urine. To compound the tragedy, the young mothers of both boys were pregnant, and Charles Atkinson — the father of the murdered two-and-half-year-old — had his birthday the day his son was abused and murdered.

"I didn't realize I was going to kill them," McCorkell said in a statement. "It was an accident. I just tried to quieten them to prevent me from being discovered."

At the Don Jail, McCorkell was segregated from other inmates by staff who feared the young man — like many pedophiles — would be the target of others and would be beaten or killed before he could be tried. McCorkell faced the same team who worked on Ronald Turpin's trial, including Justice George Gale and prosecutor Arthur Klein. McCorkell, like Turpin, was the subject of a psychiatric examination by Dr. Norman Easton, who testified he was not mentally ill when he smothered the boys. Found guilty of capital murder, McCorkell was scheduled to hang, and he entered the Don Jail to await his execution.

While on death row, Turpin and Lucas struck up a friendship with the teenaged McCorkell, whom they called "the Kid."

Although they never saw him, both men, Lucas in particular, played chess and checkers with him using numbered boards, and they became very protective of the shy killer, who spent his time reading Winston Churchill's book *Closing the Ring* when he wasn't playing games.

"Their conversation was never on a sordid or low level," said Chaplain Cyril Everitt, who regularly visited the trio at the jail. "But when McCorkell came in they were even more careful of what they said. They realized he was just a boy, and when we were discussing their execution or burial arrangements, they'd whisper to me: 'I don't want to say this out loud — McCorkell might be upset.'"[87]

Unlike Turpin or Lucas, the all-male jury recommended mercy for the teenaged killer "in the strongest possible terms," and there was a chance his death sentence could be commuted to life imprisonment. He spent his twentieth birthday in jail expecting to be hanged in a few months, and was given a sleeping pill the night Turpin and Lucas went to the gallows. Twenty years later, McCorkell spoke about his fellow death row cellmates: "I woke up the next morning, and the two were gone, and I knew that they'd been hung, and that's when it really hit … that it dawned on me for the first time that this could happen to me. And the closer it came, I guess, the more worry and fear I experienced at that time."[88]

Although found guilty as charged and with his appeal rejected by the Ontario Courts, McCorkell's capital sentence was commuted to life under the Conservative government of Prime Minister John Diefenbaker. He was the fiftieth person whose sentence had been commuted between 1957 and 1963. As he had done with Turpin and Lucas, Everitt petitioned the Minister of Justice and the Prime Minister to commute the sentence. "I, personally, am against capital punishment, with only a little reservation," Everitt told the *Globe and Mail*. He believed the young man had matured, and was "very remorseful" for the horrible deeds he had committed. Everitt admitted McCorkell needed psychiatric help, but told a Toronto newspaper the killer was not violent. "He's passive, in fact," the chaplain said of the child killer, who wanted to reform his ways, and become a leader, helping out people in difficulty as he himself had been helped.

Years later, almost immediately upon his release and after decades of therapy, the adult McCorkell would surrender to his demons and commit crimes as monstrous as the ones he carried out in 1962.

For Turpin and Lucas, there was nothing left to do but sit in their death row cells and pray somehow their lives would be saved. If they were to hang on December 11, it would be the first double execution at the Don Jail in almost ten years to the day. On December 16, 1952, Boyd Gang members Steve Suchan and Leonard Jackson dropped to their deaths on the Don's gallows. Their crime was the same as the one Turpin was convicted of. They killed a police officer.

CHAPTER 8

The Last to Hang

Within the past week two young children in Ontario tried their best to hang a baby: a dogcatcher successfully hanged a dog. There will no doubt be a great outcry over the hanging of the dog.
— Desmond Morton

In the final days leading up to December 11, 1962, newspapers and television and radio stations scrambled to feed the public as much information as possible about the upcoming hangings of Ronald Turpin and Arthur Lucas. Although legal appeals to save the lives of the two men were exhausted, the media relentlessly pursued their particular point of view, either for or against capital punishment. The decisions they made would themselves prove contentious in the years to come.

In a controversial last-minute decision, the Canadian Broadcasting Corporation decided to postpone a scheduled radio address about capital punishment until after the hangings. The program was slated to air just two days before the executions, but executives at the CBC suddenly changed their minds, stating the timing of the broadcast "would not be in good taste and serve no useful purpose." The move incensed Osgoode Hall law school professor Desmond Morton, who was about to speak his mind on Canada's national broadcaster about the perils of capital punishment.

"It is nonsense to say that to discuss the case beforehand would not be in good taste. Hanging is not in good taste,"[89] stated Professor Morton, arguing the point of the radio program was to debate the hangings *before* they were about to happen, certainly not after, when nothing more could be done. "There is no doubt that, even at this late date, something could be done to stop the hangings," he said. The CBC would not budge, and the radio broadcast would have to take place sometime after December 11. The law professor was bewildered not only by the postponement of his program but also by what he considered "the apathy of the public" and their fascination with seeing two men die at the end of the rope.

Morton was especially critical of the three major Toronto newspapers and their stance on the hangings. Two of the three came out opposing the hangings in their editorials, he said, but only in the days before December 11. The third paper's staunch support for capital punishment was "reminiscent of the fulminations of an 18th-century judge or bishop."

For the most part, the *Toronto Star*, the *Globe and Mail*, and the *Telegram* made their positions on capital punishment clear to their readers. The *Telegram*, which ran a number of articles in favour of the executions, published an uncharacteristically sympathetic piece on Turpin. In the story "P.C.'s Killer: Man Born Without A Chance," the *Telegram* attempted to explain his neglected childhood, physical and emotional abuse, and life as a small-time criminal.

"Turpin the human being is more than a cell number, more than a justice department statistic, more than a dangerous animal that society feels must be destroyed." The article spoke of Turpin's "wretched life," and how Turpin, from the age of three, "[h]as steadily been mounting the steps to the gallows."

The only person to befriend Turpin and Lucas almost a year earlier would walk with them as they took their last forty paces to meet the hangman. As the date of the executions grew closer, and the likelihood of any intervention to save their lives vanished, Chaplain Cyril Everitt increased his regular visits to the Don Jail to pray or to simply listen to the two condemned men talk for hours about their day. Taking the streetcar to the jail two or three times a day, Everitt was determined to spend as much time as possible saving the souls of the men he called friends, knowing there wasn't much time left. Although he rarely showed it in front of his spiritual charges, Everitt was mentally and physically exhausted, and close to collapse.

For jail guards walking past the death row cells and seeing the three men singing hymns together in harmony, the contrast couldn't have been greater. Here was Everitt, a lean, soft-spoken, immeasurably polite Salvationist who spent his entire adult life in the service of the Lord, praising God alongside a scrawny cop killer and a hulking black man who made his living by sending women out on the street to turn tricks. He had little in common with the two, save for the fact he and Lucas were both fifty-four years of age. It was a far cry from their first meeting months before, when Lucas looked up from his cell at Everitt, saying, "You wouldn't want to shake hands with me." Fortunately for Lucas, Everitt didn't listen. The bonds between the three were formed long before the night of the executions, as Everitt helped them believe not only in God but also in the unconditional kindness of another human being, possibly the only decent man they ever met.

It is unlikely Ronald Turpin knew the meaning of the word *repentance* prior to meeting the chaplain. On the Sunday night before the hangings, they were talking about another subject when Turpin stopped midway through their conversation. Looking puzzled, he shyly asked, "How can I meet my Maker if I hold a grudge to anybody?" Everitt explained that it was necessary for him to forgive everyone who had done him wrong. Turpin explained there was an old girlfriend in Vancouver he needed to send a message to. Everitt placed a long-distance call to the woman in Vancouver and got her address for Turpin, so he could write her his final letter. Before hanging up, she told Everitt to let Ronnie know she was thinking of him. The chaplain never divulged the name of Turpin's friend or what he wrote, only that he said, "I know you did me wrong but I can't go into eternity with feelings of resentment on my soul."[90]

Although Turpin grew up without religion, Lucas was surprisingly well-versed in the Bible. As a youngster, he attended Sunday school, which came to a halt soon after his mother and father died. In many ways, Everitt viewed Lucas as a marvel. Although his appearance was menacing, even terrifying, the chaplain rarely heard him speak a slang word, let alone a swear word. "He was a very docile sort of a man, despite his looks," said Everitt. "He looked a terrible man in pictures. He did look like a rough customer, there was no doubt about it. But in the main, he was a very, very quiet, sensible man. He'd been brought up in the Bible belt in Georgia, and knew his Bible very well, but somewhere along the line had gone astray."

In their death row cells at the Don Jail, Turpin and Lucas were considered model prisoners, never causing a fuss or creating a disturbance. Toronto detective Jim Majury sometimes guarded Lucas during the trial and escorted him to court. He still remembers Lucas vividly. "The first time I first saw him, he was lying on a cell bed with his porkpie hat under his head, sleeping," says Majury. "He got up, went into court, and when he came back, he put the porkpie hat under his head, and fell asleep again. He was the coolest man I had ever met." Although he didn't agree with his sentence of death, Lucas accepted his fate, something Turpin was unable to do until he met Everitt.

"I had told him all along that his chances of escaping the gallows were less than they were for Lucas, who had shot two drug peddlers," said Everitt. "But I don't think either of them were too surprised."

For Everitt, the hangings of Lucas and Turpin awakened harrowing memories from his childhood. Growing up on Carlaw Avenue in Toronto's east end, Everitt lived with his parents near the Don Jail. On June 13, 1919, just two days before his eleventh birthday, the young Cyril saw hundreds of spectators outside the jail. They were there to protest the hanging of Frank McCullough, who was convicted for the murder of acting detective Frank Williams. Many were there hoping to catch a final glimpse of the condemned man, and he did not disappoint them.

On his way to the gallows, Everitt remembered a great cheer bursting from the crowd as McCullough, passing one of the jail windows, stopped and waved a white flag to the crowd, which started singing, "Nearer My God to Thee." Many in the five-hundred-strong throng turned violent, and a mounted police officer was thrown off his horse when struck by a flying brick hurled by a gang of youths. At least thirteen arrests were made outside the jail, while inside, McCullough was led to the gallows.

Standing on the trap door while his black hood and noose were being adjusted, McCullough was asked if he had any last words. To his spiritual advisor, the Reverend Bertram Nelles, he said, "This is going to be harder on you, than on me. Good-bye, Mr. Nelles. God bless you."

Then the trap was sprung. Although McCullough's neck was broken instantly, he hung there for fifteen minutes while his heart continued to beat. Everitt found the entire spectacle to be repulsive, and had long since forgotten about it, until now.

Both Turpin and Lucas were up by six in the morning on their final day, hoping to receive word that their sentences had been commuted to life imprisonment. Everitt was also at the jail early that Tuesday, telling his wife, Olive, as he left their house, "If I haven't got them saved now, I guess I never will."

Another person who came by the Don Jail that morning was an anonymous-looking fellow in a business suit who used the surname Ellis. To the jail staff, he was better known by his working title: hangman. Although he was using the same pseudonym as the gentleman who had executed Frank McCullough over forty years earlier, this man was different, but the job was exactly the same.

Sometimes he was Jack, and at other times he went by James, or John. Most often, he was Arthur Ellis. A studious, scientific sort of man, Ellis arrived early at the Don Jail to make calculations about which length of rope to use for each man, based on their size, weight, and muscularity. This was nothing new, since Canada had adopted hanging as the only method of execution from Great Britain. The famous hangmen of England — from James Berry to Albert Pierrepoint — took great pride in refining the "art" of hanging over the decades, allegedly making the experience less painful. Skilled at their craft, the best of them had the condemned man positioned on the scaffold, hood over his head, noose around his neck, and hanged in under a minute.

In Britain, the "short drop" was first used, often resulting in an agonizing death by strangulation, sometimes taking the condemned man as long as half an hour to die. By 1871, hangman William

Marwood introduced the "long drop," a method designed with the intention of breaking the condemned's neck. If the rope was too short or poorly positioned around the neck, the prisoner slowly choked to death, kicking and flailing in mid-air; if the rope was too long for the man or woman's weight or build, the unthinkable sometimes happened — decapitation.

On more than one occasion, a prisoner dropped through the scaffold and a bloody rope snapped straight back up again like an enormous rubber band, the head flying one way and the body falling to the ground in a revolting heap. It had happened before in Canada, in Montreal's Bordeaux Jail in 1935, when Thomasina Sarao was hanged for the murder of her husband Nicholas. She had gained about forty pounds in prison, but the hangman was given a slip of paper with her previous weight, and she was beheaded as a result. It ended that hangman's career, and he died three years later in poverty.

Little is known about Arthur Ellis, the man who would put Lucas and Turpin to death. Unlike some hangmen, such as England's James Berry, who developed a famous "table of drops" and proudly advertised his trade on colourful business cards with his name, address, and the word "Executioner," Ellis lived an otherwise quiet, uneventful existence in Ontario. A family man who told his wife and kids he was a travelling salesman, Arthur Ellis regularly attended church on Sundays. He believed in God, the strength of his convictions, and the death penalty. He would be paid $500 each from the York County sheriff's office for hanging Turpin and Lucas, a considerable sum in 1962.

Just as Ellis was busy making his preparations for what would happen later that night, so was Everitt. The strong friendship he'd developed with Turpin and Lucas over the past months meant he didn't want any unnecessary surprises in their final hour, so he carefully calculated how many paces it would take to walk from their cells to the gallows. He also came up with a way to let his boys know the end was at hand: the 23rd Psalm.

Just days before the hangings, Turpin said to Everitt that he didn't want him to be there, since it would be "too messy." Everitt said he'd promised to be there with them until the end, and that was the last time it was ever mentioned.

The three discussed all the fine details of the hanging, from the noose that would soon be around each of their necks to the trap door that would soon give way beneath their feet. Everitt would be there with them, and he told both men he would be reading, beginning with the 23rd Psalm. Once he got to the line "My eyes have seen thy salvation," from the Book of Common Prayer, it would signal the hangman to trip the lever. The last thing they would hear was Everitt's voice, and the word "Salvation," assuming everything went as planned.

Before noon, radio reports said the death sentences of the two men would stand, and they would hang at midnight. Everitt was understandably upset by the news, since he had done everything possible to have their sentences commuted to life imprisonment. The decision was made with Don Jail governor David Dougall to wait until after Turpin and Lucas had finished lunch to tell them the bad news.

"Well, boys, we've heard from Ottawa," said Everitt.

Without letting him finish, Turpin said, "We can tell there's no hope."

There was no hope, and deep down, the three had known it all along. That afternoon and early evening were spent praying, reading the Bible, and talking about sports and horseracing, a favourite pastime of Turpin's. They sang hymns they loved the most, like "Stand Up, Stand Up for Jesus," "Love Lifted Me," "What a Friend We Have in Jesus," and "Down From His Glory." "The Old Rugged Cross" was the one Turpin liked best.

While jail staff were respectful of their privacy and came by only when necessary, they were often interrupted by ministers and "oddball preachers," according to Everitt, strangers who managed to talk their way into the jail to make sure the two men were "right with God." Their concerns were less about salvation of the condemned men's souls and more about generating publicity for themselves. Turpin and Lucas could be the last to die, after all. In his unflappable way, Everitt simply asked any religious types who came by where they had been for the last ten months. None had an answer, so they left in awkward silence.

Knowing their lives would come to an end in a few hours, Lucas and Turpin were surprisingly calm. There were no cries of self-pity, and no tears from either man. Only Everitt broke down, when a young officer came by the death cells to offer him support. It was the only time anyone had seen him cry in public since he was fourteen. The jail was silent by that time, as prisoners in cells located in corridors near Turpin, Lucas, and the gallows had already been moved, with the exception of Gary McCorkell in another death row cell. Like Turpin and Lucas, he was preparing himself to hang.

At 6:00 p.m., dinner was served, and Everitt shared their last meal of steak, potatoes, vegetables, and pie. Lucas was hoping for fried chicken, but got steak instead. Dinner was served on cardboard plates, and the three ate with spoons — forks and knives weren't allowed on death row, since they could be used as weapons.

Soon after they finished dinner, Walter Williston, the lawyer who worked on Lucas's appeal, came by the cell to see his client with the bad news. Williston, like Turpin's appeal lawyer Patrick Hartt, had received a telegram the day before from D.H. Christie, director of the criminal law section at the Department of Justice. Both telegrams were similar. Williston's read: "Governor general in council will not interfere with death sentence passed upon Arthur Lucas convicted for the capital murder of Therland Crater." The last appeal to Justice Minister Donald Fleming didn't work, and there were no options left; they would be dead in a few hours.

"If it's any consolation to you," said Williston, "you may be the last men to hang in Canada."

"Some consolation!" chortled Turpin.

Having maintained his innocence the entire time, the last thing Lucas said to Williston was, "When a man thinks he has been tricked out of his life, it's hard."

Outside the Don Jail, a crowd of protestors against the death penalty was starting to gather, and the media frenzy was well under- way. Reporters were eager to get quotes from family members and friends, politicians, religious figures, police, and anyone connected to Turpin and Lucas for their opinions about the double execution.

Constable Nash's widow, who remarried eight months after Frederick was shot and killed, would not discuss the hanging of her late husband's killer, except to say, "The judge and jury did their job. I have been much too busy with my four daughters to give it any thought." Harold Nash, brother of Frederick, was at home with his family the night of the hangings. He had no interest in going to the Don Jail, although many others tried to get inside the building's unforgiving stone walls, like Lizzie Fisher, Arthur's sister. She came from Detroit with a cousin, Albert, to see her brother one last time. Lucas refused, and passed on a one-line message to her: "Remember me as I was."

In a faltering, two-page letter written in pencil and signed and dated December 10, Lucas essentially wrote out his will, giving his sister Lizzie "permission to get the following articels [sic]." Items on the list include a dining room set with six chairs, a bar with four stools, a Ford automobile, and a portable tape recorder and TV set. A man who prided himself on his taste in clothes, Lucas was careful to detail almost every item of clothing in his possession, including "15 suits or more," four sport coats, five overcoats, six hats, an "all white leather sport coat," and five pairs of shoes.[91]

On the second page of his letter, Lucas writes about not understanding the laws of Canada.

> My lawyer who was sent to me by the crown atty [sic] didn't have time to handly [sic] my case when I couldn't raise some of $5,000 then by some reason I was given Mr. Ross mckay [sic]. I told him about my statement give to the officers and he told me he would investigate it but he never did a thing. I know somewhere in this city there is a person or persons who saw a 1958 Black cheve [sic] because the police asked me if I had ever seen such a car in the area at 116 Kendal Ave.

If there were any witnesses who saw anyone else at the murder house that cold November morning, they never came forward. For Lucas, it was already too late.

By nine o'clock that night, the crowd outside the jail had grown considerably larger, as more and more people — many of them in their late teens and early twenties — arrived with placards to protest the hangings. In the jail a few hundred feet away from the demonstrators, prison physician Dr. W.H. Hills administered a mild sedative to Turpin and Lucas, who remained unaware of the gathering outside the cold stone walls.

Smoking cigarettes, sipping coffee, and stamping their feet to stave off the biting cold, picketers stared at the looming, moonlit structure, hoping to catch a glimpse of the condemned men. Others had portable transistor radios pressed against their ears, listening for any news bulletins. Since the gallows were located on the other side of the jail, all they could see was the occasional blinking light through one or two of the Don's tiny windows.

On Gerrard Street East, the main road nearest the jail, anti-hanging protesters slowly paraded back and forth carrying homemade signs that read, "Christmas in a Grave," "Capital Punishment Revenge Not Justice," "Thou Shalt Not Kill," and "Two Wrongs Don't Make a Right." Across the street from the Don, groups of teenagers sat in the warmth of their cars, taking advantage of the moonlit night to smooch or to stare at the jail "as though sitting at a drive-in movie." Occasionally, some of the few picketers in favour of the hangings would walk past their windshields, brandishing signs like "An Eye for an Eye" and "Save the Taxpayers' Money."

For decades, reporters had not been permitted inside the jail to witness any hangings. Allowed to be witnesses at executions in the past, journalists were now racing from one demonstrator to the next, asking the same questions over and over again: What brought you here tonight? Are you here with a group, or as an individual? What do you hope to accomplish by being here?

"I hope to make people aware of the fact that men are dying merely for vengeance, but it isn't going to accomplish any good at all,"[92] one young woman told a CBC Television reporter outside the Don Jail Roadway. All across the city, journalists were making calls to get a good quote for the morning's first edition.

"The phone calls started before midnight, man, it was unbelievable," says Bram Everitt. "I don't know what the media expected, my father to be there and just come back from the hangings? He was there all day." It was decided ahead of time that nineteen-year-old Bram would stay at home with his mother the night of the hangings and take messages from reporters while his father was at the Don Jail with Turpin and Lucas. The calls continued long into the night, only stopping around three in the morning.

Inside the jail, Everitt was alone with Turpin and Lucas well into the evening. At 11:00 p.m., Everitt told the pair they had an hour left, which took them off guard — they were chatting and getting along so well that they had actually forgotten the time. It would be one of Everitt's only regrets for the rest of his life, as he was growing anxious, asking if they wanted to read scripture or sing a few more hymns.

"Just be yourself, brigadier," said Turpin, a smile creasing his face. Over the past months, Turpin had grown to have the utmost respect for the chaplain, a man who represented decency, honesty, and stability, something Turpin never had as a child.

Miles away from the jail, Rev. J. Franklin Chidsey began conducting a death watch service at the suburban Don Heights Unitarian Congregation. An outspoken opponent of hanging, Chidsey was not reticent about expressing his views. Better known as Jay to his congregation, Chidsey was a man with a strong social conscience, and years ahead of his time in his reverence for all life, not just human, as he called for legislation to stop cruelty to animals in the fur trade and laboratory experiments.

Midway through the death watch, gasps and whispers were heard as Turpin's girlfriend, Lillian White, made a dramatic entrance into the church. Dressed entirely in black from her pillbox hat to her coat and shoes, White sat in silence for over an hour alongside thirty-five parishioners as Chidsey spoke about the hangings, calling them "cold-blooded murder." Soon, the lights in the concrete-block church dimmed, and a single candle was lit, which Chidsey called "a candle of hope, not a candle of despair." White stared at it as it flickered, averting her eyes only briefly to dab at them with a handkerchief or to take a quick puff from her cigarette.

"There will never be another execution in Canada — another public murder — but that there will be, here or elsewhere, a death watch like this," said the reverend. "In one church ... in two ... in ten ... in a hundred. Those who favor this evil thing are on the defensive now. Let us keep them there."

The members remained still and silent as Chidsey spoke, and the only sound that could be heard was the faint *tick-tick-tick* of a clock as it counted down the minutes to midnight.

"The issue is not the merits of Lucas and Turpin. They may be innocent — and innocent men have been hanged; they may be as much victim as enemy of society; they may be the most ideal candidates for hanging Canada has had for a century," said Chidsey in a strong voice. "The issue is the merits of murder — calculated, cold-blooded, premeditated murder, done without passion or animus, shamefully, and behind locked doors by an anonymous civil servant, at our behest. Public murder for murder privately done."

At the same time as the death watch service was underway, the crowd outside the Don Jail grew to almost two hundred people. As midnight approached, some people began to cry, huddling together as they stared wordlessly at the jail. Above them, the full moon hung in a blue-black sky, a few slender clouds threading their way across its face. Police on motorcycles slowly drove back and forth near the crowd, in case there was a riot. On Gerrard Street, some motorists slowed down, honking their horns in protest, while others rolled down their windows and hollered "Hang 'em!" and "Why don't you wise up?" as they drove by in the night. There was only one traffic accident, when a car was rear-ended.

At 11:40 p.m. Arthur Lucas, his huge, thick-knuckled hands on the bars of his cell, spoke to Everitt: "You know, brigadier, we is lucky."

Everitt couldn't quite believe what he was hearing, wondering how a man can be lucky when, in twenty minutes, a noose will be around his neck.

"What do you mean?" asked Everitt, visibly puzzled.

"Well, if I were on the street, I could be killed by a car, and I wouldn't be ready to meet my maker," said Lucas. "But this way, because of your talking to us and leading us up through the steps to salvation, I'm ready to meet my maker."

At one minute to midnight, the stillness of the corridor leading to Hospital Nine was broken by the steady rhythm of footsteps, which came to a stop outside the jail cells. The trio had finished their final prayer minutes earlier and were chatting away casually, as if this were just any other night in the Don Jail. Standing outside in the corridor, the sheriff asked if he'd gotten the right night for the hangings. He would later tell Everitt he was amazed at how calm they were — no tears, no cursing. "Even as I heard the footsteps in the hall, footsteps of the guards coming to get them, they remained composed,"[93] said Everitt.

With the jail governor and guards standing by, Turpin and Lucas rose to their feet and were instantly handcuffed. Lucas, who was in the middle of smoking his cigarette, asked the guard if he could finish it. They told him to go ahead, and he leaned down — because of the handcuffs — and took one last drag.

As they left their cells and began the final forty paces, the reality of what was about to happen became very clear for the hanging party. Making a sharp left down the corridor, they walked through the first of three doors on the way to the gallows. Leading the men were the Don Jail governor and sheriff, followed by Lucas with two guards, then Everitt, then Turpin with two guards. As they walked the doors slammed shut behind them, first one, then another. The third and final door was a flat metal plate with no handles. Locked by a large nut, it could only be opened with a wrench. It was open when the procession arrived. Inside, painted an ugly utility green, were the gallows.

Above the scaffold, the two nooses looked almost transcendent as they dangled in mid-air, starkly illuminated by the stark yellow glow of a spotlight. The hangman, Arthur Ellis, unmasked and dressed in a plain suit, was waiting for them.

In seconds, the two ascended the steps of the gallows.[94] Unlike the often-used thirteen steps to the scaffold, the Don Jail gallows were only slightly raised, dropping down to the floor below. At 12:01 a.m., their feet were manacled, and they were told to stand back to back on the chalk-marked area of the platform.

"Do you have anything to say?" asked the hangman.

"No," was the response from both men. Everitt then wished the men he had befriended over the past ten months goodbye.

"I will see you in heaven," said the chaplain, as black hoods were slipped over their heads. Lucas whimpered softly, and Everitt commenced reading the 23rd Psalm as the hangman drew the ropes over their hooded heads and around their necks. He had been over this time and time again with them and the hangman, and they waited for the word.

"The Lord is my shepherd, I shall not want," read Everitt. Then he moved on to the Book of Common Prayer: "… for mine eyes have seen thy salvation."

What happened next is the stuff of nightmares.

Turpin and Lucas never heard the end of the word *salvation*. The hangman sprung the trap, the platform falling beneath their feet with a deafening crash that echoed throughout the room as they plummeted to their deaths. No one who was at the hangings revealed what happened that night for many years, and newspapers at the time were not given the full story.

"The hanging was bungled. Turpin died clean, but Lucas' head was torn right off. It was hanging just by the sinews of the neck. There was blood all over the floor. The hangman had miscalculated his weight. What a way to die!"[95] said Everitt in an interview published just before his own death many years later.

In what would become the eeriest coincidence of his life, Julian Porter and his wife, the former Susan McCutcheon, were downtown at the famous O'Keefe Centre the same time as the double hanging. The performance that evening was the musical *Oliver!* Porter was grateful to be there, hoping the show would take his mind off what was happening at the Don Jail. As a law student, Porter assisted Walter Williston with Lucas's appeal and went to Ottawa to see Justice Minister Donald Fleming about having the sentence commuted to life imprisonment.

Porter and his wife sat close to the stage, which was designed to look like the tenements and streets of London. The performance was running late. The audience watched as one of the key characters on stage was chased by an angry crowd and ran above the safety curtain. Quickly checking his watch, Porter saw that it was midnight. The moment he looked up, it happened. "Suddenly, from behind and down under the safe curtain, a gallows rope falls with a six-foot rag body, and the body falls down and jerks up, and I must have jumped out of my seat by three feet. So help me God, it was at the same time that it happened."

Knowing the approximate time of the hangings, many protestors outside the Don Jail fell silent. Picketers stopped walking and stood absolutely still, while one young woman's piercing cries broke the silence as she collapsed to the cold pavement in tears. Downtown at Toronto police headquarters, switchboard operators and detectives were flooded with dozens of anonymous calls. Some screamed "Murderers!" into the phone before slamming down the receiver. Other callers were even more disturbing and perverse, wanting to know exactly what was going to happen to Turpin's body and wanting to claim his remains. Inside the jail, all was quiet, except for the gallows area, where the gruesome spectacle of the double hangings was far from over.

"Everybody was taken aback by the spray of blood, a horrendous display of blood that was literally like a water pipe had burst, and the walls were sprayed with blood," said Toronto homicide detective Jim Crawford, who attended the double hanging of Turpin and Lucas that cold December night. Crawford was connected to both cases. He had sometimes escorted Arthur Lucas to and from Courtroom 33 at Toronto's City Hall to the Don Jail. Death threats had been made against Lucas by members of the Detroit underworld, and the authorities wanted to ensure he made it to and from court safety.

When it came to Ronald Turpin, Detective Crawford's involvement ran much deeper. He rushed to the crime scene on the Danforth when Nash was shot and went to the East General Hospital afterwards with partner Irvine Alexander to question Turpin. He testified at Turpin's trial and was present at Nash's autopsy, when bullets from the slain constable's body were handed to him as evidence. He knew Frederick Nash and his police officer brother, Harold, and remembered Turpin's shrug of the shoulders and flippant comment when told Fred Nash was dead: "Everybody's gotta go sometime." Needless to say, Turpin was not one of Crawford's favourite people.

For years after the hangings, many were convinced Lucas's near-decapitation occurred because Ellis the hangman miscalculated Lucas's weight, because the rope was too long, or because he was drunk. Crawford spoke to Ellis after the hangings and says the hangman was "sober as a judge." A big man, Lucas lost a great deal of weight over the ten months he spent in the Don Jail — fifty pounds by his own estimate — making a slip-up of his weight unlikely. The hangman explained to Crawford that the most probable reason for Lucas almost being beheaded was because he had syphilis, a sexually transmitted disease that can affect the bones, joints, internal organs, heart, and major blood vessels, such as those found in the neck.

As the black-hooded bodies of Turpin and Lucas swayed in mid-air, Dr. Hills had the unenviable task of checking if the two were still alive. Walking down the wooden spiral staircase to where the bodies hung, Dr. Hills climbed a stepladder, his stethoscope around his neck. Minutes passed as the doctor pressed his cold instrument to the chest of one man, then the other, listening to their faint, dying heartbeats. At 12:18 a.m., they were pronounced dead by chief coroner Harold Beatty Cotnam and Dr. Hills. Cotnam was later quoted by newspapers as saying that unconsciousness on the rope was "actually instantaneous." No mention was made of Lucas almost losing his head.

Once it was determined Turpin's and Lucas's hearts had stopped beating, the ropes that held them aloft were cut and their bodies were lowered to the floor. Still wearing their grey prison shirts and blue trousers, the two men were wrapped in white sheets by undertaker Jack Jerrett, laid on metal gurneys, and wheeled into another room for one of the last steps of the execution, the coroner's jury.

Outside the jail, the atmosphere of the crowd remained relatively calm, except for a few drunks staggering around here and there among the protesters. The mood changed immediately at 12:25 a.m., when the official typed declaration notice of the executions — one for Turpin, and one for Lucas — were tacked to the Don's massive oak front doors.

"Let's read it!" they shouted, advancing to the door. Motorcycle police tried to hold back the surging crowd.

"You've murdered them, we've got a right to read it," they yelled, taunting police with challenges like, "Why don't you draw your guns? Then we'd have a complete police state." When it was over, Toronto police arrested four men, two for causing a disturbance, the other two for being drunk. Later, some of the demonstrators complained of strong-arm tactics outside the Don Jail that night, claiming they were threatened and shoved around by police. "One policeman tried to make me move on by running me down with his motorcycle," complained one man, who said the police then threatened to "get" him before four of them threw him off the road.[96]

The notices posted on the door were signed by the sheriff of York County Philip Ambrose and David Dougall, the governor of the Don Jail. It read: "We the undersigned hereby declare that judgment of death was this day executed on Arthur Lucas, in the common gaol in the County of York, at Toronto, in our presence." The other note was the same, except for Turpin's name in place of Lucas's.

At the same time as the execution notices were tacked to the enormous wooden doors of the jail, Reverend Chidsey's death watch service at Don Heights Unitarian Congregation was nearing its conclusion. A woman softly asked Turpin's girlfriend, Lillian White, if she'd like a cup of coffee. Tears running down her face, White refused. When the service ended at 12:50 a.m., she rose to her feet and walked out of the church. No one offered White sympathy or a kind word as she left the warmth of the church for the bitterly cold night, where she was faced with reporters hungry for a quote for the morning newspapers about her feelings for Turpin.

"He was the most wonderful man on earth and just because he made one bad mistake ..." she said, bursting into tears. At that moment, two of White's friend grabbed her by the arms and led her to a waiting car, which quickly drove off into the darkness.

At the jail, the coroner's jury was about to start. Just before it began, Crawford's partner, Irvine Alexander, saw two metal gurneys with the bodies of Turpin and Lucas. Both were covered with white sheets, except from under one sheet, a pair of oxblood-coloured shoes poked out. Crawford was known around the station for his highly polished oxblood shoes, and by coincidence, Lucas went to his death wearing a similar pair of shoes. Detective Crawford and Lucas were about the same large build, and Alexander — who did not witness the hangings — thought his partner had fainted during the hangings and had to be wheeled out on a gurney.

"We got a kick out of that," said Crawford. The shoe incident would become a joke the two detectives shared for many years afterwards.

In a damp, chilly room on the ground floor near the execution chamber, the coroner's juries were waiting. The atmosphere was visibly tense, as none of the men gathered to view the remains of the newly dead Turpin and Lucas wanted to be there. At the time, being called to attend a coroner's jury was much like receiving a letter for jury duty. Members of the public were picked at random and had no choice but to show up or face contempt of court charges. The only exception that night came from one member of the Turpin jury, who showed up so drunk that assistant coroner Jack Hills had to take his place. Dr. Cotnam was the coroner for both juries; one was to view the remains of Turpin, the other the body of Lucas, with a total of six men for each jury, including Cotnam.

The purpose of the juries was to inquire for the Queen when, where, and by what means Ronald Turpin and Arthur Lucas came to their deaths. Around the same time, Sheriff Ambrose sent a letter to justice minister Donald Fleming in accordance with Section 649 of the Criminal Code regarding Turpin and Lucas, which included a certificate from Dr. Hills that the men were indeed dead, along with a declaration from the sheriff and governor that the men were executed in their presence and a copy of the coroner's inquisition.

After being briefed by Dr. Hills, the inquest began. The bodies were still covered by their white sheets. The point was to determine an official verdict of death by hanging. The sheets were flipped back, revealing only the head and neck of each man. Some jury members glanced at each body for only as long as necessary, while others craned their necks, taking a good, long look. Each inquest took about half an hour to determine that the men were dead, and that they died as the result of judicial hanging, "in accordance with the sentence under which he lay in the said Gaol," as the statement the witnesses signed read. After the inquest, each jury member wrote his name and address on an official form, and a small red seal was placed next to each name. Sheriff Ambrose would later tell the *Toronto Star* about the last minutes of Turpin and Lucas. "They died quietly and calmly and seemed to be at peace. I believe they'd come to realize it was inevitable," he said. "These people had died at least five times before — when the police caught them, when they were tried, when they were found guilty, when they were sentenced, with each appeal and when cabinet refused to commute their sentence."

Once the inquest was over, the bodies were placed, unembalmed, in plain pine coffins, still wearing the clothes in which they died. The coffins were loaded into a white Ford van deliberately smeared with mud to disguise it and taken to their final resting place, two unmarked graves in Prospect Cemetery. By the time the remains were driven to the cemetery, the large crowd outside the jail had all gone home, except for one unknown man, who continued to pace back and forth along Gerrard Street. He carried no sign, instead wearing a white trenchcoat with red letters on the back reading, "Forgive us."

CHAPTER 9

The Aftermath

I do not say that Lucas was innocent, but I believe
there are serious doubts as to his guilt.
— Walter Williston

The controversy surrounding capital punishment and the double hanging on December 11, 1962, did not die with Ronald Turpin and Arthur Lucas. In the weeks and months following their executions, the press and public alike kept asking if the "right thing" was done at Toronto's Don Jail that eerily moonlit night, when a petty criminal with no history of violence and an African-American with an I.Q. bordering on retarded were sent to their deaths based on largely circumstantial evidence or witness testimony coming from characters of questionable integrity.

Was Turpin acting in self-defence that frigid February evening when he shot and killed Toronto police officer Frederick John Nash, or was he just another anti-social low-life who would weave and spin a story into a lie, any lie, as long as it saved him from the gallows? Did Arthur Lucas, a soft-spoken but monstrous-looking hulk of a man, possess the necessary mental capacity to plan and carry out a double murder that bore the qualities of a professional hit, or was he the dupe of an elaborate set-up by Detroit gangsters?

Opinions about the guilt of both men and the morality of the death penalty — which had divided the city's newspapers before the executions

— continued long after the two were buried in their unmarked graves in Prospect Cemetery. The *Toronto Star* made its stance against capital punishment clear when it printed editorials questioning the secrecy surrounding the hangings, calling them "a tacit acknowledgment that capital punishment performs no useful deterrent function." Society, said the paper, would *not* be worse off if murderers were housed in penitentiaries or mental hospitals instead of being killed by the government.

"A hanging such as last night's is simply a barbaric and degrading survival from the past. Everyone involved is ashamed of it and wants, instinctively, to conceal it from public view."[97] Next to the editorial, the paper printed a cartoon showing a man reading on the subway; instead of handrails above his head, nooses dangled from the subway ceiling. In another editorial entitled "Relic of Barbarism," the *Toronto Star* said the majority of Canadians no longer believed in capital punishment and that it served no useful purpose.

> Essentially, capital punishment is nothing more than a ritual of vengeance inherited from the dark past. It degrades the community which practices it by making every citizen an accomplice in a cold-blooded killing. It undermines that respect for the sanctity of human life which the criminal law is supposed to promote. Its abolition is a mark of advancing civilization. Canada has unquestionably reached that point in civilization.[98]

Other newspapers maintained the same pro-capital punishment stand long after the hangings. An editorial in the *Telegram* spoke of society exacting the "supreme forfeit" from Turpin and Lucas, calling the manner of their deaths repugnant but necessary. "The formal, almost ritualistic killing of a man by hanging is ugly, but there are occasions when there is no justifiable alternative to the execution of a criminal for the murder he has committed."

Rather than take sides for or against the death penalty, Canada's national newspaper, the *Globe and Mail*, published an exhaustive, six-part series in October and November 1963 on the Lucas case. While Turpin's crime was relatively straightforward — shooting and killing a police officer — the trial of Arthur Lucas was full of questions from the beginning, rumblings that grew to a roar in the months following his execution.

Less than a year after his death, reporter Betty Lee created her series based on trial transcripts and numerous interviews. It was a well-crafted, thoroughly researched account that raised serious doubts about Lucas's conviction and execution, and it remains valid decades later: "The Lucas case was sordid and sensational. It involved drugs, prostitution, international crime, gangland revenge. Yet it did not arouse the public interest that was instantly generated by the more cut-and-dried Turpin affair. Nor was there any vigorous public discussion as to whether Lucas should be executed."[99]

Some facts of the case, wrote Lee, were puzzling, even suspicious. All the evidence introduced during the trial was circumstantial. Not only didn't any of the fifty-four witnesses who testified see Lucas shoot Therland Crater or slash Carolyn Newman's throat, no one came forward claiming to see him in, at, or anywhere near 116 Kendal Avenue when the murders were committed. Even when he was ascending the gallows and felt Ellis the hangman slipping the noose over his black-hooded head, Lucas did not stray from his alibi, maintaining his innocence to the very end.[100]

Many of the individuals involved in Lucas's trial and the appeals to have his death sentence commuted to life imprisonment expressed their doubts about his guilt to the reporter. Chaplain Cyril Everitt, one of the only decent men Lucas ever knew in his life, could not shake the feeling as he walked the forty paces to the gallows with the condemned that he was walking with an innocent man. At the very least, Lucas should have been granted a new trial, Everitt told Lee, or had his sentence commuted. And though Lucas's appeals were rejected and just one out of seven Supreme Court Justices said he would have allowed a new trial, justice minister Donald Fleming spoke of the unprecedented and "exhaustive consideration" given to the Lucas case.

Lee created a detailed chronology for *Globe* readers outlining details of the crime, from the arrival of Crater and Newman in Toronto to post office employee Frank McGuire discovering Crater's bloody, still-warm body in the hallway of the Annex-area house. Tracking the trail of evidence, from the large gold ring found on the bed next to Newman's body to Lucas's arrest in Detroit and extradition to Canada, the reporter then raised her concerns about Crown attorney Henry Bull's impartiality.

The "vast majority of sinners" in court are found guilty, said Bull, and "it would be far more reasonable to presume accused persons guilty — in fact we did so in the early stages of our legal history."[101] Bull's comments are disturbing, coming from a prosecutor whose intention should have been to bring out the facts for the for the jury, not consider the majority of individuals facing charges to be "sinners."

Lee detailed just how neophyte lawyer Ross MacKay took on the Lucas case, the first capital case he ever defended. He was not the first choice to represent Lucas; another lawyer, George Wooten, had to drop the case, and MacKay carried on in his place, with virtually no help and no money to create an adequate defence. It was while MacKay was working on Lucas's case that he was asked to take on Ronald Turpin's case, and he said yes, assuming it would not take place until the fall of 1962.

Soon after MacKay agreed to take on Turpin as a client, the Crown said they would not delay the Turpin trial, which found MacKay shouldering the monumental task of defending a *second* man's life less than three weeks after the conclusion of his first murder trial. Lee estimated that for the two and a half month period it took MacKay to prepare both cases, he received a paltry $700 from Legal Aid, with another $1,500 being spent on Lucas's behalf. In comparison, a group of Toronto lawyers estimated the Crown spent somewhere between $30,000 and $40,000 to prosecute Arthur Lucas.

Resurrecting details that were overlooked or deliberately ignored during Lucas's trial, Lee wrote about the fate of the battered and bloodstained .38-calibre Ivor Johnson revolver found on the Burlington Skyway Bridge. The weapon was not discovered until approximately fifty hours after the murders. During that time, employees from Ontario's Department of Highways made regular round-trip safety patrols of the bridge, driving from one end to the other, looking for such things as stalled vehicles, debris on the road, and other driving hazards. Defence attorney Ross MacKay estimated that patrols driving back and forth across the bridge would have passed the revolver at least one hundred times, if it had indeed been there since the early hours of November 17. "Crown ballistics experts were extremely uncooperative about identifying it positively as the weapon that fired the bullets found in Crater's body," wrote Lee, who also criticized much of the blood evidence linking Lucas to the murders, stating that some of it could not even be identified as human blood.

Lucas's appeals were also the subject of some controversy, as Lee interviewed Everitt, who not only befriended Lucas but never stopped believing in his innocence until the day he died in 1986. It was Everitt who'd placed a telephone call to Walter Williston, one of Toronto's best-known trial lawyers, urging him to present the condemned man's case to the Ontario Court of Appeal. "I took the case because it annoyed me," Williston told Lee. Upon meeting Lucas, Williston felt his annoyance with the guilty verdict was justified. In Arthur Lucas, he discovered not a fearsome killer but a placid, uneducated man who was always respectful to him and grateful for his help.

Since he did not attend any of the trial, the first thing Williston did was turn to the transcripts, where he discovered what he considered "disturbing points" about the Crown's circumstantial case, such as the knife wounds to the victims. Doctor Chester McLean, who performed the autopsies on Crater and Newman, testified the injuries inflicted to the throats of both victims were "strikingly similar and effective wounds" executed with near-surgical precision, the hallmark of a professional killer.

At age fifty-four, Arthur Lucas was out of shape and slow moving, with chronic bad knees, sore feet, and varicose veins. He did not demonstrate the mental or physical characteristics of a hired hit man, a quick thinker light on his feet, someone able to shoot and slash the throat of a much smaller but extremely fit forty-four-year-old, run up the stairs to corner and kill his lithe twenty-year-old girlfriend, then calmly leave the house, unseen and soaked with the blood of his victims.

Assuming Lucas was the killer, wrote Lee, would he be so incredibly foolish as to sign into the Waverley Hotel using his own name and real address? Would he phone Crater at 116 Kendal from the hotel phone, when there were plenty of coin-operated and anonymous pay phones in the area? Why would he wear bloodstained clothes on the return drive to the United States, when they could easily have been discarded in Toronto? Would a professional hit man use an old and unreliable weapon like a .38-calibre Ivor Johnson revolver to kill someone, a gun considered second-rate even when it was new?

Lee probed other information which should have been made available to the defence at Lucas's trial, but wasn't. Why, for example, was blood not taken from others connected to the case, such as Gus Saunders — who allegedly ordered Therland Crater's murder —Wesley Knox, and Morris Thomas? A self-confessed heroin user, Thomas's needle-scarred arms would have undoubtedly shown the jury the character and calibre of the man they were dealing with; instead, Ross MacKay's request was denied by Justice McRuer. Although he considered himself Arthur Lucas's friend, Morris Thomas's testimony about Lucas owning guns, his gold ring, and his involvement with drugs was inflammatory and far-fetched, as was the man himself.

Concluding her series, Lee questioned the more obvious aspects of the investigation into the murders. Why wasn't Lucas's alibi about drinking coffee at Wong's Café on Dundas Street at the time of the murders explored in more detail? Why were police on both sides of the border unable to track down the shadowy Willie White? After sharing drinks and a room with him, Lucas left White standing outside the Waverley Hotel before proceeding to Wong's Café, making White the perfect alibi witness for the defence. Most incredible of all, would any assassin be so remarkably stupid as to leave an easily identifiable ring in full view on the bed just inches from the body of his dead victim? If Lucas was the killer, why couldn't he find the ring and take it with him, when police detectives discovered it in a matter of seconds?

Betty Lee's controversial series concluded with what reads like an open-ended epitaph:

> Arthur Lucas is, indeed, buried in an unmarked grave in Toronto. There can be no retrial now. But after considering his story, every Canadian — who might well find himself in the same circumstantial position one day — should surely ask one vital question: in a country which advocates the noose, was this man served

unquestionably and impeccably by the processes of law
that lead to the ultimate?![102]

Immediately, the *Globe* series on Lucas drew attention from readers in equal parts complimentary and critical. Letters flooded the newspaper, many saying Lucas received a fair trial and justice was served. After the series was published, Lee began receiving strange calls at her east end Toronto apartment. Many were just hang-ups, but she was disturbed enough by these calls to mention them to the man who handled Lucas's appeal, Walter Williston.

In an unpublished letter sent to Williston, Quebec lawyer Gilles Belanger wrote that justice was denied to Lucas: "I have the uneasy feeling that the majority who delivered the judgment of the Supreme Court in this case did not scrutinize sufficiently the record and therefore, as it appears to me, your grounds of appeal were dealt with, in a sort of manner that overthrows well settled principles dealing with the appreciation of circumstantial evidence."[103]

For a time, Lucas's older sister, Lizzie Fisher, considered bringing a suit against the Canadian government "concerning taking the life of my Brother." Nothing ever came of her wish to seek justice for her dead sibling.

Lee's articles expressing serious doubts about the guilt of Arthur Lucas would not be the last on the subject, as questions about the trial continued for many years afterwards. In 1966, the *Globe*, under the banner headline "No reversing that mistake," paralleled the Lucas case to that of Timothy John Evans. A young Englishman who may have been slightly retarded, Evans was hanged in 1950 for the murder of his infant daughter. Despite a confession, Evans's guilt was widely disputed at the time, and his death led to the abolition of capital punishment in the United Kingdom.

Sixteen years after he plunged through the gallows, Evans was granted a posthumous pardon by the Queen. "Although Arthur Lucas was found guilty of a particularly sordid murder, and although all his appeals were denied, lingering doubts of his guilt have remained and they have never been resolved," stated the *Globe*. That same year, the *Toronto Star* published "Arthur Lucas — executioner or victim?" The article stated many of the points Lee raised in her *Globe* series: that Everitt felt "he was walking with an innocent man" to the gallows; that the evidence against Lucas was "entirely circumstantial" and he never wavered in his alibi; that Lucas had no money for an adequate defence; and that appeal lawyer Walter Williston tried to have two new pieces of evidence accepted by the court, which were refused. Williston, like many others, continued to doubt Lucas's guilt for years afterwards.

When he was made Chief Justice of Canada in 1967, five years after the hangings, the soft-spoken, scholarly seventy-two-year-old John Robert Cartwright was interviewed about his new position at the pinnacle of Canada's judicial system. Cartwright was the Supreme Court justice who cast the sole dissenting vote and would have permitted Lucas a new trial. Newspapers resurrected the case: "Mr. Justice Cartwright in his dissent said the jury might have convicted Lucas even if errors had not been made in the Crown's presentation of the case, but that the conviction would not have been certain. He also questioned whether a murderer would sign the guest book in his victim's house, as Lucas did in Crater's apartment."[104]

In the final days of 1967, as the year of the country's centennial came to a close, Canadians were again questioning condemning a man to death when a bill was put forward to abolish the death penalty, except for the murder of policemen or prison guards. On New Year's Eve, the CTV television news magazine program *W5* aired a program on major events of the past 365 days, including the war in Vietnam, Expo '67, the Beatles and Maharashi Mahesh Yogi, and the bill to abolish the death penalty in Canada.

Through gritty, overexposed black and white footage, *W5* host Ken Cavanaugh took viewers through the crime scene at 116 Kendal filmed in November 1961, starting with the front door with its tombstone-shaped glass panel and moving to a close-up on a small square of paper tucked above the black electric doorbell with "Jean Rochelle," Carolyn Newman's prostitute alias, printed in upper-case letters.

Inside the house we see the front hallway where Therland Crater's dead body recently laid; in its place is a ghostly white sawdust silhouette, soaking up blood from the hardwood floor. The camera crawls unsteadily up the stairs to the bedroom where Newman was killed, the stained sheets already removed for evidence, leaving just the naked mattress saturated with an enormous bloodstain. In the background, a November wind blows through the drapes, probably opened by police to air out the dead woman's room.

The program then cuts to Arthur Lucas being escorted by police guards into the courtroom at Toronto's City Hall. Accompanied by suit-wearing detectives and a court officer, Lucas walks down the hallway, a head taller than some of the men guarding him. Wearing an open-jacketed dark grey suit, a striped shirt buttoned to the top, and a black porkpie hat atop his head, Lucas somehow manages to appear comical and menacing at the same time. Turing to look at the camera, his face shows no emotion until one of the detectives says something to him. As he turns to enter Courtroom 33, he cracks a faint smile.

Five years after Lucas was hanged and nearly decapitated, *W5* tracked down and interviewed four members of the all-white, all-male jury. Although they were willing to appear on camera, none are named. Three of the four jurors expressed grave doubts about Lucas's guilt.

"My reaction is that I wish I had never been on the jury that hung this man, that said he was guilty," said one juror. "And certainly I will never go on another one if I can possibly avoid it." A second man, eyes downcast, said, "I just felt that … it's always bothered me, really, that I was part of eventually having this guy hung. I'll tell you one thing: I would never do it again." Several said they would refuse if called to serve on a jury again. Another man said he still has a hard time thinking about Lucas's death sentence, five years after the execution: "I think that the whole thing was — from my personal point of view — was to find a way to convict this man, and not to find a way to find out if he was guilty or not. I never had any proof, as far as I'm concerned, that he ever committed this crime."

Most telling is the juror who remembered Lucas — whom he refers to as a "gentleman" — sitting in the witness box:

> He was a huge-shouldered man, a fairly good-looking
> fellow, I thought, and rather a placid type. It was hard
> to understand that this man had actually committed
> a murder. And, he seemed to have no friends at all,

and would periodically look at the jury with eyes that suggested, "You know, look, I'm in a spot, you guys, will you listen to my story? Can you do something for me?" And I think many of us perhaps thought that maybe we could.

Even in 1976, the year capital punishment was abolished in Canada and fourteen years after Arthur Lucas and Ronald Turpin were hanged at the Don Jail, newspapers raised doubts surrounding the Lucas case. "Was Arthur Lucas guilty of murder?" asked an editorial in the *Globe and Mail*. "Fourteen years after his conviction there are many people, some of them distinguished members of the bar, who believe that he was not. Or who believe that he did not have a fair trial, who believe as one judge of the Supreme Court of Canada believed, that Lucas should have been tried again."[105]

The deaths of Ronald Turpin and Arthur Lucas may have marked the end of capital punishment in Canada, but the lives of many involved in their trials and executions were never the same afterwards. At the tender age of nineteen, Gary Alexander McCorkell was the third man on death row in Toronto's Don Jail. Classified by psychiatrists as a homosexual pedophile, McCorkell was sentenced to be hanged in February 1963 for the murder of two young boys, and he moved into Cell No. 1 on death row after the double execution of Lucas and Turpin.

McCorkell would likely have become the last man executed in Canada, but his life was spared because the jury recommended mercy for the gangly teenager "in the strongest possible terms," a consideration not made for Turpin or Lucas. As a result, his death sentence was commuted to life imprisonment. Many, including senior homicide officers who investigated the crime scene where toddlers Michael Atkinson and Ronald MacLeod were found and saw their tiny bodies carried out to the coroner's office on just one stretcher, felt justice would be have been better served if McCorkell were not among the living.

After twenty years of psychiatric treatment in prisons and mental institutions, the teenager who heard imaginary voices and violently bashed his head against walls was released from Toronto's Queen Street Mental Health Centre in 1981. Living at his West Toronto home with his mother, McCorkell briefly worked as an electrician. Fast approaching age forty, and after spending half his life in correctional facilities and mental hospitals, McCorkell was, like many pedophiles, never truly cured. Instead, his unnatural infatuation with very young boys had bubbled and simmered over the decades, as he'd struggled trying to convince psychiatrists he saw anything other than lithe young bodies in the inky black Rorschach Tests he took over the years.

In May 1982, a man abducted two boys from a West Toronto construction site, raping them and threatening to kill them if they talked. A week later, an unsuspecting eleven-year-old male was snatched from a railway bridge and raped. Horribly beaten to the point of unconsciousness, the youngster then had his own shoelaces tied around his neck before he was flung face first into the Etobicoke Creek and left to drown. Miraculously, the child survived his ordeal, and he — along with the other two boys — picked out their attacker, a "raspy-voiced man," from police photos. Even with his black hair receding, face growing paunchy, and a thick, dark moustache, McCorkell's mug shot showed the same vacant, unrepentant eyes as when he was arrested in 1962.

A Canada-wide warrant was immediately issued for thirty-nine-year-old McCorkell, and his mother, Blanche, made appeals for her son to surrender. He didn't, and fled to the United States, where he sexually assaulted a boy at knifepoint in Tennessee's Natchez Trace State Park. McCorkell was finally captured in Texas when he flagged down a car — a police cruiser — to ask for directions.

In 1983, McCorkell was sentenced to sixty years in a Tennessee prison for aggravated rape and aggravated kidnapping. Although McCorkell was still wanted by police for his crimes in Toronto, Tennessee prosecutor Jerry Woodall boldly stated, "I will resist any move by Canada of getting him if there is even a chance of him receiving parole up there." McCorkell remained in Tennessee. The convicted child killer, said psychiatrists, longed for the father figure which was denied him in his childhood, a feeling of loss that attracted him to young boys.

Balding, unshaven, and sickly pale, McCorkell was interviewed by Hana Gartner for *The Fifth Estate* soon after he was apprehended in the United States. During the interview, he freely admitted he convinced Canadian parole boards he was ready to be released because he felt he could "make it on society." It was soon after his release that McCorkell picked up exactly where he left off twenty years earlier, attacking and molesting young boys.

Gartner:	How do you think of yourself?
McCorkell:	Sometimes I think I'm rotten to the core. Sometimes I feel, given the chance, the help I need, I'm a pretty good guy, who likes to help people. But I haven't had much chance in doing that.
Gartner:	Is it better that you are locked up, rather than in the streets where you could possibly attack another little boy?
McCorkell:	[long pause] If there's a chance of attacking another boy, I prefer to be locked up. If I'd be on the street and be safe, I'd like to be on the street. But not with that over my head.[106]

Today, McCorkell is inmate 99143 at the Tennessee Department of Correction, and no longer the gangly, wavy-haired teenager he was when he sexually abused and smothered toddlers Ronald MacLeod and Michael Atkinson to death in 1962. Overweight, bald, and with a gray, grizzled beard, McCorkell more closely resembles a deranged Santa Claus than the twenty-year-old who beat death by the noose in his native Canada. Assuming he survives to a ripe old age, Gary Alexander McCorkell will be eligible for release in 2032, when he will be almost ninety years old.

McCorkell narrowly escaped death partly through the dedicated efforts of Chaplain Cyril Everitt, who did everything possible to spare McCorkell the same fate as Turpin and Lucas. In February 1963, when McCorkell's death sentence was commuted to life by the newly elected Liberal Cabinet of Prime Minister Lester B. Pearson, Everitt spoke to the media about McCorkell.

"It's my policy, and I think it should be the police of all spiritual advisers, to do the best for the body as well as the soul of these people," said the chaplain. "I, personally, am against capital punishment, with only a little reservation." Everitt regularly visited McCorkell in his death row cell at the Don Jail, talking to the young man as he had to Turpin and Lucas, or playing games of chess or checkers with him. After finishing Winston Churchill's book *Closing the Ring*, he asked Everitt to get him Churchill's *The Valiant Years*. Everitt obliged, and enrolled McCorkell in a Salvation Army course entitled *Science and the Bible*.

Salvation Army Chaplain Cyril Everitt was a man who believed in the redemption of man's body and soul, and he served as chaplain at the Don Jail until 1965. He believed religious training, if instilled in children at a young age, would significantly reduce the rate of crime. Helping others was in his blood from a very early age. The child of Salvationist parents, Everitt was born in the small village of Great Wakering, Essex, in England, and came to Canada at the age of five in 1913. Entering the Toronto Training College at age twenty-two, he soon became a Salvation Army officer, and served as a divisional youth secretary and chancellor in Manitoba, British Columbia, Ontario, and Quebec before becoming chaplain at the Don Jail in 1959.

A gifted piano and organ soloist, Everitt used his skills as a musician to promote the word of God, and claimed one of his happiest moments came when he played the organ at the Royal Albert Hall in London. A humble, unassuming man, Everitt regularly conducted services, and helped run the Salvation Army Camp in Toronto for underprivileged city children. When he left his position at the Don Jail, Everitt became administrator of the Isabel and Arthur Meighen Lodge in Toronto, where he and his wife, Olive, helped the aged until he retired in 1973.

Although his efforts to spare the lives of Turpin and Lucas were unsuccessful, Everitt never stopped helping others, especially inmates. As he had with McCorkell, Lucas, and Turpin, the chaplain also petitioned the government to save the lives of other condemned men like John

Charles Byrnes and Harry Wilson. With the exception of McCorkell, who reoffended soon after his release, the cases of Byrnes and Wilson were tragic errors of judgment that almost cost them their lives.

Byrnes was sentenced to hang on May 12, 1965, for the murder of Mrs. Avis Slack, a forty-one-year-old mother of four who had arrived in Canada with her family from England less than a year before her death. Walking home after working the late shift at a doughnut store one night, Byrnes attempted to steal Slack's purse. Instead of surrendering her handbag she screamed. In a panic, Byrnes stabbed her five times with an ice pick, with Slack bleeding to death on the sidewalk. At the time, she had been working late shifts to raise enough money to fly back to England to attend her daughter's wedding.

"He just wanted her purse," wrote Everitt in an unpublished letter to John Diefenbaker. By this time, Diefenbaker was no longer prime minister, but leader of the opposition. Everitt was quick to remind Diefenbaker of their past history: "It seems as though I write you only when there is someone awaiting execution on the gallows!" He told Diefenbaker of his concerns about Byrnes's upcoming execution, and although no one had been hanged in Canada with a jury recommending mercy, "none of us who are deeply concerned with the case are anxious for it to set a precedence!"

On the same day, May 4, Everitt also wrote a letter to Prime Minister Lester B. Pearson on Byrnes's behalf, and reminded him that the jury recommended mercy in the Byrnes case. "I am the Chaplain of the Don Jail in Toronto, and visit Mr. Byrnes every day," wrote Everitt. "While my purpose is primarily Spiritual, we do discuss other subjects, sometimes at great length. I am convinced that the prisoner did not realize the enormity of his act, and do trust that you and the members of your Cabinet will take this fact into consideration when you make your final decision."

As he had with Byrnes, Everitt made appeals to spare the life of Harry Wilson, a forty-four-year-old unemployed electrician's assistant who murdered William Fox Young in a snow-covered Toronto lane in late January 1963. Young was savagely beaten following a barroom brawl and died from head wounds and exposure. To Prime Minister Pearson, the chaplain described Wilson as a man who "has no friends or relatives whatever"; he had even attempted to contact family members in the U.S., to no avail. "Every cent spent during his incarceration for personal requirements (tobacco, magazines, etc.) has been supplied by us. Really, sir, he is a poor soul. I would personally appreciate anything you can do for him, and on his behalf I can assure you *he* will." As a postscript, Everitt added. "I was also the spiritual advisor to Arthur Lucas and Ronald Turpin, accompanying them to the gallows last December. However, the jury did not recommend mercy in either case."

For many years after the deaths of Turpin and Lucas, individuals present at the double hangings were interviewed by the press, especially on the anniversary of the executions or when the subject of abolition came up prior to 1976. The person sought out most often was Everitt, who would accompany reporters to Prospect Cemetery and patiently pose for photos by the unmarked graves as a reporter asked him what it was like to be at the last hangings in Canada. He never wavered in his opinion on how much he genuinely missed Turpin and Lucas. "If men can love men, I think I loved those two," Everitt told the *Globe and Mail* in 1985. "I knew they had no other friends and I wondered how quickly they had been forgotten." He continued to visit the graves for many years after their deaths, until old age made him unable to do so.

Although he never wavered in his belief in Lucas's innocence, the "little reservation" Everitt felt about capital punishment changed as he aged, especially when his grandchild was born. Adamantly against the death penalty at the time of the hangings, Everitt modified his stance to allow for hangings of child molesters, dope dealers, and murderers of prison guards.

"I love my work and I believe in the dignity of it. What greater dignity is there than to restore a human life back to society?" said Everitt, who died in Toronto in 1986 at age seventy-eight.

One man who had absolutely no regrets over the hanging of Arthur Lucas was the judge who sentenced him to death. For James Chalmers McRuer, the trial of *Regina vs. Lucas* was not particularly memorable, just one of many over which he presided. In many ways, McRuer is better remembered for his involvement with the controversial spy trial of Igor Gouzenko and with the grisly Evelyn Dick "torso" murder case, which saw Dick prosecuted for the brutal murder of her estranged husband.

In his biography on McRuer, Patrick Boyer writes the hanging of Lucas was no different to McRuer than that of any other man he had sentenced to death. The morning of the executions, he read about the upcoming hangings in the newspaper, and made no comment to his wife. "Instead, he simply went back to work, unaware that he would never again have to send a man to his death."[107]

Through his long and distinguished career, McRuer served on numerous royal commissions examining the textile industry, the penal system, the law and sexual psychopaths, civil rights, and the use of insanity as a defence in capital cases. A chief justice of the Supreme Court of Ontario, McRuer was often asked about what it was like to sentence a man to death; invariably, his answer was the same: he was simply doing his duty.

In his last interview of his life with author Jack Batten at age ninety-five, McRuer had a final comment about capital punishment. "There was one good thing about Lucas' hanging," said McRuer. "It was the last. Parliament ended the death penalty, and sentencing a man to hang is one part of the administration of justice that judges need have no fear of now."[108]

McRuer's death from a heart attack in 1985 brought an end to the life of a legal legend, and though the Lucas trial was not as complicated as others in his court, it forever linked McRuer to the end of capital punishment in Canada.

Like McRuer, the judge presiding over the trial of Ronald Turpin was involved with some of Canada's most controversial criminal cases in his thirty years on the bench. Threatened with physical violence numerous times, George Alexander Gale once had a man armed with a club arrested in his home.

Born in Quebec City and raised in Vancouver, Gale spent most of his adult life in Toronto. In 1951, he incensed labour leaders when he overturned a decision by the Ontario Labour Relations Board, and in 1968, he presided over a lawsuit between two companies fighting over $2 billion of iron ore. The case lasted a staggering sixteen months, making it one of the longest in Canadian history. An expert in court procedures, Gale was made editor-in-chief of and completely revised text for the Rules of Court in Ontario.

Appointed chief justice of Ontario in 1964 and retiring in 1976, Gale soon became vice-chairman of the Ontario Law Reform Commission. He was made a companion of the Order of Canada in 1977. In the 1970s, he donated a trophy to a national university debate, which became the Gale Cup, a prized forum for legal debate. Gale died in 1997 at the age of ninety-one.

Fearless and intimidating, Henry Herbert Bull prosecuted the case against Arthur Lucas. Born in Windsor, Ontario, in 1911, the ambitious Bull attended Trinity College at the University of Toronto, and graduated from Osgoode Hall in 1938. By 1939, he rose to the position of assistant Crown attorney, leaving for three years to serve his country during the Second World War. A member of the Canadian Bar Association, the Advocate Society, the County of York Law Association, and the Lawyers' Club of Toronto, Bull was chosen as one of only two Canadian lawyers to lecture at a course for prosecutors at Northwestern University in Chicago.

A prosecutor for three decades, Bull was an aggressive, fast-thinking man, not at all reserved when it came to berating others for their mistakes. In 1967, Bull told a committee that evils in the Canadian bail system were not a fault of the law but came from poor administration by officials. He was also not shy about his position on the media, telling the press in no uncertain terms that they should improve their coverage of trials.

An intense and determined man in and out of court, Bull was discussing staff replacements with his deputy when he collapsed from a heart attack in his Toronto office in 1968; he died en route to hospital. He was fifty-seven years old.

The counterpart to Henry Bull, Arthur Otto Klein was the Crown prosecutor for the trial of *Regina vs. Turpin*. Born the son of a barrister in Walkerton, Ontario, Klein completed his studies at the University of Toronto, and was called to the bar in 1933. He articled with his father before serving as a flight instructor with the Royal Canadian Air Force during the Second World War. He was appointed assistant Crown attorney for the County of York in 1945.

During his lengthy career, Klein prosecuted a number of well-known Canadian cases, including Boyd Gang members, Louis Fisher, and Robert Fitten, who strangled schoolgirl Linda Lampkin to death. Two years after the Turpin trial, he was appointed chief magistrate for Toronto, later becoming provincial chief judge. His greatest wish was to see a central Toronto courthouse, with an adjacent jail used for the sole purpose of housing persons awaiting trial.

"At present our courts are a maze of antique facilities which are quite inadequate," said Klein, hoping for some improvement, and believing a jail next to the courts would speed up the process of justice.

Retiring in 1979, Klein was a life member of the Law Society for fifty years, passing away in 1997 at age eighty-seven.

Along with his partner John Bassett, homicide detective Jack Webster helped solved the Lucas case, and he remains the Toronto police force's longest serving member. Beginning his lengthy career the same day he was discharged from the Canadian army in 1945, "Copper Jack" Webster served under nine chiefs of police, receiving more merit citations than any other officer.

Towards the end of his career, Webster investigated the controversial bombing at Litton Systems Canada in 1982, which was making parts for the Cruise missile. By the time he retired in 1988 as staff superintendent, Webster had more than eighty-five solved murders to his credit. Even after he officially retired, Webster kept busy doing what he loved most, educating others as historian of the Toronto Police Museum. Webster passed away from a heart attack at age seventy-eight in 2002.

A highly respected Toronto detective-sergeant, John Bassett was one of the key homicide officers who helped track down Arthur Lucas. Along with fellow homicide detective Kenneth Evans, he was sent to Montreal at the last minute to testify in the murder trial of a Quebec grocer. Tragically, Bassett's life was cut short when the plane they were on, Trans-Canada Air Lines flight 138, crashed in the foothills of the Laurentians near Ste. Thérèse, killing all 118 passengers and crew on November 29, 1963. The crash of the Douglas DC-8 remains one of Canada's worst aircraft disasters.

A distinguished Toronto homicide detective, Jim Crawford helped solve many of the city's high-profile murder cases. The murder of Fred Nash was one of hundreds Crawford investigated during his thirty-eight years on the force. Other high-profile cases include child-killer Gary Alexander McCorkell and Wayne Ford, who killed his mother, Minnie, sinking her body in a box in Lake Couchiching, where it didn't surface for several years.

In October 1954, Crawford, along with contractor Herb Jones, saved at least fifty people from drowning when Hurricane Hazel hit Toronto. Flood waters from the Humber River reached housetops, and the two men went from rooftop to rooftop in a small boat selflessly rescuing others. In 2006, "Big Jim" was on hand for the dedication of the Crawford-Jones Memorial Park. Only years later did Crawford learn that Jones, the man who helped him save dozens from drowning, couldn't swim.

As one of the officers investing a rash of fur thefts in the early 1960s, Jim Majury encountered Arthur Lucas a week before the murders of Therland Crater and Carolyn Newman. While investigating the Kendal Avenue crime scene, Majury was instrumental in remembering details about his earlier conversation with Lucas that helped police track him down in Detroit.

Serving the Toronto Police Force for thirty-three years before retiring in 1985 as a staff inspector, Majury always had a keen eye for detail, which he used to create drawings of criminal suspects. Producing drawings for the police department that were second to none, Majury was one of Canada's first sketch artists, even before the term existed. Thanks to Majury, the success rate for capturing criminals based on his drawings increased dramatically, with more than half of the wanted men he sketched being captured.

Today, Majury dedicates himself to his first love: wildlife art. World-renowned for his work, Majury's highly detailed paintings sell as limited editions, while his originals often command thousands of dollars. He loves all animals, especially wolves, and prefers to paint animals in situations.

"I usually create a story in there, whereas other people just paint the animal in a kind of a portrait, and I like to put some kind of a story in it that may or may not be apparent," says Majury. "We have a lot of fun with the titles; they are a very important part of the painting, and we spend a lot of time getting the right title. I have fun explaining the titles, too," he says, laughing.

On June 15, 1962, forty-four-year-old Gus Saunders was sentenced to twenty years in prison in Detroit. The man who ordered the hit on Therland Crater, who was going to be the star witness against him in a drug trial, was sentenced as a second offender, having already served a five-year prison term after being convicted on narcotics charges.

Zygmunt Turlinski, owner of the rooming house at 116 Kendal Avenue where Therland Crater and Carolyn Newman were brutally murdered, died in 1989.

"Justice had been done and I never lost a moment's sleep over the hangings," said Minister of Justice Donald Fleming following the hangings. Fleming died in 1987.

The lawyer who defended the last two men hanged in Canada, Ross MacKay was young, brilliant, and forever affected by the deaths of Arthur Lucas and Ronald Turpin. His daughter, Alison, followed in her father's footsteps, and is a criminal lawyer in Ontario. Sadly, MacKay died on Thanksgiving Day in 1983, the first month his daughter was in law school.

When the subject of capital punishment came up again in 1987, the *Toronto Star* interviewed a number of lawyers about the subject, and Ross MacKay's name invariably came up. Defence attorney Earl Levy was a friend of MacKay's and saw how the deaths of Turpin and Lucas affected him. "He gave his all to defend those two men, and then they died," said Levy. "It got to him. He had been a drinker before, but his problems really accelerated. He couldn't stand the thought that the state had executed two men — it was a very painful experience for him. Perhaps he got too close to them; it would be hard not to, when you're spending that much time with a client."[109]

MacKay continued to practise law in Ontario following the trials of Turpin and Lucas, and his magnetic presence and expertise at cross-examination continue to inspire others. Nancy Morrison, who sat in the courtroom for both trials as a law student, is today Madame Justice Morrison, a Supreme Court judge in British Columbia. She still remembers Ross MacKay.

"Those trials changed my life," said Morrison. "I fell in love with the courtroom. Within just a couple of days, I said to myself, 'This is where I belong, in the courtroom, this is where I want to be.'"

Even today, MacKay's daughter is approached by lawyers and judges who speak fondly about her late father. Says Alison, "A lot of the older fellows have this phrase: 'Who are the two best criminal lawyers in the country? Ross MacKay drunk, and Ross MacKay sober.'"

Following the murder of Toronto police officer Fred Nash, his wife, Dorothy Nash, and their four young daughters were left without a husband, a father, or any long-term financial resources. Generously opening their hearts and wallets to the Nash Fund, Toronto's citizens provided some immediate relief, but it would not be enough to take care of the children as they grew older. Although Mrs. Nash had worked as a supply teacher in the past, she spent years at home raising her growing family and was not employed at the time of her husband's death, when the awarding of a pension to the family of a slain police officer was virtually unprecedented. While the public and newspapers like the *Toronto Star* and the *Telegram* felt a pension for the widow of a police officer killed in the line of duty was appropriate and necessary, others at Metro Council were unwilling to grant Dorothy a pension.

In October 1962, eight months after her husband's murder, Dorothy received the Metro Police Commission's Medal of Honour, which was awarded posthumously to her late husband. It was also the same month Toronto newspapers reported that Dorothy was about to remarry another police officer, John Kryskow, the same man who brought her deceased husband's belongings to her from his police station locker and who assisted at his funeral. The Nash children already knew of Kryskow, who occasionally worked as a crossing guard, helping them and other children safely cross Albion Road on their way to Beaumonde Heights Public School. The pension Dorothy fought so hard to get only lasted a few months, and stopped the day she married Kryskow in November of 1962. The pair had two children of their own, bringing the number to six, and remained happily married until John's death in 1999.

The scene of the last judicial hangings in Canada, Toronto's Don Jail remains an integral part of the country's legal and architectural history. Notorious as a hotbed for diseases like tuberculosis due to overcrowding, the Don was the subject of numerous grand jury investigations over the years, with one calling the facility "an insult to humanity."

From the time it opened in 1864, the Don Jail was where seventy men and women died on the gallows. Countless others succumbed to illness and disease over the decades, or chose to take their own lives rather than spend another day in the "black cesspool unfit for human habitation." Every year, at least 23,000 men and women entered the Don. Although a new addition was created in 1958 and still operates today, the original brick and stone Don Jail, with its eerie metal brackets cast in the form of dragons and serpents, is what most people remember, especially those who served time behind bars.

From the moment it was conceived by architect William Thomas, the Don Jail has never been without controversy. Even when it finally shut its doors amid much fanfare in 1978, the storm surrounding the old structure never subsided. Correctional Services Minister Frank Drea came under attack at the closing ceremony when it was revealed he had ordered the infamous gallows where Turpin and Lucas and sixty-eight others met their maker destroyed. Fearing their could become part of a "historic restoration project," Drea's move was made without consultation, with the city's historical board calling Drea "extremely irrational and paranoid."

Fortunately, the original building has been spared, and will soon see a new life as hospital administration offices.

In a rare interview taped a few months prior to the abolition of capital punishment in 1976, CBC Television's *Take 30* spoke to the man who put Turpin and Lucas to death. Using the name John Ellis for the interview, Canada's hangman spoke to Paul Soles about his memories of the last hangings in Canada. Sitting comfortably on a studio sofa, left leg crossed over his right, Ellis wears a suit, his head draped with a black hood similar to the kind placed over the heads of Lucas and Turpin. Two feline-looking angled holes are crudely cut through the fabric, pale white eyes peeking out behind the black material. Even as Ellis assures host Paul Soles that he does not wear a mask when he conducts a hanging, Soles squirms in his seat, visibly uncomfortable in the presence of the hooded executioner. He is quick to explain that the hood he wears for the interview is to conceal his identity and is not part of his normal attire.

"All I wear is a black suit, black bow, white shirt, and black shoes," Ellis tells Soles, reassuringly. "I'm not there to frighten him — I'm there to execute him."

His voice cracking with age, the hangman spends the next few minutes explaining how he takes a life, and his views on capital punishment. It remains an eerie, disturbing interview with a man who does not seem to have softened in any way over the years.

"I don't follow a case," says Ellis. "If a man is found guilty by a judge and jury, then I'm an instrument of the court to carry out the sentence."

The hangman then explains how humane a hanging is, assuming it is properly done. He is critical of other methods of execution, especially electrocution, telling Soles the man in the electric chair is not dead right away, but burned. In what remains one of the strangest demonstrations ever broadcast on Canadian television, Ellis pulls out a noose and reveals to the camera how the spine and spinal cork breaks, if the knot is placed behind the left ear. "And that man is dead from the time he hits the bottom of the rope," says Ellis. "His heart will beat — it varies with the physical condition the man's in — but his heart will beat for 20, maybe 40 seconds after that, but no longer."

With the end of capital punishment and his employment as Canada's hangman in the very near future, Soles asks Ellis about his feelings on the end of an era.

Paul Soles:	If the vote goes for abolition, and there is no longer a need of the hangman, how do you think you personally will feel?
John Ellis:	Well, I'll feel that I've served the country in the best way that I know how — maybe I shouldn't say that. I've met the requirements that the country required. I've done my job, and I'm retired.
Paul Soles:	You won't feel years younger or pounds lighter because of the vote?
John Ellis:	No, no.
Paul Soles:	Will you feel concerned if abolition is passed that this will bode ill for the country?
John Ellis:	Yes, I will, in that respect to myself, but I won't divulge it. As far as I'm concerned now, people seem to think that the trap is not a deterrent. In any case, if you go to a life imprisonment, I have met people that

just wanted … in fact, you're heard it in the paper of people who want to die, rather than spend life in prison.

Paul Soles: That is more inhumane, a life internment rather than execution?

John Ellis: Yes, the torture they go through. Plus, it's a burden on the taxpayer of about $13,000 to $14,000 per year per man that is in death row, or is serving life term.[110]

Around the same time, the CBC also interviewed Dr. Guy Richmond, who considered hanging inhumane as a form of execution. A former senior medical officer with the British Columbia Corrections Branch, Richmond worked at the province's Oakalla Prison, and X-rayed bodies of hanging victims. Contradicting the hangman, Richmond did not find broken vertebrae, and said the heart kept beating for ten to twelve minutes after death, much longer than the twenty to forty seconds of which Ellis spoke.

Whatever became of Canada's hangman, the mysterious little fellow known to the men and women he was about to execute as Jack, James, Arthur, even John Ellis? To them, the face of this polite, meticulous, and nondescript man was the last they would see before the black hood was placed over their heads, the noose secured around their necks, and the platform gave way beneath their feet, dropping them into eternity. To the condemned, Ellis was an instrument of death, as much as the noose and the gallows; to his wife and children, he was a salesman who sometimes went out of town on business trips. To the Canadian government, he was an employee who did his job, and did it well.

The last laugh belongs to the hangman. In a macabre example of government overspending, a report from the auditor general revealed that Ellis, who hanged Turpin, Lucas, and dozens of others, was kept on the payroll until 1985, almost a decade after the abolishment of capital punishment in 1976. An investigation revealed the decision to continue to pay him $200 every month came from Philip Ambrose, the sheriff of York County, who believed there was a still a great deal of public opposition against abolition. Although his services were not required for many years, Ellis undoubtedly looked forward to his $200 cheque every month.

Long after the hangings of Ronald Turpin and Arthur Lucas at the Don Jail, Sheriff Ambrose told reporters he would never throw away the hangman's name and contact information, just in case. "Politicians being what they are, you never know if they'll bring it back again."[111]

Bibliography

Books

Abbott, Geoffrey. *The Executioner Always Chops Twice: Ghastly Blunders on the Scaffold*. New York: St. Martin's Press, 2004.

Anderson, Frank W. *Hanging in Canada: Concise History of a Controversial Topic*. Heritage House Publishing Company Ltd., 1982.

Atholl, Justin. *Shadow of the Gallows*. John Long Limited, 1954.

Atholl, Justin. *The Reluctant Hangman: The Story of James Berry, Executioner 1884-1892*. John Long Limited, 1956.

Bailey, Brian. *Hangmen of England: A History of Execution from Jack Ketch to Albert Pierrepoint*. Barnes & Noble Books, 1992.

Batten, Jack. *Judges*. Toronto: Macmillan of Canada, 1986.

Batten, Jack. *Lawyers*. Toronto: Penguin Books Canada Ltd., 1985.

Batten, Jack. *The Annex: The Story of a Toronto Neighbourhood*. Erin, Ontario: Boston Mills Press, 2004.

Boyd, Neil. *The Last Dance: Murder in Canada*. Seal Book, 1992.

Boyer, Patrick. *A Passion for Justice: The Legacy of James Chalmers McRuer*. Published for the Osgoode Society by the University of Toronto Press, 1994.

Capote, Truman. *In Cold Blood*. Modern Library Edition, 1992.

Carrigan, D. Owen. *Crime and Punishment in Canada, A History*. Toronto: McClelland and Stewart Limited, 1991.

Chandler, David. *Capital Punishment in Canada*. Toronto: McClelland and Stewart Limited, 1976.

Dernley, Syd with Newman, David. *The Hangman's Tale: Memoirs of a Public Executioner*. Pan Books Limited, 1990.

Drimmer, Frederick. *Until You Are Dead: The Book of Executions in America*. Citadel Press, 1990.

Duff, Charles. *A Handbook on Hanging*. New York: New York Review Books Classics, 2001.

Duff, Louis Blake. *The County Kerchief*. The Ryerson Press, 1949.

Ellis, John. *Diary of a Hangman*. Forum Press, 1997.

Engel, Howard. *Lord High Executioner: An Unashamed Look at Hangmen, Headsmen, and Their Kind*. Toronto: Key Porter Books Limited, 1996.

Faverau, Guy. *Capital Punishment: Material Relating to Its Purpose and Value*. Information Canada, 1965.

Gardiner, Gerald. *Capital Punishment As a Deterrent: And the Alternative*. Lowe and Brydone, 1961.

Gowers, Sir Earnest. *A Life for a Life: The Problem of Capital Punishment*. Chatto and Windus, 1956.

Haines, Max. *Canadian Crimes*. Toronto: Signet, 1998.

Hann, Robert G. *Deterrence & The Death Penalty*. Decision Dynamics Corporation; Communication Division of the Ministry of the Solicitor General, 1977.

Hustak, Alan. *They Were Hanged*. Toronto: James Lorimer & Company, 1987.

Jayewardene, C.H.S. *After Abolition of the Death Penalty*. Crimcare Inc., 1989.

Jayewardene, C.H.S. *The Penalty of Death*. D.C. Heath and Company, 1977.

Kettle, John and Walker, Dean. *Verdict! Eleven Revealing Canadian Trials*. McGraw-Hill Company of Canada Limited, 1968.

Koestler, Arthur. *Hanged by the Neck*. Penguin Books Ltd., 1961.

Mackey, James P. *I Policed Toronto: An Autobiography by James P. Mackey, Chief of Police, Metropolitan Toronto, 1958–1970*. Jas. P. Mackey, 1985.

McArthur, Glenn and Annie Szamosi. *William Thomas: Architect, 1799-1860*. Archives of Canadian Art, 1996.

Mencken, August. *By the Neck: A Book of Hangings*. Hastings House, 1942.

Pierrepoint, Albert. *Executioner: Pierrepoint.* Coronet Books, 1977.

Prejean, Helen. *Dead Man Walking: An Eyewitness Account of the Death Penalty in the United States.* New York: Random House, 1993.

Shapiro, His Honour Judge B. Barry. *Report of the Royal Commission on the Toronto Jail and Custodial Services Vols. 1–4.* Queen's Printer for Ontario, 1978.

Vallée, Brian. *Edwin Alonzo Boyd: The Story of the Notorious Boyd Gang.* Doubleday Canada Limited, 1998.

Webster, Jack with Rosemary Aubert. *Copper Jack.* Toronto: Dundurn Press, 1991.

Video

The Last Hanging in Canada: The Moral Question. 1981, Ontario Educational Communications Authority.

The Fifth Estate. Canadian Broadcasting Corporation, aired May 13, 1987.

W5 News Magazine. CTV, aired December 31, 1967.

Rogers *Structures*, on Don Jail, aired December 27, 2001.

Endnotes

1   A British man, Arthur Bartholomew English, became Canada's official hangman in 1913. His use of the pseudonym "Arthur Ellis" was later adopted by his followers, who would occasionally use Jack, James, or John in place of Arthur.

2   Frank W. Anderson, *Hanging in Canada: Concise History of a Controversial Topic* (Heritage House Publishing Company Ltd., 1982), 53.

3   Commons Debates, June 15, 1976, 14500.

4   Ipsos-Reid, "Support for Capital Punishment Plummets," February 15, 2001.

5   There are a few notable exceptions, including *Hanging in Canada: Concise History of a Controversial Topic* by Frank W. Anderson (1982), *They Were Hanged* by Alan Hustak (1987), and *The Last Dance: Murder in Canada* by Neil Boyd (1992).

6   Department of Justice Canada fact sheet, Capital Punishment in Canada, http://canada.justice.gc.ca/en/news/fs/2003/doc_30896. html.

7   Carolyn Strange, "The Half-Life of the Death Penalty: Public Memory in Australia and Canada," *Australian-Canadian Studies*, 19 2 (2001): 90–91.

8   Dr. W. Arthur Blair's two-hour psychiatric examination of Turpin, Don Jail, October 13, 1962.

9   Some sources, including Lucas himself, contradict his date and place of birth, which is sometimes given as Daytona Beach,

Florida, August 18, 1910.

10   Memorandum to Cabinet, Minister of Justice, November 12, 1962.

11   Federal Bureau of Investigation report on Arthur Lucas, September 20, 1956.

12   Federal Bureau of Investigation report on Arthur Lucas, October 26, 1956.

13   Federal Bureau of Investigation report on Arthur Lucas, January 25, 1957.

14   To this day, the murder of Lorne Gibson remains unsolved.

15   *Regina vs. Ronald Turpin*, 1858–1859. Turpin's account of the events of the night of February 11, 1962, are still disputed. To the author, it seems extremely unlikely that Nash, or any experienced police officer, would hold a loaded pistol and a cumbersome flashlight in one hand and use the other hand to strike a suspect. In court, Turpin testified, "I said, 'What the "f'" — referring to the word — are you doing?' and I brought my arms up, like this (indicating), he had his revolver — his own revolver — in his hand, and he was bringing it down."

16   *Regina vs. Turpin*, 1861–1863.

17   The *Toronto Star*, February 12, 1962, 2.

18   RG 13 C-1 Vol. 762, Vol. 1842, 133.

19   The *Telegram*, February 12, 1962, 1.

20   The *Globe and Mail*, February 13, 1962, 1.

21   The *Toronto Star*, February 16, 1962, 19.

22   The *Toronto Star*, November 18, 1961, 4.

23   The *Toronto Star*, November 18, 1961, 4.

24   John D. Webster case synopsis, 1961, 2.

25   The *Telegram*, November 18, 1961, 1.

26   Undated Toronto Police Department file, 2.

27   The *Toronto Star*, November 20, 1961, 6.

28   The *Telegram*, November 17, 1961, 1.

29   The trial of Arthur Lucas was held in what is today referred to as Toronto's Old City Hall, which opened in 1899.

30   The *Globe and Mail*, September 4, 1968, 38.

31   The *Toronto Star*, January 6, 1962, 45.

32   The *Globe and Mail*, March 29, 1962, 5.

33   *Regina vs. Arthur Lucas*, 44.

34   *Regina vs. Lucas*, 96–97.

35   The *Toronto Star*, May 1, 1962, 2.

36   *Regina vs. Lucas*, 190–191.

37   *Regina vs. Lucas*, 222.

38   *Regina vs. Lucas*, 251–252.

39   Report of J. P. S. Cathcart, Metropolitan Jail, Toronto, June 9, 1962, 2.

40   *Regina vs. Lucas*, 1076–1077.

41   *Regina vs. Lucas*, 1172.

42   *The Scales of Justice*, "End of the Rope," 38.

43   *Regina vs. Lucas*, 1436.

44   The *Globe and Mail*, May 10, 1962, 5.

45   *Regina vs. Lucas*, 1568.

46   *Regina vs. Lucas*, 1571.

47   *Globe and Mail*, April 17, 1962, 4.

48   *Regina vs. Turpin*, 15.

49   *Hush*, March 10, 1962, 7.

50   *Regina vs. Turpin*, 473.

51   *Regina vs. Turpin*, 482.

52   *Regina vs. Turpin*, 544.

53   *Regina vs. Turpin*, 1717.

54   *Regina vs. Turpin*, 1084.

55   *Regina vs. Turpin*, 1366–1367.

56   *Regina vs. Turpin*, 1581.

57   *Regina vs. Turpin*, 181.

58   *Regina vs. Turpin*, 1741–1742.

59   *Regina vs. Turpin*, 1768.

60   *Regina vs. Turpin*, 1819–1820.

61   *Regina vs. Turpin*, 1861–1863.

62   *Regina vs. Turpin*, 1871.

63   *Regina vs. Turpin*, 1950–1951.

64   *Regina vs. Turpin*, 1995.

65   Department of Health report from Dr. N.L. Easton to Dr. C.H. Lewis, April 19, 1962.

66 Department of Health report from Dr. J. Grodsinski to Dr. C.H. Lewis, May 24, 1962.

67 *Regina vs. Turpin*, 2696.

68 Unfortunately, only one of the four daughters was able to benefit from the endowment fund.

69 *Telegram*, February 14, 1962, 7.

70 *Toronto Star*, July 19, 1962 6.

71 Two-man cruisers for Toronto police between the hours of 8:00 p.m. and 8:00 a.m. were not brought in until ordered by court in 1974. As always, cost was cited as the key prohibitive factor.

72 "Since Turpin was listed as 'wanted' on various police bulletins; and since he further admits. that P.C. Nash recognized him as 'wanted.'" From an undated document by Patrick Hartt.

73 *Regina vs. Turpin*, Memorandum of Fact and Law, 12.

74 CC 904, thirteen-page report, June 18, 1962.

75 A.O. Klein to D.H. Christie, July 12, 1962.

76 Dr. W. Arthur Blair, psychiatric report on Ronald Turpin, October 13, 1962, page 11.

77 Letter from J.P.S. Cathcart to D.A. Christie, June 12, 1962.

78 Arthur Lucas appeal, 29–30.

79 Memo from Julian Porter to Walter Williston, October 15, 1962.

80 *Globe and Mail*, June 11, 1987, A07.

81 *Globe and Mail*, November 24, 1962, 6.

82 *Maclean's*, April 9, 1960, 63.

83 Letter from Donald Fleming to Walter Williston, December 10, 1962.

84 Letter from Walter Williston to John Diefenbaker, December 7, 1962.

85 Glenn McArthur and Annie Szamosi, *William Thomas: Architect, 1799–1860* (Archives of Canadian Art, 1996), 124.

86 *Telegram*, February 18, 1963, 5.

87 *Toronto Star*, January 15, 1963, 14.

88 *The Fifth Estate*, Canadian Broadcasting Corporation, aired May 13, 1987.

89 *Globe and Mail*, December 8, 1962, 5.

90 *Toronto Star*, December 10, 1962, 15.

91   Arthur Lucas letter, December 10, 1962.

92   CBC Television, broadcast December 10, 1962.

93   *Globe and Mail*, December 12, 1962, 5.

94   There remains some debate concerning Turpin's last moments of life. In the 1981 documentary *The Last Hanging in Canada: The Moral Question*, Chaplain Cyril Everitt claims Turpin did not make it to the gallows on his own. "Turpin, remember, he was the younger of the two. He didn't walk to the gallows. Poor fellow. He was so nervous at the end, he went unconscious. They had to carry him. Lucas never made a sound, except when they put the rope around his neck. He whimpered a little — not a cry, just a whimper — but Turpin never regained consciousness." According to Everitt's son Bram, his father stated Turpin fainted. However, Everitt did not mention Turpin fainting in earlier interviews, and others say he walked to the gallows unassisted.

95   Rights & Freedoms, March 1985, 16.

96   *Toronto Star*, December 13, 1962, 99.

97   *Toronto Star*, December 11, 1962, 99.

98   *Toronto Star*, December 10, 1962, 9.

99   *Globe and Mail*, October 28, 1963, 7.

100   Days before the hangings, Everitt confronted Lucas about his guilt or innocence, giving him a chance to repent. Bram Everitt reports his father said, "'Arthur, you've got to tell me now, all the appeals are gone. What are you going to tell me when you're standing up there? Are you going to tell me then that you were actually there [at the murder scene]?' Lucas replied: 'Cy, I'm telling you, I didn't do this.' And that's how he qualified it. He said he'd done a lot of other stuff, but as far as [what] he was charged with, he didn't do it."

101   *Globe and Mail*, October 30, 1963, 7.

102   *Globe and Mail*, November 2, 1963, 9.

103   Gilles Belanger to Walter Williston, January 15, 1964.

104   *Globe and Mail*, August 16, 1967, 3.

105   *Globe and Mail*, June 19, 1976, 6.

106   *The Fifth Estate*, Canadian Broadcasting Corporation, aired May 13, 1987.

107 Patrick Boyer, *A Passion for Justice: The Legacy of James Chalmers McRuer* (published for the Osgoode Society by the University of Toronto Press, 1994), 223.
108 Jack Batten, *Judges* (Toronto: Macmillan of Canada, 1986), 270.
109 *Toronto Star*, March 28, 1987, B4.
110 *Take 30*, CBC Television, broadcast February 24, 1976.
111 *Globe and Mail*, February 7, 1973, 52.